ENOCHIAN MAGIC
for BEGINNERS

Open the Gates of Understanding

Begin with a clear and comprehensive overview of the entire system of Enochian magic—not just another rehash of previously published material. *Enochian Magic for Beginners* presents the authentic system of angelic magic taught to Dee and Kelley in its natural order, and places these teachings in their historical context. Drawing upon such obscure and hard-to-find sources as Dee's *Heptarchia Mystica, Liber Scientiae Auxillii et Victoriae* and others, Donald Tyson has painstakingly reconstructed the most accurate and accessible version of Enochian magic published to date.

Here are all the essential parts of the original system of Enochian magic, as it was delivered to John Dee—completely restored and corrected. All of the sigils, seals, and other magical symbols have been carefully re-drawn based upon photographs of Dr. Dee's original drawings and various plates in Causabon's *True and Faithful Relation.* Everything you need to become a practitioner of Enochian magic—or to learn what it's all about—is provided in an easy-to-use format, in simple language.

About the Author

Donald Tyson resides in Halifax, Nova Scotia, Canada. Early in life he was drawn to science by an intense fascination with astronomy, building a telescope by hand when he was twelve. He began university seeking a science degree, but became disillusioned with the aridity and futility of a mechanistic view of the universe and shifted his major to English literature. After graduating with honors he has pursued a writing career.

Now he devotes his life to the attainment of a complete gnosis of the art of magic in theory and practice. His purpose is to formulate an accessible system of personal training composed of East and West, past and present, that will help the individual discover the reason for one's existence and a way to fulfill it.

To Write to the Author

If you would like to contact the author or would like more information about this book, please write to him in care of Llewellyn Worldwide. We cannot guarantee that every letter will be answered, but all will be forwarded. Please write to:

Donald Tyson
c/o Llewellyn Publications
P.O. Box 64383, Dept. K747–1
St. Paul, MN 55164-0383, U.S.A

Please enclose a self-addressed, stamped envelope for reply or $1.00 to cover costs. If ordering from outside the U.S.A., please enclose an international postal reply coupon.

ENOCHIAN MAGIC for BEGINNERS

The Original System of Angel Magic

Donald Tyson

1997
Llewellyn Publications
St. Paul, Minnesota 55164-0383

FIRST EDITION
First Printing, 1997

Cover design: Lisa Novak
Editing and layout: Ken Schubert
Illustrations and Enochian fonts: Donald Tyson

Library of Congress Cataloging-in-Publication Data
Tyson, Donald, 1954–
     Enochian magic for beginners : the original system of angel magic
  / Donald Tyson. – 1st ed.
         p.   cm.
     Includes bibliographical references.
     ISBN 1–56718–747–1   (trade paper)
       1. Enochian Magic. 2. Dee, John, 1527–1608 3. Kelly, Edward,
  1555–1598. 4. Enochian language.   I. Title.
  BF1623.E55T97 1997   97–42043
  133.4'3–dc21   CIP

Llewellyn Publications
A Division of Llewellyn Worldwide, Ltd.
P. O. Box 64383, St. Paul, Minnesota 55164-0383, U.S.A.

Contents

Introduction

Legacy of the Angels

The Original Enochian Magic

This book contains the complete and original system of Enochian magic. It was transmitted to the Elizabethan sage Dr. John Dee through his seer the alchemist Edward Kelley by a group of spiritual beings who presented themselves as the same holy angels who had instructed the patriarch Enoch. Whether they were really angels is a moot point, since they ceased to speak with humankind after Dee and Kelley separated in 1589, but their legacy is without question the most remarkable artifact in the entire history of spirit communication.

It is both a system of theurgy (a method for summoning and commanding angelic beings) and goety (a method for summoning and commanding demons). Although the angels gave Dee strict instructions that he should never use the magic for evoking evil spirits, the names of evil spirits are provided in Enochian magic nonetheless, along with techniques for summoning them. In the following pages I put forth the premise that Enochian magic may have a deeper and darker purpose that was never revealed by the angels to Dee. It is my belief that the angels intended it to serve as a magical trigger for the chaotic transition—generally referred to as the apocalypse—between the present aeon and the next.

ORIGIN OF THE SYSTEM

The practical efficacy and ultimate purpose of this system depends in large measure on its origin. For centuries it was dismissed by scholars as either a conscious fabrication by Kelley to deceive Dee or a device Dee created to conceal a technique of cryptography he used in his political espionage. The evidence is persuasive that Dee was indeed a secret agent working for the English government, and he did possess an extensive knowledge of ciphers. Kelley, for his part, was a rogue who had engaged in numerous criminal activities including forgery, counterfeiting, and black magic before entering Dee's employ as a seer. Yet there is no evidence that Enochian magic was ever used to encode espionage ciphers, nor is it likely that Kelley was intellectually capable of creating so complex and beautiful a system of magic.

Anyone who makes a serious study of Dee's magical diaries is forced to conclude that Enochian magic is a genuine phenomenon of spiritualism. Whatever the true nature of the angels—messengers of God or shadow personalities within the unconscious minds of the two men—they clearly intended the information they transmitted to serve some higher purpose: one which they never explicitly revealed to Dee. On several occasions they told Dee and Kelley that the men had been brought together to act as key agents in a divine plan, and that united they were greater than the sum of their parts. They informed Kelley that his amazing talent as a psychic was a gift they had bestowed upon the alchemist, a gift that would be withdrawn should Kelley ever leave Dee's service.

One thing is beyond question—there exist levels of mystery and power in Enochian magic that no scholar and no ritualist has even begun to exploit. Much of the system, including the complex set of magic squares that makes up Dee's *Book of Enoch* and the numbering that appears in the hauntingly beautiful poetry of the Enochian Keys, persists as a complete enigma to this day. For centuries Enochian magicians have made use of parts of the system. Other parts remain beyond their reach, just as they were beyond the understanding of Dee and Kelley. The angels reserved to themselves many secrets.

THE DIVISION OF FATE

Enochian magic falls into two parts. This structure was not intentional, but an accident of fate. Originally the angels transmitted the system in bits and pieces that were not in any logical order, but were scrambled together. This may have been the result of the angels' difficulties in dealing with linear time, or it may have been a deliberate way of concealing the magic from casual eyes. Dee was able to sort out some of the confusion in his manuscripts, but after his death his Enochian papers became split into two collections.

The papers that concern the latter half of Enochian magic were published in 1659 by Meric Casaubon. This is the material that is generally known as Enochian magic. It contains the four Watchtowers, the Enochian Keys or Calls, and the vocabulary of the Enochian language. It was this second half of the system that found its way into the magic of the Victorian occult society known as the Hermetic Order of the Golden Dawn. Through the teachings of the Golden Dawn, Enochian magic has spread widely in the English-speaking occult community over the last century.

The papers that address the first half of the Enochian system remained unpublished until modern times. They were available to serious researchers in the original manuscripts by Dee and early handwritten copies by others, but were virtually unknown to the average working ritualist. They deal with the invocation of planetary angels using a system of sigils and magic squares. This early portion of Enochian magic known as the *Heptarchia Mystica* is still widely regarded as a separate system, more or less unrelated to the magic of the Watchtowers and the Enochian language. This is incorrect, however. Enochian magic is a single, complex entity that can only be understood as a whole.

THE REASONS FOR THIS BOOK

I wrote this book for two reasons. The first purpose was to present the entire spectrum of Enochian magic as an integrated system. Because of its early division into two parts, and because of the sheer complexity of the subject, it has been the tendency of writers to treat single aspects (such as the Watchtowers) in great detail, but to ignore other aspects. This can be disorienting to the novice, who is unable to place the topic under examination into the context of Enochian magic as a whole.

Too often, Enochian magic is presented as something eternally existent. There is no serious attempt to give a detailed history of Dee and Kelley during their partnership, or to show the technical elements revealed by the angels in a wider context. Usually no more than a few pages is devoted to the ritual method by which the communications were received, to what the angels actually said to Dee and Kelley on a personal level, or to the significance of their philosophical teachings. While I have treated the ritual mechanics of Enochian magic with great thoroughness, I have not neglected the larger picture. Those who wish to know what Enochian magic is all about will find their questions answered here, insofar as such questions have an answer.

The second reason I wrote this book was to give, perhaps for the first time, the original system of Enochian magic as revealed by the angels and recorded by John Dee. Most works focus exclusively on the form of Enochian magic that was taught in the order papers of the Golden Dawn, which is *not* the Enochian magic of Dee and Kelley. Golden Dawn Enochian magic deals almost exclusively with a modified version of the Great Table of the Watchtowers and the Enochian Keys—important elements of the system, but only a small part of the whole. To this essential nut of Enochian material the leaders of the Golden Dawn grafted a complex set of magical associations derived from the general Golden Dawn system of magic. These occult correspondences have nothing whatsoever to do with the original system of Enochian magic revealed by the angels.

When the Enochian material in the papers of the Golden Dawn represented all of the system generally available to the public, there was some rationale for favoring it. But since most of the surviving original Enochian manuscripts have now found their way into print in one form or another, it has become inexcusable to treat the restricted, modified portion of Enochian material used in the Golden Dawn as the whole of Enochian magic. This work is dedicated to illuminating the whole of the original system.

NEW FINDINGS

Some of what I present here will not be found outside my works. It is the result of my intense personal studies of the Enochian system. This includes the reformed ordering of the Watchtowers on the Great Table, the assignment of the Enochian Keys to the subquarters of the Table, the completely rewritten *Book of Spirits* by which the angels are to be initially contacted, the final version of the Heptagon Stellar (the great seal of the angelic heptarchy), the illustrations showing the flow of elemental currents in the Round House, and much more.

In the course of writing this book I created two new Enochian typefaces, one for Enochian print characters and the other for script or cursive characters. This was necessary since the standard Enochian typeface contains numerous serious and obvious errors. These new Enochian fonts appear in my illustrations of sigils and tables, all of which have been redrawn and corrected after comparing them with multiple sources. It is my belief that my illustration of the Sigillum Aemeth is the most accurate version currently available.

SECRETS OF THE ANGELS

Enochian magic is complex. Aspects of it remain obscure to this day. This situation is made worse by the loss of some of John Dee's manuscripts, and the damage time has done to those that survive. Even if we possessed all of Dee's magical writings in pristine condition, we would not fully understand Enochian magic because the angels did not transmit all the details of its working. Dee did the best he could to make sense out of the communications, but was forced to rely on an incomplete model.

Without question, some of what appears in this book is faulty. On key topics for which there is no complete explanation I have been forced to speculate. These speculations are clearly labeled as my own interpretation of the material, and you should treat all of these personal interpretations as unproven. I have given them because I believe them to be the best available understanding of the material. Other writers would give you nothing for fear that they might be discovered at some later date to have made mistakes, and indeed, I have probably committed errors in my personal interpretation of obscure parts of the Enochian system, but I believe the value of these speculations outweighs their liability.

For example, in redrawing the ensigns of the heptarchical angels I relied mainly on the plate that appears in Meric Casaubon's *True and Faithful Relation,* which shows the ensigns spread in a circle on top of the Table of Practice. It is my conviction that the ensigns were actually painted on the table (an alternative method of presentation allowed by the angels). Since the artist who made the plate for Casaubon worked from Dee's actual table, which has since vanished from the face of the Earth, I judge his illustration to be the most valuable, even though it conflicts in many details with other versions of the ensigns published by Robert Turner in his book *The Heptarchia Mystica of John Dee.*

Dee may well have made deliberate modifications to the ensigns when he came to paint them onto the surface of his Table of Practice, and these changes may not have been retroactively made in his manuscript drawings. Nonetheless, I closely referred to the ensigns in Turner's work, and where it seemed likely that the engraver may have committed an error (i.e., mistaking Dee's handwritten "ll" for "u"), I have included these changes in my illustrations of the ensigns.

This process of comparison, judgment, and compromise was followed throughout this book. I believe it has resulted in a high degree of accuracy, but due to the very nature of the Enochian material, complete accuracy is impossible. In many cases we simply do not know what the angels intended—or even what Dee intended—with absolute certainty. Bear this fact in mind when you encounter details in the system that seem to contradict what you have seen elsewhere.

A COMPLETE COMPENDIUM OF ENOCHIAN MAGIC

I wrote this work to orient the novice to Enochian magic and to provide in a logical and accurate form all the key aspects of the original system delivered to Kelley by the angels. However, experienced Enochian magicians will also find a great deal that is of interest, because I have been able to treat familiar parts of the system in fresh and insightful ways. Even though the Great Table of the Watchtowers is the most frequent subject of writers on Enochian magic, its essential nature has never really been examined. Writers get lost in the details of its construction and use, and forget to ask what it actually *is*.

Enochian magicians should not be misled by the title of this work. It is written for beginners, but it is not a superficial treatment of Enochian magic. It is a comprehensive examination of the full range of original Enochian magic set in the wider context of all of the Enochian communications. I have been able to encapsulate a great deal of useful information in the form of images and tables. My hope is that the work will serve not only as an overview for beginners, but also as a source for working Enochian magicians.

I am deeply indebted to those writers who have published accurate transcriptions of portions of Dee's magical diaries. Noteworthy among them are Robert Turner, Geoffrey James, and, most of all, Meric Casaubon. Without their work and the work of others like them this book would not have been possible. They have my sincere thanks.

CHAPTER ONE

Enochian Magic

THE WISDOM OF ENOCH

Enochian magic is a system of theurgy, or angel magic, psychically conveyed to the Elizabethan alchemist and seer Edward Kelley by a group of spirits that came to be called the Enochian angels. Over the years 1582–1587 the spirits dictated various parts of this magic to Kelley, or presented it in the form of visions while Kelley scried into a crystal ball.

Kelley repeated the words of the spirits and described the visions to his friend and employer, the great mathematician, geographer, and astrologer Dr. John Dee. Dee sat beside Kelley during the scrying sessions with a pen in his hand and papers spread before him. Everything that Kelley said, Dee recorded verbatim. Thanks to Dee's careful method, the communications of the spirits have been preserved with the accuracy of a court transcript.

The angels identified themselves to Kelley as the same angels who had instructed the patriarch Enoch in the angelic language and the wisdom of God. Enoch was the only patriarch of the Old Testament to be elevated into heaven while still alive—at least, this was the interpretation of the Jewish rabbis and Kabbalists of *Genesis* 5:24: "And Enoch walked with God: and he was not; for God took him." All the other descendants of Adam

1

down to Noah mentioned in the Bible are explicitly said to have died, but not Enoch.

Over the centuries, a wisdom tradition grew up around Enoch. Along with Adam, Noah, Solomon, and a few others, he is said to have been one of those responsible for passing the primal teachings of the angels on to humanity. The apocryphal *Book of Enoch* arose from this tradition. The key event in this book is a description of how the rebellious angels, lusting after the daughters of men, descended to Earth and taught humankind all the arts and sciences of adornment, magic, and warfare that sow strife throughout the world.

THEURGY AND GOETY

According to the angel Ave, these evil angels were permitted to descend upon the Earth and spread false and destructive teachings because the kings of the Earth had grown arrogant through the use of the wisdom bequeathed to them by Enoch. As a punishment, God sent false and deceiving angels to teach what is presently known as black magic. In this way, God allowed humankind to be the instrument of its own punishment. However, Ave tells Kelley, God has decided to permit the true wisdom of Enoch, as preserved in his heavenly books, once again to be known upon the Earth. Dee and Kelley are to be the instruments of its dissemination.

> The Lord appeared unto Enoch, and was merciful unto him, opened his eyes, that he might see and judge the earth, which was unknown unto his Parents, by reason of their fall: for the Lord said, Let us shew unto Enoch, the use of the earth: And lo, Enoch was wise, and full of the spirit of wisdom.

And he sayed unto the Lord, Let there be remembrance of thy mercy, and let those that love thee taste of this after me: O let not thy mercy be forgotten. And the Lord was pleased.

And after 50 days Enoch had written: and this was the Title of his books, let those that fear God, and are worthy read.

But behold, the people waxed wicked, and became unrighteous, and the spirit of the Lord was far off, and gone away from them. So that those that were unworthy began to read. And the Kings of the earth said thus against the Lord, What is it that we cannot do? Or who is he, that can resist us? And the Lord was vexed, and he sent in amongst them an hundred and fifty Lions, and spirits of wickednesse, errour, and deceit: and they appeared unto them: For the Lord had put them between those that are wicked, and his good Angels: And they began to counterfeit the doings of God and his power, for they had power given them so to do, so that the memory of Enoch washed away: and the spirits of errour began to teach them Doctrines: which from time to time unto this age, and unto this day, hath spread abroad into all parts of the world, and is the skill and cunning of the wicked.

Hereby they speak with the Devils: not because they have power over the Devils, but because they are joyned unto them in the league and Discipline of their own Doctrine.

For behold, as the knowledge of the mystical figures, and the use of their presence is the gift of God delivered to Enoch, and by Enoch his request to the faithfull, that thereby they might have the true use of Gods creatures, & of the earth whereon they dwell: So hath the Devil delivered unto the wicked the signs, and tokens of his error and hatred towards God: whereby they in using them, might consent with their fall: and so become partakers with them of their reward, which is eternal damnation.

These they call Characters: a lamentable thing. For by these, many Souls have perished.

Now hath it pleased God to deliver this Doctrine again out of darknesse: and to fulfill his promise with thee, for the books of Enoch: To whom he sayeth as he said unto Enoch.

Let those that are worthy understand this, by thee, that
it may be one witnesse of my promise toward thee.[1]

God directly pledges to John Dee, through his mes-
senger the angel Ave and through Dee's scryer Edward
Kelley, that the system of magic being revealed to Dee
is the genuine wisdom of Enoch by which may be had
"the use of the earth." The one hundred and fifty lions,
"spirits of wickednesse, errour, and deceit" are the
same fallen angels who, in the *Book of Enoch*, sin with
mortal women and teach corrupting sciences to
humankind. According to Ave, this false teaching consisted mainly of demonic magic, or goety.

It is common for the proponents of a system of reli-
gion, philosophy, or magic to claim that theirs is the only
legitimate practice, and that all methods that differ from
it are corrupting and false. By slandering other forms of
magic the angels hope to elevate their own teachings and
give them a greater importance in Dee's eyes.

Kelley, who before his association with Dee had considerable firsthand knowledge of necromancy and other
forms of black magic, tells Ave that the wisdom of Enoch
seems very like common magic to him, but Ave assures
Kelley, "Nay, they all played at this,"[2] meaning that all
forms of magic other than Enochian magic are mere
playthings—that Enochian magic is the only true theurgy
approved by God and accepted by the angels of heaven.

THE GATES AND THE KEYS

It is important to understand that Enochian magic is solely
concerned with the ritual summoning and command of
angels and lesser spirits. When speaking about the formal
Enochian evocations known as the Calls or Keys, the angel
Mapsama tells Dee:

These Calls touch all the parts of the World. The World may be dealt withall, with her parts; Therefore you may do anything. These Calls are the keyes into the Gates and Cities of wisdom. Which Gates are not able to be opened, but with visible apparition.[3]

The gates to the cities of wisdom are forty-nine in number. However, one of the gates is too holy to be opened, so the actual Keys number forty-eight. The cities of wisdom are spiritual realms inhabited by different hierarchies of angels with distinct functions on the earth. These heavenly cities are represented by forty-nine extremely complex number/letter squares that contain forty-nine rows and forty-nine columns. Taken together, the angels refer to these squares as the *Book of Enoch*. One of the squares is represented in a plate at the beginning of Meric Casaubon's *A True and Faithful Relation*. Concerning these magic squares, Nalvage tells Dee:

You have 49 Tables: In those Tables are contained the mystical and holy voices of the Angels: dignified: and in state disglorified and drent in confusion: which pierceth Heaven, and looketh into the Center of the Earth: the very language and speech of Children and Innocents, such as magnifie the name of God, and are pure.[4]

The forty-nine tables do not play a direct part in Enochian magic. They serve as the chaotic ground from which the words of the Keys were drawn letter by tortuous letter during the scrying sessions. Kelley would watch in the crystal as an angel pointed to one cell or another of the relevent table, then call out the position of the cell to Dee, who would then look up the cell in his copy of the table and write down the letter he found there. The Keys were delivered in this way, backwards and one letter at a time.

The occult energies of these tables are embodied collectively in a single letter table with four quadrants called the Great Table. It is a magical schematic diagram of the Enochian universe. Each quadrant on the Great Table is known as a Watchtower. The Keys open the gates to the cities of the angels whose names are written in the Watchtowers and call them forth, along with their numerous servants. Taken together, the forty-eight Keys and the Great Table of the four Watchtowers form the heart of Enochian magic.

THE BOOK OF SILVERED LEAVES

There is another book spoken about by the angels that is undoubtedly connected with the book of magic squares. Dee is directed to construct it with blank leaves in preparation to receive the writing of the angels. They will inscribe the book directly during the initial ritual working that will establish contact with the Enochian hierarchies:

Mapsama: Bind up together, 48 leaves; whose skin shall bear Silver: Whose Perimeter shall be 30 inches: in length, 8; in breadth 7.

Dee: do you require it to be parchment, or paper?

Mapsama: I have said.

Dee: What shall I, then, do, after I have caused 48 leaves to be bound?...

Mapsama: The fourteenth day of your rest, even this Table-Cloth, and none other shall be spread for a Banket. Whereunto, you shall invite the Angels of the Lord: In the middest of the Table lay down the book and go forth; make also the doors after you. That the heavens may justifie your faith, and you may be comforted. For, man is not worthy to write that shall be written: neither shall there be found many worthy to open book.[5]

The Book of Spirits is a common feature of medieval angel magic.[6] It contains the names, sigils, and occasionally images of the spirits who are bound in service to the magician—usually after an involved and intense ritual working that achieves the initial evocation of the spirits.

The spirits write the book themselves, sign it with their marks and signatures, or at the least swear obedience to it. Of course, spirits are not actually capable of writing in the book. This is accomplished by possessing the magician without his or her awareness and using the body of the magician to write or sign the Book of Spirits.

In Dee's case, the angels of the forty-eight spiritual cities that may be opened by the Keys are to be represented by occult symbols that probably contained letter and number combinations. However, we will never know what the Book of Silvered Leaves was intended to contain since Dee's copy, if he ever made it, was not inscribed by the angels and has not survived. These mysterious signs were to be inscribed on silvered parchment by the potent Mother of many of the Enochian angels, a being so exalted she identifies herself only with the title I AM, which is equivalent to the Hebrew name of God, Eheieh. She appears to be the same angel as the Queen of Heaven of *Revelation* 12:1.

THE ENOCHIAN WORKING

The inscription of Dee's Book of Silvered Leaves was to occur after an eighteen-day period of ritual working during which an original evocation composed by Dee and Kelley was to be spoken on each day. For the first four days of the working, Dee was instructed by Ave to address his evocation only to the names of God; for the following fourteen days Dee should evoke the hierarchies of angels by the specific names of God that rule each:

> Four dayes ... must you onely call upon those names of God, or on the God of Hosts, in those names:
>
> And 14 dayes after you shall (in this, or some convenient place) Call the Angels by Petition, and by the name of God, unto the which they are obedient.
>
> The 15 day you shall Cloath your selves, in vestures made of linnen, white: and so have the apparition, use, and practice of the Creatures. For, it is not a labour of years, nor many dayes.[7]

The Creatures that Ave refers to would seem to be the angels of the Thirty Aethers or Airs, who are represented by the last thirty Keys. These keys are really a single call or summons to thirty different angelic zones or spheres called Aethers. Only the names of the Aethers change in the last thirty Keys—they are otherwise identical. For this reason, the nineteenth Key is known as the Key of the Thirty Aethers. The Princes of the Aethers rule over the lesser spirits of the regions or kingdoms of the world. It was these geographical spirits that Dee most wanted to control.

About the robes and the book used during this working, Ave says: "You must never use the Garment after, but that once only, neither the book." Kelley quite reasonably objects: "To what end is the book made then, if it be not to be used after." Dee somewhat testily reproves Kelley: "It is made for to be used that day onely."[8]

There is some ambiguity here about which book is being discussed. Kelley means the book of names and invocations that he and Dee are ordered to create themselves. About this workbook, which I will call Dee's Book of Spirits, Ave tells Dee: "The Book consisteth [1] of Invocation of the names of God, and [2] of the

Angels, by the names of God: Their offices are manifest."[9] This would seem to have a function throughout the eighteen days of the working, and perhaps thereafter. Dee actually created the model for this Book of Spirits invoking the names of God and the angels. It forms Dee's manuscript *Liber Scientiae Auxilii et Victoriae Terrestris,* which still exists and is kept in the British Library.

The angel Ave probably means the book of blank, silvered leaves that is to be supernaturally inscribed by his Mother. This Book of Silver would be used only on the single day the angels pledged obedience to Dee. The silvering of the leaves suggests that the Mother of the angels is a lunar goddess, and that Enochian magic is lunar in nature. Monday (the day of the Moon) appears to be the Enochian sabbath.[10]

ENOCHIAN MAGIC FORBIDDEN TO DEE AND KELLEY

There is no evidence that Dee and Kelley ever conducted this working to initiate the power of the Enochian angels. They were waiting for permission to do so from the angels, but that permission was never granted.

> *Mapsama:* You called for wisdom, God hath opened unto you, his Judgement: He hath delivered unto you the keyes, that you may enter; But be humble. Enter not of presumption, but of permission. Go not in rashly; But be brought in willingly: For, many have ascended, but few have entered. By Sunday you shall have all things that are necessary to be taught; then (as occasion serveth) you may practice at all times. But you being called by God, and to a good purpose.

> Dee: How shall we understand this Calling by God?
> Mapsama: God stoppeth my mouth, I will answer thee no more.[11]

It is evident to me from a close study of the Enochian transcripts that the angels intended Dee to have the system of Enochian magic, but never intended to permit him to actually use it. Dee and Kelley served as human instruments through which the angels were able to transmit Enochian magic to the human race. Gabriel tells Dee and Kelley, "But in you two is figured the time to come."[12] The angels assure Dee and Kelley that they will continue to prosper and be secure for as long as they remain together, because they are two parts of a single whole. "The Seer let him see, and look after the doing of him that he seeth; For you are but one body in this work."[13]

Kelley has been granted the gift of second sight solely so that he can assist Dee in receiving Enochian magic.

> Shall a dark seller brag or boast of her beauty? because she receiveth light and cleernesse, by a Candle brought into, or shinning into her.
> No more canst thou, [E.K.] for the ripennesse of thy wit and understanding is through the presence of us, and our illumination.
> But if we depart, thou shalt become a dark seller, and shall think too well of thy self in vain.[14]

Elsewhere the angel Uriel, speaking in the voice of God, tells Kelley: "I will make thee a great Seer: Such an one, as shall judge the Circle of things in nature. But heavenly understanding, and spiritual knowledge shall be sealed up from thee in this world."[15] Kelley is regarded by the angels as little more than a psychic telephone through which they may reach the conscious mind of John Dee. The angels barely tolerate his suspicions and verbal abuse. They know that Kelley detests them and considers them to be deceivers.

The angels respect Dee for his great piety and wisdom, but even he will not be permitted to attain the full understanding of Enochian magic. The angel Gabriel tells Dee this, and makes further reference to the necessity of Dee and Kelley remaining together as one organic unit (even to the extent of sharing their wives in common, a future event foreshadowed here):

> "Thou shalt never know the mysteries of all things that have been spoken. If you love together, and dwell together, and in one God; Then the self-same God will be merciful unto you: Which bless you, comfort you, and strengthen you unto the end."[16]

Dee and Kelley were two halves of a human machine for receiving and recording the mysteries of the angelic communications. Kelley had the ability to perceive the angels and their teachings. Dee had the intelligence to understand and transcribe them accurately, and to correct any errors that occurred during their transmission. Neither man could have generated the system of Enochian magic alone. Each acted as a catalyst to the other.

CHAPTER TWO

John Dee and Edward Kelley

AN UNLIKELY PARTNERSHIP

To understand the origin of Enochian magic, it is necessary to know something about the strange partnership from which it germinated. There has never been a more unlikely pairing of personalities than Dee and Kelley. They were as different as day and night. Yet they shared an irresistible fascination for the forbidden wisdom of the angels.

Dee sought the teaching as an instrument through which he could serve his nation and revolutionize human knowledge. Kelley single-mindedly pursued the secret of alchemical transformation that would give him personal wealth and power. Each man needed the other to make his dream a reality. Although they often disagreed, they remained throughout their years together, and for many years after, genuine friends.

"MY UBIQUITOUS EYES"

John Dee (1527–1608) was the elder of the two men by twenty-eight years. His father, Rowland Dee, a minor and relatively poor nobleman of Welsh descent, worked as a Gentleman Server in the household of King Henry VIII.

This office consisted of supervising the royal kitchens and carving the meat at the King's table. The young Dee was brought up to be proud of his remote blood connection with the ancient Welsh kings.

Early in life Dee showed a precocious talent for mathematics. At age fifteen he became a student at St. John's College at the University of Cambridge. He excelled at scholarship and pursued it with a fanatical zeal, writing: "in the yeares 1543, 1544 and 1545 I was so vehementlie bent to studie that for those yeares I did inviolably keep this order: only to sleep four houres every night; to allow to meate and drink (and some refreshing after) two houres every day; and of the other eighteen houres all (except the time of going to and being at divine service) was spent in my studies and learning."[1]

In 1546 he graduated Bachelor of Arts from St. John's College, and later in the same year became one of the original Fellows of Trinity College, newly founded by Henry VIII. Although he earned his Master of Arts degree from Trinity, and subsequently won great acclaim for his studies and lectures at the universities of Louvaine and Paris, there is no evidence that he was ever awarded a doctorate from any university in Europe. The "Doctor" attached to his name may have been an honorary title.

It was during his graduate years at Trinity that he first acquired the label of "sorcerer" that was to follow him throughout his life. For a student production of Aristophanes' play *Peace* he contrived a mechanical flying beetle that carried one of the actors up into the air. The stage mechanism was so well designed that many in the audience thought Dee had achieved the effect through supernatural means.

When Elizabeth came to the throne in 1559, it was Dee who astrologically chose the date for her coronation.

Dee was later summoned to investigate a waxen witch doll in the image of the Queen found in Lincoln's Inn Fields with a great pin thrust through its heart. Throughout her life, Elizabeth maintained the highest respect and affection for Dee—although this seldom translated into desirable political appointments or lavish gifts.

In part, the Queen's favor was repayment for Dee's loyalty to her during her house arrest under Bloody Mary Tudor. Dee once showed Elizabeth a horoscope he had cast for Queen Mary and compared it unfavorably with Elizabeth's own horoscope. This imprudent act caused him to be denounced as a sorcerer by one of Mary's spies and arrested. He was tried for treason, but was acquitted due to lack of evidence. This shared persecution by Mary bonded him more closely to Elizabeth.

But there was no condescension in Elizabeth's attitude toward Dee, who at the time was widely regarded as the foremost bright young man in England. He was skilled in Latin, Greek, and Hebrew, knowledgeable in medicine, a gifted mathematician, a philosopher, a practical astronomer as well as an astrologer, a historian, and a respected author. He had studied cartography and navigation under Gerhardus Mercator and was responsible for introducing some of the latest scientific instruments into England. During his trips to the Continent while a university student he had garnered great acclaim as a public lecturer.

Precisely what Elizabeth's true relationship with Dee may have entailed is not known for certain, but there is evidence that he acted as an espionage agent for the Queen during his Continental travels. Elizabeth referred to Dee as "My Noble Intelligencer" and "my Ubiquitous Eyes."[2] It is only coincidence, but a very curious one, that Dee signed his letters to the Queen with the symbols 007.[3]

Dee also instructed the Queen in arcane matters. Besides teaching her astrology and astronomy, he gave her private lessons in the mysteries of his 1564 work *The Hieroglyphic Monad* at her own request. After revealing the secret keys of the *Monad* to Elizabeth, Dee records in his diary her reaction: "Whereupon her Majestie had a little perusion of the same with me, and then in most heroicall and princely wise did comfort and encourage me in my studies philosophicall and mathematicall."[4]

Dee acted as her astrological counselor in personal and state affairs, and probably erected protective barriers for her against occult attacks. Elizabeth thought so highly of Dee she defended his reputation against those in her court who criticized him during his absence from England. She privately assured Dee that he should feel free to continue with any magical experiments he chose, regardless of their nature—that there would be no danger of prosecution during her reign.

Dee was among the greatest social and political visionaries of the Elizabethan Age. He encouraged the quest for a Northwest Passage and supplied geographical and navigational resources to such English explorers as Drake and Frobisher. He promoted the concepts of a strong English navy to counter the dominance of Spain and foresaw a globe-spanning British Empire. He delved deeply into the genealogical history of the Tudors to prove that Elizabeth had legal claims to lands in the New World. He promoted the reform of the English calendar. When Elizabeth made no effort to carry forward the proposal he had made to Mary for founding a national library, Dee proceeded to amass his own library. At one stage, this became the largest collection of scientific and philosophical books and manuscripts in England. The biographer John Aubrey called Dee "one of the ornaments of his age."

The Quest for the Red Powder

Edward Kelley (1555–1597) was born at Worcester the same year that John Dee faced charges of treason in the court of the Star Chamber. We know this because Dee cast Kelley's horoscope. The events of Kelley's life are uncertain. He is said to have served as an apothecary's apprentice,[5] perhaps under his own father. His true family name may have been Talbot, and he may have attended Oxford University for a short period around the age of seventeen before leaving "under a cloud."[6]

The rumors surrounding his early life are unsavory. He is reported to have been pilloried at Lancaster, either for forging land title deeds or coining (counterfeiting). He is also supposed to have had his ears cropped (that is, cut off) as punishment for one or the other of these crimes, although there is no real evidence to support this story. Perhaps two separate incidents were involved.

However, he is most notorious for having, in the company of his friend Paul Waring, dug up the corpse of a pauper buried in the graveyard of Walton-le-Dale church in the county of Lancashire and invoked the spirit of the dead man to inquire into the future prospects of a young nobleman. There is reason to believe this necromancy actually took place, particularly since Kelley later admitted to Dee a knowledge of goetic magic.

It may have been the unfavorable notoriety surrounding this desecration that forced Kelley to abandon his profession as legal scribe and set out on an extended visit to Wales. While walking through Wales, as the story goes,[7] Kelley bought from an innkeeper two caskets containing the white and red powders of alchemy and an alchemical manuscript titled the *Book of St. Dunstan*. The innkeeper is supposed to have obtained these powders from tomb robbers who stole them from the crypt of a Catholic bishop. When properly used, the white powder turned base metal into silver and the red powder turned base metal into gold.

There is another version of the story that asserts that Kelley and Dee went together to Glastonbury, and that this was the site where Kelley discovered the powders and the book.[8] This fanciful tale derives from Elias Ashmole, who wrote:

> 'Tis generally reported that Doctor Dee, and Sir Edward Kelly were so strangely fortunate, as to finde a very large quantity of the Elixir in some part of the Ruines of Glastenbury-Abbey, which was so incredibly Rich in vertue (being one upon 272330.) that they lost much in making Projection, by way of Triall; before they found out the true height of the Medicine.[9]

The elixir of life is here confused with the red powder of projection. The meaning of Ashmole is that one part of the powder could convert 272,330 parts of base metal into pure gold. About this romantic excursion of Dee and Kelley to Glastonbury, Charlotte Fell Smith comments: "Another version of this discovery is that Dee and Kelley together found the powder at Glastonbury. This we may dismiss."[10]

I am inclined to dismiss both versions of the story. The only certainty is that when Kelley arrived at the house of John Dee at Mortlake, he had in his possession both an alchemical manuscript that he referred to as the *Book of Dunstan* and a small quantity of what he sincerely believed was the red powder of projection.

Alchemy was Kelley's lifelong passion. He probably became interested in the subject as a young child while watching his father mix medicinal remedies with mortar and pestle. There is a natural connection between the desire to manufacture alchemical gold and the crime of coining, which involved counterfeiting silver or gold coins with adulterated metals. Kelley was drawn to John Dee for one purpose only—to learn how to decipher the meaning of his *Book of Dunstan* and manufacture more of the miraculous red powder.

THE COMING OF THE ANGELS

As can be seen from these narrations, Dee and Kelley had almost nothing in common. Dee was a nobleman, a scholar, a nationalist, a visionary, an agent of the Queen, and a man noted for his extraordinary goodness and piety. Kelley was a commoner, a forger, a coiner and a necromancer. His world was the murky realm of under-the-table dealings and trickery. He acknowledged loyalty to no one but himself.

Yet Kelley was not, at root, evil. He was merely a romantic dreamer who longed to unearth arcane secrets for his own betterment. He was drawn like a man entranced by the siren spell of magic. This lust to unlock the hidden secrets of the spirit world he shared with Dee. Kelley sought them for his own personal gain, while Dee sought them for the benefit of his Queen and his nation—but both hunted the same prize. Neither could know at that first meeting that their destinies had already been shaped by the Enochian angels, and were inextricably entwined.

Kelley arrived at Mortlake on March 8, 1582. He was introduced to Dee by a mutual friend named Clerkson. Kelley called himself Edward Talbot, and this may well have been his real name. Dee's fame, and that of his personal library, had by this time spread throughout Europe. Scholars frequently traveled to Mortlake from far places to consult with him or study his books. Their relationship might have ended after only a few days or weeks, but Kelley possessed a talent that Dee sorely needed—the gift of second sight.

> One Mr. Edward Talbot cam to my howse, and he being willing and desirous to see or shew some thing in spirituall practise, wold have had me to have done some thing therein. And I truely excused my self therein, as not in that, vulgarly accounted Magic, neyther studied, or exercised. But confessed my self long tyme to have byn desyrous to have help in my philosophicall studies through the Company and information of the blessed Angels of God.[11]

Dee was greatly preoccupied with the spirit world. Precisely one year before Kelley's arrival he had been troubled by a strange knocking in his bedroom. This visitation made so strong an impression, he recorded it in his personal diary:

> March 8th, [1581] it was the 8 day, being Wensday, hora noctis 10, 11, the strange noyse in my chamber of knocking; and the voyce, ten tymes repeted, somewhat like the shrich of an owle, but more longly drawn, and more softly, as it were in my chamber.[12]

This was not an isolated incident. Elsewhere in the same year Dee records: "Aug. 3rd, all the night very strange knocking and rapping in my chamber. Aug. 4th, and this night likewise."[13]

Dee became convinced that these spirit noises were an attempt to communicate with him. He began to scry into a crystal globe, and had some limited success. On May 25, 1581, he wrote, "I had sight in chrystallo offered me, and I saw."[14] He was a cautious man, even in the bounds of his own house and in the pages of his private diary—"chrystallo" is written in Greek. Unfortunately,

Dee was a terrible seer. He acknowledged this himself on a number of occasions.

"HIM THAT IS ASSIGNED THE STONE"

Almost immediately after these spirit rappings started, he began to employ a man of dubious reputation named Barnabas Saul as his private scryer. Saul is said to have been a "licensed preacher"[15] who professed abilities as a spirit medium. On October 8, 1581, Dee records: "I had newes of the chests of bokes fownd by Owndle in Northamptonshyre; Mr. Barnabas Sawle told me of them, but I fownd no truth in it," and directly after, "Oct. 9th, Barnabas Saul, lying in the ... hall was strangely trubled by a spirituall creature abowt midnight."[16]

What Charlotte Fell Smith calls the "first real *seance*" between Dee and Saul occurred December 21, 1581. Its content is almost chilling for the way it fore-shadows the coming union between Dee and Kelley:

> The scryer was bidden to look into the "great crystalline globe," and a message was transmitted by the angel Annael through the precipient to the effect that many things should be declared to Dee, not by the present worker, "but by him that is assigned the stone."[17]

In February of 1582, an attempt was made to indict Saul on some unknown charge at Westminster Hall in London. It seems probable this charge was one of sorcery, since on March 6 Saul tells Dee that he "neyther hard or saw any spirituall creature any more."[18] If Saul was under the watchful eye of the Church, it is unlikely he would continue with his scrying. On the other hand, the task of scrying for Dee was just about to pass from Saul to Kelley, and it may be that the Enochian angels withdrew their support of Saul and shifted it to Kelley as their preferred instrument.

Kelley immediately set about poisoning the waters for Saul. Whether this was a conscious attempt to gain employment as Dee's seer or an honest account of his psychic visions cannot be known, but the day after his arrival at Mortlake Kelley began to give evil reports about Saul's motives.

> March 9th, Fryday at dynner tyme Mr. Clerkson and Mr. Talbot declared a great deale of Barnabas nowghty dealing toward me, as in telling Mr. Clerkson ill things of me that I should mak his frend, as that he was wery of me, that I wold so flatter his frende the lerned man [Kelley] that I wold borow him of him. But his frend told me, before my wife and Mr. Clerkson, that a spirituall creature told him that Barnabas had censured both Mr. Clerkson and me. The injuries which this Barnabas had done me diverse wayes were very great.[19]

The results obtained by Kelley scrying in the crystal were so spectacular that Dee immediately gave up all interest in having any other seer. The men continued to work together in the closest association both in England and on the Continent until 1587, when they at last began to drift apart, separating completely in 1589. Dee heeded the command of Queen Elizabeth and returned to England, leaving Kelley to continue trying to manufacture gold for Emperor Rudolph II in Bohemia.

This rupture was Kelley's doing, not the work of Dee. Kelley died in a fall attempting to escape his imprisonment in one of Rudolph's castles. Until the day he learned of Kelley's death, Dee always hoped to be reunited with his seer and continued to refer to him as "my good friend."

CHAPTER THREE

In the Thrall of the Angels

THE CARROT AND THE STICK

During the years Dee and Kelley spent together, the Enochian angels exerted a profound effect on the lives of the two men and on the lives of their families. Indeed, from the night Dee first heard the rapping of the spirits in his bedroom, he became their unknowing instrument. Kelley was drawn into their hidden purposes the day he met Dee at Mortlake. It is frequently speculated that Kelley manipulated Dee for his private reasons, feeding him false visions that aided Kelly's pursuit of the secret of the red powder. This is not supported by Kelley's attitude toward the angels, one of mistrust and loathing.

In the fall of 1583, Dee and Kelley left England in the company of a Polish nobleman named Count Albert Laski, Palatine of Saradia. Laski had first visited Mortlake on March 18 that same year seeking arcane wisdom, and was soon pulled into the Enochian communications. The angels predicted great political advancement for Laski, who quite naturally was flattered and excited by the prospect of gaining the Polish crown. However, on July 2 the speech of the angels took a menacing turn:

> *Madimi:* The Lord Treasurer and he [Walsingham] are joyned together, and they hate thee. I heard them when

they both said, thou wouldst go mad shortly: Whatsoever they can do against thee, assure thy self of. They will shortly lay a bait for thee; but eshew them.

Dee: Lord have mercy upon me: what bait, (I beseech you) and by whom?

Madimi: They have determined to search thy house: But they stay untill the Duke [Laski] be gone.

Dee: What would they search it for?

Madimi: They hate the Duke, (both) unto the death....

Dee: Lord, what is thy counsel to prevent all?

Madimi: The speech is general, The wicked shall not prevail.

Dee: But will they enter to search my house, or no?

Madimi: Immediately after the Duke his going they will.

Dee: To what intent? What do they hope to finde?

Madimi: They suspect the Duke is inwardly a Traytor.

Dee: They can by no means charge me, no not for so much as of a Trayterous thought.

Madimi: Though thy thoughts be good, they cannot comprehend the doings of the wicked. In summe, they hate thee. Trust them not...

Dee: I pray you make more plain your counsel.

Madimi: My counsel is plain enough.

Dee: When, I prey you, is the Duke likely to go away?

Madimi: In the middle of August.

Dee: If in the midst of August he will go, and then our practises be yet in hand, what shall be done with such our [ritual] furniture is prepared, and standing in the Chamber of practise?

Madimi: Thou hast no faith. His going standeth upon the determined purpose of God. He is your friend greatly, and intendeth to do much for you. He is prepared to do thee good, and thou art prepared to do him service.[1]

Neither Dee nor Kelley had any wish to leave England, but they were manipulated into doing so by the carrot and stick of the angels. They thought they would be serving God and would gain worldly benefit if they accompanied Laski, but that Dee would be arrested for treason if he remained at Mortlake. The threat to Dee was completely false, but he believed it. Throughout his life he suffered from a persecution mania. He was always ready to believe that men in high places plotted against him. Kelley's fortunes were bound up with Dee, his employer. He hoped to use Dee to help him, through the revelations of the angels, to discover the making of the red powder. Since Dee was determined to leave England, Kelley felt compelled go with him.

The angels have little to say about how Dee is to find the money to close up his house and move his wife, children and servants to Poland, although he asks them with a tone that borders on desperation:

> Dee: Because it hath been said, that in the beginning of our Country troubles we should be packing hence into his [Laski's] Country; What token shall we have of that time approaching, or at hand?
> Madimi: Your watchword is told you before: When it is said unto you, Venite, &.
> Dee: But (I beseech you) to be ready against that watchword, hearing what is to be done, as concerning our wives and children into his Country.
> Madimi: Miraculous is thy care (O God) upon those that are thy chosen, and wonderful are the wayes that thou hast prepared for them.[2]

KELLEY BETAKES HIMSELF TO THE WORLD

Kelley had already experienced the manipulations of the angels in his private life. When he first met Dee, he was a bachelor. On April 29, 1582, the angel Michael commanded him to betake himself "to the world." Explaining this curious commandment to Dee, Kelley says: "It is that I shall marry, which thing to do I have no natural inclination, neither with a safe conscience may I do it contrary to my vow and profession."[3] Presumably, he referred to the vow of celibacy and the profession of alchemy. On May 4 Dee records of the angels, "they willed him [Kelley] to marry."

The angels had their way. Kelley married a nineteen-year-old named Joanna (or Joan) Cooper, a girl from Chipping Norton—a town near Oxford that Richard Deacon calls "one of the most notorious haunts of witchcraft in England in Tudor times."[4] Kelley must have known this girl previous to the command of the angels that he wed, and it may be conjectured that she shared some of his occult interests, although there is no evidence that this was their common bond. Francesco Pucci, writing to Dee in 1586, described Joanna Kelley as "a rare example of youthful holiness, chastity and all the virtues."[5]

Since Kelley had never wanted the marriage, it quickly became unbearable to him. On July 4, 1583, Kelley admitted in a rage to Dee: "I cannot abide my wife, I love her not, nay I abhor her; and there in the house I am misliked, because I favour her no better."[6] After Kelley stormed out of Dee's house, Dee remarked to his own wife, "Jane, this man is marvallously out of quiet against his Wife, for her friends their bitter reports against him behind his back, and her silence thereat, &."[7] This row was smoothed over, but the unwanted marriage was never really happy.

IN THE TONGUE OF ANGELS

Besides compelling Dee and Kelley to move all over central Europe for the next several years, the angels cast Dee into the unwilling role of prophet. He was to travel about and meet with the great leaders of Poland and Bohemia and declare the teachings of the angels. It mattered little to the angels that those teachings were heretical.

Very much against his desire and better judgment, they compelled him to seek out an audience with the Emperor Rudolph II at Prague on September 3, 1584, and to deliver a lecture on morals. That he did so showed great courage, since the power of Rudolph was almost absolute, and Dee's magical activities were of a kind likely to get him burned at the stake for witchcraft. Rudolph must have been a remarkably patient man, restraining himself as Dee declared to him:

> The Angel of the Lord hath appeared to me, and rebuketh you for your sins. If you will hear me, and believe me, you shall Triumph: If you will not hear me, The Lord, the God that made Heaven and Earth, (under whom you breath, and have your spirit) putteth his foot against your breast, and will throw you headlong down from your seat.
>
> Moreover, the Lord hath made this Covenant with me (by oath) that he will do and perform. If you will forsake your wickednesse, and turn unto him, your Seat shall be the greatest that ever was: and the Devil shall become your prisoner: Which Devil, I did conjecture, to be the Great Turk, (said I) This my Commission, is from God: I feigne nothing, neither am I an Hypocrite, an Ambitious man, or doting, or dreaming in this Cause.[8]

It is easy to imagine the sheer astonishment of Rudolph at the crazy audacity of Dee in saying such things to his face. Perhaps he dismissed Dee as a madman. Dee was unable to secure future audiences, even though the angel Uriel ordered Dee to write to Rudolph saying he possessed the secret of the Philosopher's Stone, which he would reveal to the Emperor at their next meeting. Rudolph sent one of his spies, a Doctor Curtz (or Kurtz) to find out more details about the magic used by Dee and Kelley and to obtain Dee's diaries of the scrying sessions and Dee's crystal. Fortunately, Dee was cautious enough not to send his books and instruments to the Emperor.

When the angels ordered Dee and Kelley to go from Prague to Cracow to meet with the Polish king Stephen Bathori, Dee hesitated until after he received letters from Laski inviting him to Cracow. The angels were furious that Dee should doubt their command, and cursed him:

> When the Lord bad thee go, if thou had'st so done, and had'st not taken thine own time, more had been given unto him [Laski], and more had been added unto thee.
>
> But now Letters came, that have passed through the hands of Sodomites and Murderers, (through whose hands they are accursed,) you rejoice, you receive comfort, you determine to goe.
>
> But if you had left those letters behind you, had come when I bad you go. Then had my Name been untouched.
>
> Therefore is the Lord angry, and forgetteth not this offense.
>
> For he that dealeth with me, dealeth not as with a man, for I have nothing in me tied to time, much lesse hath he that sent me.[9]

The angels then cursed Dee and his children for five generations because of his slowness in obeying their command. Utterly terrified, Dee begged that the curse be lifted, crying: "Lord, I am heartily sorry, I bewaile with teares this great offence, thou seest my contrite heart, O God, O God, O God." Apparently, this groveling worked. Dee was greatly relieved as the angels lifted the curse.

> After this we [Dee and Kelley] sat and considered, and perceived, and confessed the greatnesse of our offence, how it concerned much the Honour and Glory of God, if we had gone without receiving the advertisement of those Letters; So should they hear (the [Polish nobles]) and the King St[ephen] have perceived that we had the direction of God, and of his good Angels, and not to have depended upon mans letters, or perswasions...[10]

"USE THEM IN COMMON"

The strangest and most interesting example of the authority exerted by the Enochian angels over Dee and Kelley is the infamous wife-swapping affair. In the spring of 1587, Kelley grew increasingly reluctant to scry into the stone. He wanted to turn all his efforts to alchemy, and advised Dee to employ his eldest son Arthur as seer. Several times in their relationship he had threatened to leave Dee in Bohemia and return alone to England, but this time he was emphatic. Dee reluctantly tested the seven-year-old Arthur as a scryer.

The boy proved completely unfit for the job. Dee begged Kelley to resume his duties, and Kelley allowed himself to be persuaded. He confessed the real reason for his latest dislike of the angels. They had ordered him to inform Dee that he and Dee should use their wives in common. They told him that if he refused this command, he was free to cease all communications with them.

When the angel Madimi appeared to Kelley after young Arthur's failed attempt to scry, Kelley was incensed:

> Madimi openeth all her apparel, and her self all naked; and sheweth her shame also.
> *E.K.:* Fie on thee, Devil avoid hence with this filthiness, &.
> *Madimi:* In the Name of God, why finde you fault with mee?
> *Dee:* Because your yesterdayes doings, and words are provocations to sin, and unmeet for any godly creature to use.
> *Madimi:* What is sin?
> *Dee:* To break the Commandement of God.
> *Madimi:* Set that down, so. If the self-same God give you a new Commandement taking away the former form of sin which he limited by the Law; What remaineth then?[11]

At first Dee would not believe that the command was intended in a carnal sense. Kelley knew better.

I was glad that an offer was made of being every seventh day to be taught the secrets of the books already delivered unto us: Thinking that it was easie for us to perform that unity which was required to be amongst us four; understanding all after the Christian and godly sense. But E.K. who had yesterday seen and heard another meaning of this unity required, utterly abhorred to have any dealings with them farther, and did intend to accept at their hands the liberty of leaving off to deal with them any more..."[12]

Dee required some clear proof that the angels really did intend that each should have intercourse with the other's wife. The command appeared written in Latin on a white crucifix. Dee was shocked. The faith he had placed in the angels seemed to crumble away beneath his feet.

Hereupon we were in great amazement and grief of minde, that so hard, and (as it, yet seemed unto me) so unpure a Doctrine, was popounded and enjoyned unto us of them, whom I alwayes (from the beginning hitherto) did judge and esteem, undoubtedly, to be good Angels: And had unto E.K. offered my soul as a pawn, to discharge E.K. his crediting of them, as the good and faithful Ministers of Almighty God. But now, my heart was sore afflicted upon many causes: And E.K. had (as he thought) now, a just and sufficient cause, to forsake dealing with them any more.[13]

It did not take Dee long to reconcile himself to this strange doctrine, however. That same night when he left Kelley and went to his bedroom he discovered his wife lying awake, waiting to hear the latest teachings of the angels. "I then told her, and said, Jane, I see that there is no other remedy, but as hath been said of our cross-matching, so it must needs be done. Thereupon she fell a weeping and trembling for a quarter of an hour: And I pacified her as well as I could; and so, in the fear of God, and in believing of his Admonishment, did perswade her that she shewed herself prettily resolved to be content for God his sake and his secret Purposes, to obey the Admonishment."[14]

The four signed a solemn covenant on April 18, 1587. They agreed to "this most new and strange doctrine" and enjoined the angels to fulfill their part of the bargain and deliver the final teachings in Enochian magic as they had promised. They pledged: "we will for thy sake herein captivate and tread under foot all our humane timorous doubting of any inconvenience which shall or may fall upon us, or follow us (in this world, or in the world to come) in respect, or by reason of our embracing of this Doctrine..."[15]

In return, they expected the angels to reward them for their obedience. Dee writes:

> Now it was by the women as by our selves thought necessary to understand the will of God and his good pleasure, Whether this Covenant and form of words performed, is and will be acceptable, and according to the well liking of his Divine Majesty: And that hereupon, the act of corporal knowledge being performed on both our parts, it will please his Divine Majesty to seal and warrant unto us most certainly and speedily all his Divine, Merciful and bountiful Promises and Blessings; and also promises us wisdome, knowledge, ability and power to execute his justice, and declare and demonstrate his infallible verity amongst men, to his honour and glory.[16]

How long the four continued in their communal marriage is not known. The account of the wife-swapping Covenant is almost the final incident recorded concerning the occult partnership between Dee and Kelley. It has been speculated that the cross-matching was unsuccessful, but there seems no basis for this belief, other than the fact that Kelley and Dee drifted apart soon after the Covenant was signed. However, the reason for this may have been Kelley's growing acclaim as an alchemist, which caused him to spend more time in the company of the Emperor Rudolph and other Bohemian nobility. Kelley put on a good enough show for Rudolph to persuade the King to give him the title *eques auratus*, which in England was later interpreted as a knighthood. Dee referred to Kelley as a "Baron of the Kingdom of Bohemia."[17]

It might be speculated that if the angels fulfilled the promises made to the two men, Kelley was gifted with the ability to manufacture the genuine red powder, at least for a short period. As fanciful as this notion may be, it would explain Kelley's sudden success as an alchemist. Dee's eldest son, Arthur, always maintained in later life that he had actually seen Kelley make gold in Bohemia,[18] and had played on the floor with the new gold bars. Whatever the truth, Kelley enjoyed a sudden fame and wealth in Bohemia that attracted the attention of the Emperor.

There is no record of how Joanna Kelley felt about the cross-matching arrangement, but she was probably just as horrified as the other three partners. The exchange of wives (or husbands, depending on how you look at it) was carried out only because of the great gifts of knowledge and power promised by the angels if Dee and Kelley would, once and for all, prove their faith. There is little evidence to suggest that lust was the motivating factor, at least on the part of the human beings involved.

A GNOSTIC UNION?

It is common for modern critics to regard the whole affair as a trick by Kelley to sleep with Jane Dee. They say the incident is out of character with the rest of the

Enochian communications, that Kelley was deeply unhappy with his own wife, and perhaps infatuated with Jane Dee. This is to view the matter from a jaded, modern perspective which dismisses the sanctity of the marriage vow. Adultery was a serious crime in Elizabethan times, particularly to those men and women who considered themselves good Christians.

I see no reason to suspect that Kelley is any less sincere in his expression of horror than Dee or his wife. As for it being out of character for the angels, they had previously delivered several radical doctrines to Kelley that can only be described as Gnostic, or at least non-Christian:

  – That Jesus was not God.
  – That no prayer ought to be made to Jesus.
  – That there is no sin.
  – That mans soul doth go from one body, to another childes quickening or animation.
  – That as many men and women as are now, have always been: That is, so many humane bodies, and humane souls, neither more nor lesse, as are now, have alwayes been.
  – That the generation of mankind from Adam and Eve, is not an History, but a writing which hath an other sense.
  – No Holy Ghost they acknowledged.
  – They would not suffer him to pray to Jesus Christ; but would rebuke him, saying, that he robbed God of his honour, etc.[19]

The question then becomes, what was the motive of the angels? In my opinion, it was to bring about a symbolic union between Dee and Kelley. Remember, the angels regarded Dee and Kelley as two halves of a single living unit that would transmit their system of magic to humanity. Both were necessary, and neither could succeed without the full dedication of the other. Since neither Dee nor Kelley would ever have agreed to a homosexual union to bind themselves together spiritually with the occult energies of sex, the angels chose the next best option and used the wives as surrogates. Each wife represents her husband. In Christianity, husband and wife are one flesh. By lying with Jane Dee, Kelley was uniting with an extension of Dee himself; similarly, by taking Joanna Kelley to his bed, Dee joined in a symbolic manner with Kelley.

There is a great deal of Gnostic imagery in the Enochian communications and Keys, and one of the features of Gnosticism is the use of sexual energy to bring about a union with the divine in order to achieve a heightened spiritual awareness and an enlightened mind. This technique of using sex for spiritual awakening is common around the world. It is employed in European shamanism, in Voudoun, and in Tantric sects in India, China, and Tibet. It also finds frequent occurrence among some schools of modern Western magic such as the Odo Templi Orientis, which is closely associated with the teachings of Aleister Crowley.

It is frustrating that the Enochian diaries break off so soon after the exchange of the wives. Suitably empowered with sexual energy, the revelations of the subsequent scrying sessions probably contained many profound secrets. Perhaps the teachings on how to actually employ the Watchtowers and Keys of Enochian magic so earnestly sought by Dee were delivered in the weeks and months following the union of the four. Perhaps, as I suggested above, Kelley learned the manufacture of the red powder. If so, the transcription of those conversations have never been discovered. If there was any such record, it appears to have been lost forever.

CHAPTER FOUR

Enochian Magic and the Apocalypse

THE PURPOSE OF THE ANGELS

Why did the angels deliver Enochian magic to John Dee? It seems this question is never asked by those who study Dee and his angelic transcripts. Scholars tend to dismiss the teachings of the angels as either deliberate conscious deceptions by Kelley, or airy fantasies called up from the depths of his unconscious mind during the scrying sessions. Modern Enochian magicians, when they consider the matter at all, seem content to accept the explanation of the angels that the magic was a fulfillment of the patriarch Enoch's wish that the wisdom of the angels be taught to the human race.

Knowing why the magic was given to Dee is central to understanding its real purpose. Dee believed the magic was a reward for his service to the angels in conveying their message to the rulers of Europe. He saw himself as their prophet, and thought that at some time in the near future the angels would give him permission to perform the initial eighteen-day ritual of evocation that would allow him to use the spirits of the Watchtowers for his own personal ends.

A Covenant Unfulfilled

In essence, Dee regarded his dealings with the angels as a legal contract. Enochian magic was payment for services rendered. This is a familiar pattern in medieval magic. The witch's pact with the Devil (if it ever truly existed) involved acts of evil performed in exchange for occult powers the witch might then use to fulfill his or her desires. The black pact between ceremonial magicians and the Devil is essentially the same as the witch's pact, save that the magician usually got the power first and pledged to turn over his soul to the Devil after the date of his death (the time of which might be specified in the pact).

The Book of Spirits mentioned in Chapter One is another form of binding agreement between magician and spirits. By signing the Book, the spirits evoked by the magician pledge their obedience. The Book of Spirits is separate from the black pact. A magician, if he or she was spiritually pure, could gain the sworn obedience of spirits merely by calling upon the authority of God without having to offer services or sacrifices in return. This is how John Dee understood his blank book of forty-eight silvered leaves.

Dee viewed his arrangement with the Enochian angels as similar to the Covenant between the ancient Hebrews and IHVH. Indeed, he may have seen himself as a latter-day Moses. God, through his messengers, talked to Dee, and Dee carried these divine teachings and commandments to the kings and leaders of different peoples. He regarded the "cross-matching" of the wives as a test of his faith, similar to the test of Abraham's faith when God commanded Abraham to sacrifice his first-born son Isaac (*Genesis* 22:2). He specifically calls the letter to God signed by himself, Kelley, and their wives, in which they agree to exchange bed partners, a "Covenant," and mentions in it their "Abraham-like faith and obedience unto thee our God."[1]

There is no mention made in the Covenant of specific payment by God for the obedience of Dee, Kelley and their wives, but previously the spirit Madimi sets forth the form of compensation:

> Behold, if you resist not God, but shut out Satan (through unity amongst you) thus it is said unto you, Assemble your selves together every seventh day, that your eyes may be opened, and that you may understand by him that shall teach you, what the secrets of the holy books (delivered you) are: That you may become full of understanding, and in knowledge above common men."[2]

Every seventh day is Monday, the Sabbath or holy day of the Enochian angels.

"INSTRUMENTS OF THRASHING"

It seems implausible that the angels, who throughout the conversations show concern only for their own purposes, should convey with great difficulty over a period of years the system of Enochian magic purely for the benefit of Dee and Kelley. When Dee and Kelley request aid from the angels on personal matters, the angels either put them off with vague promises or tell them outright that human concerns do not interest them. With the possible exception of Madimi, who came most often in the form of a young girl and formed a close personal relationship with Dee, the angels show no affection for the men.

The Enochian angels manipulated Dee and Kelley as unwitting instruments to achieve their own higher purpose. The angels planted the system of Enochian magic among humankind for angelic reasons. These had nothing whatsoever to do with the wishes of either Dee or Kelley. Indeed, they have nothing to do with the desires of mortal humanity, and it is extremely naïve for any modern Enochian magician to believe that Enochian magic was delivered to the earth for his or her personal benefit.

The angels intend that Enochian magic be used to initiate the process of violent and destructive transformation linking our present aeon, which is ending, with the new aeon that is about to dawn—a transformation like that described in the biblical book of *Revelation*. In many places throughout the angelic conversations, the words of the angels are filled with apocalyptic imagery. Gabriel expresses this higher purpose very clearly while speaking with the authority of God, although Dee probably failed to gather the full implications of his words.

> I have chosen you, to enter into my barns: And have commanded you to open the Corn, that the scattered may appear, and that which remaineth in the sheaf may stand. And have entered into the first, and so into the seventh. And have delivered unto you the Testimony of my spirit to come.
>
> For, my Barn hath been long without Threshers. And I have kept my flayles for a long time hid in unknown places: Which flayle is the Doctrine that I deliver unto you: Which is the Instrument of thrashing, wherewith you shall beat the sheafs, that the Corn which is scattered, and the rest may be all one.
>
> (But a word in the mean season.)
>
> If I be Master of the Barn, owner of the Corn, and deliverer of my flayle: If all be mine. (And unto you, there is nothing: for you are hirelings, whose reward is in heaven.)
>
> Then see, that you neither thresh, nor unbinde, untill I bid you, let it be sufficient unto you: that you know my house, that you know the labour I will put you to: That I favour you

so much as to entertain you the labourers within my Barn:
For within it thresheth none without my consent[3]

THE BLINDNESS OF JOHN DEE

Dee firmly believed that the angels intended to honor
him as their prophet and spokesman to the princes and
potentates of the world. He seems never to have asked
himself why the angels chose to bestow upon him the
precious system of Enochian magic, but simply
accepted it as a reward for his lifelong piety. He
regarded himself as chosen by God, and did not question the choice. Kelley, on the other hand, always
believed the angels were deceiving and using them. He
judged they were demons in disguise.

It is difficult to understand how Dee could have
remained ignorant of the implications of Enochian magic.
The reason the angels chose Dee as the human instrument to record its details was his intellectual genius, his
extensive knowledge of ciphers and his skill in the mathematical magic of the Kabbalah. Dee was one of the few
men of his age willing and able to receive such a transmission, and clever enough to make sense of it.

OPENING THE GATES

The primary action of the magic is the opening of the
gates of the four Watchtowers that stand at the corners
of the world. Each Watchtower has twelve gates, which
lead to twelve angelic "cities" or dimensions of reality.
The gates of the Watchtowers are opened by means of
the forty-eight Keys or Calls (the angels use both
names). They may be termed Calls because they evoke
the angelic hierarchies from the cities, through the gates

of the Watchtowers, and into our universe. The leader of each hierarchy (named on the squares of the Watchtowers) and his numerous followers have specific functions recorded by Dee in his Latin manuscript *Liber Scientiae Auxilii et Victoriae Terrestris*.[4]

Dee was aware of the angelic teaching that the disobedience of Adam was responsible for the curse of God upon the Earth. The Earth is regarded by the angels as a goddess. The Watchtowers were established at the moment time began, which was when Adam was expelled from the Garden: "But in the same instant when Adam was expelled, the Lord gave unto the world her time, and placed over her Angelic Keepers, Watchmen and Princes."[5] We know that the Watchtowers are equivalent to the Watchmen from Kelley's great vision of the Watchtowers, expounded by the angel Ave: "The 4 houses, are the 4 Angels of the Earth, which are the 4 Overseers, and Watch-towers...."[6]

The universe of time, in which exists human consciousness, is established and maintained like a little bubble in the vast sea of eternity. It is the Watchtowers that sustain the bubble's cohesion. The Watchtowers are equivalent to the four pillars of Egyptian mythology that support the sky and keep it from crashing chaotically down upon the earth. The four ruling angels in the towers (who are not really separate from the towers but part of them) are time keepers—they maintain and regulate the laws of cause and effect.

To open the gates of the Watchtowers is to mingle the eternal with the temporal, to admit the angels into our world: not only the holy angels who follow God's plan and execute his judgment during the transformation known as the apocalypse, but the fallen angels who sinned with the daughters of men, and who will act as instruments of punishment. It is in this sense that Enochian magic is the "instrument of thrashing." Elsewhere, the angel Mapsama tells Dee: "You called for wisdom, God hath opened unto you, his Judgement: He hath delivered unto you the keyes, that you may enter...."[7] A gate, once opened, permits travel in either direction.

THE DOCTRINE OF THE ANGELS

Both the language of the Keys and the conversation of the angels are filled with apocalyptic imagery. The angels seem to introduce it in an almost random way when Dee is asking about the health of distant friends or trying to get money to travel, or when Kelley is attempting to wheedle from them the secret of the red powder. However, this description of the manner in which the goddess Earth will be punished and tormented because she harbors sinful humankind is the true doctrine of the angels, as Mapsama tells Dee:

> The heavens are called righteous, because of their obedience. The earth accursed, because of her frowardnesse. Those therefore, that seek heavenly things, ought to be obedient; lest with their frowardnesse, they be consumed in the end, burnt to ashes with fire, as the Earth shall be for her unrighteousnesse.[8]

This, in a nutshell, is the doctrine the angels have Dee preaching to the crowned heads of Poland and Bohemia. The forwardness, or impudence, of the goddess Earth lies in her providing sustenance and shelter to incarnated human souls. The goddess Earth offers bits of her own body to human souls, and from these bits they form their bodies of flesh. At the same time, they become one flesh with the goddess, and thus her children. The stated necessity to punish her, and erring human souls, is the justification the Enochian angels offer for the coming apocalypse.

Dee understood the apocalypse in the traditional Christian sense. This is not exactly the same as the way the Enochian angels understand it. To Dee, the apocalypse was to be a series of physical disasters brought about by the angelic agents of God at the will of God and at a preordained time. However, it is implicit from the Enochian conversations that the apocalypse will begin with the opening of the gates of the Watchtowers, and that these gates can only be opened by humankind from the inside. Enochian magic is the tool delivered by the angels that will enable humankind to open the gates.

"INVOCATION PROCEEDETH OF THE GOOD WILL OF MAN"

We know that the angels cannot open the gates from the outside because to open them requires the use of evocation (or as the angels term it, invocation). This is not within the power of angels, as Ave tells Dee:

> *Dee:* As for the form of our Petition or Invitation of the good Angels, what sort should it be of?
> *Ave:* A short and brief speech.
> *Dee:* We beseech you to give us an example: we would have a confidence, it should be of more effect.
> *Ave:* I may not do so.
> *Kelley:* And why?
> *Ave:* Invocation proceedeth of the good will of man, and of the heat and fervency of the spirit: And therefore is prayer of such effect with God.
> *Dee:* We beseech you, shall we use one form to all?
> *Ave:* Every one, after a divers form.

    Dee: If the minde do dictate or prompt a divers form, you mean.

    Ave: I know not: for I dwell not in the soul of man.[9]

Evocation (calling out) and invocation (calling in) are functions of human free will. Spiritual beings must be invoked into our reality by human beings. We must open the gates and admit the servants of Coronzon (the Enochian name for Lucifer) ourselves. Evocation and invocation are not a part of the business of angels, but of humans.

The angels can manipulate the time of the apocalypse by veiling or revealing the true knowledge of the Watchtowers and the Keys as it suits their purposes. They made very clear to Dee that he was not to work the ritual evocation of the Keys without their express permission, which was never granted in Dee's lifetime. To be doubly sure, they withheld details of the working. Although they promised to reveal these details after the fulfillment of the Covenant, there is no evidence that they kept their word. If they did, the manuscript appears to have been lost.

"I Have Nothing in Me Tied to Time"

The understanding of the apocalypse held by fundamentalist Christians is that it will be primarily a series of physical disasters provoked by physical agents. The angels of judgment will appear upon the surface of the Earth in unpleasant physical bodies and sow material plagues, cause volcanic eruptions, earthquakes, and so on. This is a painfully materialistic understanding. The agents of the apocalypse are spirits, and spirits have no bodies. They exist in the astral world and cannot directly affect the physical world.

For angels to affect the physical world, they must use human beings as their fleshy instruments. They do this by controlling the behavior of human beings through the unconscious mind. By manipulating humans they are then able to cause those humans to change the physical world. Indeed, it is only through the media of human perceptions that angels are able to perceive the physical universe. That is why it was necessary for souls to incarnate in the first place. Human beings are incarnated angels.

The limitation of angelic awareness is indicated by the angel Gabriel, who, when asked by Dee for some information about Albert Laski (who was not present), states: "When we enter into him, we know him; but from him, he is scarce known unto us..."[10] The difficulty arises because angels dwell in eternity and men dwell in time. An unnamed angel says to Dee: "For he that dealeth with me, dealeth not as with a man; for I have nothing in me tied to time, much lesse hath he that sent me."[11] This great difficulty the angels have in handling time may account for the nonsequential way the Enochian teachings were received.

In my opinion, the apocalypse prepared by the Enochian angels must be primarily an internal, spiritual event, and only in a secondary way an external physical catastrophe. The gates of the Watchtowers that stand guard at the four corners of our dimension of reality are mental constructions. When they are opened, they will admit the demons of Coronzon—not into the physical world, but into our subconscious minds.

Spirits are mental, not material. They dwell in the depths of mind and communicate with us through our dreams, unconscious impulses, and more rarely in waking visions. They affect our feelings and our thoughts beneath the level of our conscious awareness. Sometimes they are able to control our actions, either partially as in the case of irrational and obsessive behavior patterns, or completely as in the case of full possession. Through us, by using us as their physical instruments, and only through us, are they able to influence physical things.

THE DEMONS WITHIN OURSELVES

The Enochian communications teach us that not only must humanity itself initiate the cosmic drama of the apocalypse through the magical formula delivered to John Dee and Edward Kelley more than four centuries ago, but humans must also be the physical actors that bring about the plagues, wars, and famines described with such chilling eloquence in the vision of St. John. We must let the demons of Coronzon into our minds by means of a specific ritual working. They will not find a welcome place there all at once, but will worm their way into our subconscious and make their homes there slowly over a period of years or even decades. In the minds of individuals that resist this invasion they will find it difficult to gain a foothold, but in the more pliable minds of those who welcome their influence they will establish themselves readily.

Once they have taken up residence, we will be powerless to prevent them turning our thoughts and actions toward chaotic and destructive ends. These apocalyptic spirits will set person against person and nation against nation, gradually increasing the degree of madness and chaos in human society until at last the full horror of *Revelation* has been realized upon the stage of the world. The corruption of human thoughts and feelings may require generations to bring to full fruition. Only after the wasting and burning of souls is well advanced will the full horror of the apocalypse achieve its final fulfillment in the material realm.

APOCALYPSE IS NOT PREORDAINED

What the Enochian angels intended the Keys to accomplish, and what the Keys are actually able to do, may be entirely different. Spirits are not infallible. They often deceive human beings, and sometimes even themselves. Simply because the angels believed this system of magic could trigger the apocalypse does not necessarily mean it can do so. It does not even mean that there is, or will be, such a thing as an apocalypse.

However, it seems clear that it was the intention of the angels that the Keys be ritually applied to the Watchtowers, not so that human beings could learn divine secrets of nature, as Dee believed, but to open the way for the demons of Coronzon to enter into our unconscious minds. Once firmly established in our personal unconscious, these spirits would then be able to gain an increasing control over our physical world by manipulating our perceptions, emotions and thoughts.

Enochian magic has been used for over a century by modern magicians working in the Golden Dawn tradition and its derivatives without any obvious signs of initiating a universal Armageddon. It is evident that it can be employed for personal reasons, even though this is not the primary function intended by the angels who delivered it. Modern magicians do not perform the full eighteen-day invocation that was to be the catalytic trigger of the apocalypse. The details of this complex Apocalypse Working (as I call it) were probably never delivered to Dee and Kelley, although it may be possible to reconstruct its outline. Instead, modern magicians nibble at the edges of Enochian magic, using various aspects of it in their ritual practices. Even incomplete and misapplied, it is a highly potent form of magic.

It may be that Enochian magic was deliberately designed by the angels to be an effective system of personal magic in order to insure its survival and continuous use by human beings. What better way to guarantee that the system will still be understood in a practical way when the angels at last determine that the time has come to nudge some chosen magician, through visions and insights, into performing the Apocalypse Working? In the meantime, individual Enochian magicians have been able to use the system for their own private ends, and will go on doing so.

CHAPTER FIVE

The History of Enochian Magic

ROBERT COTTON BUYS A LIBRARY

After Dee's death in 1608, his library was sold to the antiquarian Sir Robert Bruce Cotton (1570–1631). Cotton also acquired at least some of Dee's magical apparatus, including his scrying table, one of his crystals, and the wax seals used to support both the crystal and the legs of the table. Some of these objects afterwards made their way into the British Museum collection via the Cottonian Library. The stone was acquired by the British Museum in later years. The table was extant in Meric Causabon's day. The brass engraving of its top, pictured at the beginning of *A True and Faithful Relation*, was copied from the original design. This table has since disappeared.

The history of the transcript of the angelic conversations is curious, since it reveals an almost supernatural survival of some of the manuscripts. Those acquired by Cotton (part of Dee's *Liber Mysteriorum*) make up the content of Casaubon's *A True and Faithful Relation*. Charlotte Fell Smith called these "the last thirteen books" of the transcript.[1] They cover the period from May 28, 1583, to April 2, 1587, with increasingly large gaps of time toward the end of the record. They resume again, briefly, in the year 1607 from March 20 to

September 7. During this latter period, Dee relied on the inferior scrying services of Bartholomew Hickman. The 1607 transcripts contain nothing of value. The gap between the last scrying session with Kelley and the first recorded session with Hickman is called by Casaubon "a vast chasma or hiatus."[2]

About the books of the transcript that were published by Casaubon, John Aubrey wrote: "Meridith Lloyd sayes that John Dee's printed booke of Spirits is not above the third part of what was writt, which were in Sir Robert Cotton's library; many whereof were much perished by being buryed, and Sir Robert Cotton bought the field to digge after it."[3] About this burying of the manuscripts, Casaubon states: "The Book had been buried in the Earth, how long, years or monethes, I know not; but so long, though it was carefully kept since, yet it retained so much of the Earth, that it began to moulder and perish some years ago, which when Sir Thomas C. [Robert Cotton's son] ... observed, he was at the charges to have it written out, before it should be too late."[4]

BURIED IN THE EARTH?

The notion that Dee's magical books were buried in a field to prevent discovery is very romantic, but seems too far-fetched to be taken seriously. More likely, the mold on the transcript was the result of careless storage before Cotton acquired it. However, it is possible that Dee or his eldest son Arthur (1579–1651) took the extreme measure of interment to ensure that the angelic conversations remain secret. Arthur was upset about Casaubon's book, which was published eight years before his own death. This annoyance had nothing to do with the content of the book, since Arthur himself was involved in occult and alchemical experiments. He simply did not want the teachings of the angels known, and did not wish his father's name associated with them.

Some of Dee's lost diaries and other papers passed into Arthur's hands. Apparently, Arthur searched diligently for any instructions Dee might have left describing how to actually use Enochian magic. Deacon writes: "Arthur spent much time in his later years trying to recover his father's missing manuscripts, which were supposed to be scattered as far afield as Prague, Rome, Brussels and Amsterdam."[5] After Arthur's death "his remaining notes and any manuscripts belonging to his father seem to have been dissipated among his numerous children ... and, except for odd scraps of information here and there, to have been lost to posterity."[6]

THE SECRET DRAWER IN JOHN DEE'S CHEST

The survival of Dee's transcript of the angelic conversations that took place prior to May 28, 1583, is even more remarkable. Casaubon knew nothing about their existence. Thirteen years after the publication of *A True and Faithful Relation,* the earlier papers fell into the hands of the antiquarian Elias Ashmole. Ashmole, who was well known around London as a buyer of old manuscripts, bartered them in exchange for a book from one of the warders of the Tower of London, who in turn had acquired them from his wife.

While courting her first husband, the wife of the warder had bought an old chest with a "very good lock and hinges of extraordinary neat work" from a shop. It had formerly belonged to the surgeon John Woodward, who probably bought it at Dee's estate sale in 1609. She kept the chest for twenty years without noticing anything odd about it. Then, while moving it one day, she heard a rattle inside. Her second husband pried up the bottom and discovered "a large secret drawer stuffed full of papers, and a rosary of olivewood beads with a cross, which had caused the rattle."[7]

The papers in Dee's chest covered the conversations with the angels from December 22, 1581, down to the beginning of Casaubon's book. They also contained the manuscripts *48 Claves Angelicae, De Heptarchia Mystica* and *Liber Scientiae Auxiliis et Victoriae Terrestris*—a truly extraordinary treasure. Since some of it is written in Latin and the rest in Dee's rather crabbed hand, the Tower warder probably considered it of little value. Ashmole, of course, was delighted.

EARLY ENOCHIAN SCHOLARS

Thanks to the scholarly care of Cotton and Ashmole, these manuscripts have survived to the present day. Ashmole spent considerable energy understanding the system of Enochian magic. Peter French writes about Ashmole that "he seems to have studied the 'Spiritual Diaries' seriously as a means of contacting angels. Ashmole's biographer, C. H. Josten, conjectures that he may even have attempted to repeat the angelic experiments."[8] Like Arthur Dee before him, Ashmole was, in the end, baffled by the missing instructions concerning the actual application of the Keys to the Watchtowers.

From time to time other scholars with occult inclinations have attempted to unravel the transcripts. There is an interesting section concerning the tables of Enoch in British Library manuscript Harley 6482. It is part of a larger magical workbook (Harley 6481–6) ascribed to the seventeenth-century Hermetic magician

Thomas Rudd, who published Dee's famous Preface to Euclid's *Elements* in 1651.

ENOCHIAN MAGIC IN THE GOLDEN DAWN

Since the mini-revival of Enochian magic that took place in the middle of the seventeenth century, there does not appear to have been any serious attempt to understand and practice the teachings of the angels until the efforts of the Hermetic Order of the Golden Dawn. A secret Victorian society dedicated to the practice of ritual magic, the Golden Dawn was founded in London in 1887 by three Freemasons determined to revive the intellectual magic of the Renaissance and create a true Rosicrucian society.

One of the founders, Samuel Liddell "MacGregor" Mathers (1854–1918), spent much of his time as a young man burrowing through the piles of dusty manuscripts in the library at the British Museum, where many of Dee's writings were kept. He undoubtedly read some of the angelic conversations in their original form, but seems to have derived most of his personal system of Enochian magic from the *True and Faithful Relation*. There is no mention in Golden Dawn Enochian magic of the material in Dee's *Heptarchia Mystica,* which is made up of angelic teachings recorded before the point where Casaubon's book begins.

The Enochian magic of the Golden Dawn is almost completely concerned with the Great Table of the four Watchtowers and the forty-eight Keys or Calls, which Mathers was perceptive enough to relate to the Table. It deals only with the angels or spirits whose names may be extracted from the Watchtowers by a specific set of rules—there is no mention of the spirits of the Thirty

Aethers, or the ninety-one geographical genii who rule the different regions of the world. Thus, Golden Dawn Enochian magic is only a portion of the magical system received by Dee and Kelley.

To his credit, Mathers was able to add, in a more or less intelligent way, many details concerning the Watchtowers that are not clearly stated in the angelic conversations. In Golden Dawn magic, the Watchtowers are explicitly connected with colors, signs of the zodiac, directions, letters of Tetragrammaton, and occult elements. These correspondences have immense usefulness in practical rituals that employ the Watchtowers. The Keys were related by Mathers (or one of his associates) to different parts of the Great Table, and to the spirits located in those parts, so that speaking a particular Key in Enochian evokes a particular spirit. The system of Enochian magic used in the Golden Dawn will be the subject of a later chapter.

ALEISTER CROWLEY

One of the young members of the Golden Dawn was Aleister Crowley (1875–1947). Crowley is the most famous magus of the twentieth century. When he was a young child, his mother (a member of the fanatical Plymouth Brethren sect) referred to him as the Beast. His young mind seized on this label as a revelation. In his autobiography he writes: "But my mother believed that I was actually Anti-christ of the Apocalypse...." [and above on the same page,] "I have never lost sight of the fact that I was in some sense or other the Beast 666."[9] Here, the Beast and the Antichrist are confused, but the confusion was his mother's, not Crowley's, who always understood himself to be merely the herald of the Antichrist.

Crowley eagerly devoured Golden Dawn magic. He was strongly drawn to the magic of the dark side—the goetia. His mentor in the Golden Dawn, Allan Bennett, warned him against this line of study, but Crowley paid no heed. This attraction to evil, coupled with his Bohemian habits, made him unpopular among the conservative leaders of the Order. Eventually, Crowley and the Golden Dawn parted company, but he continued to use the Golden Dawn teachings for the remainder of his life. More than with any other aspect of Golden Dawn magic, he was fascinated with the Enochian language and the Keys to the Watchtowers. Crowley considered himself a reincarnation of Edward Kelley, and to some extent he shared Kelley's scrying ability.

While wandering through Algeria in 1909, Crowley invoked the Enochian Aethers in reverse order from the twenty-eighth to the first, using the nineteenth Key for all of them. The Key for all thirty of the Aethers is the same save for the name of the Aether involved. Thus, the last thirty Keys are really a single Key that is applied to the thirty Aethers. Previously, while visiting Mexico in 1900, he had invoked the thirtieth and twenty-ninth Aethers, so he was merely taking up where he had left off.

CROWLEY'S INVOCATION OF THE AETHERS

His method of working was similar in some respects to that of Dee and Kelley. He would find a private place where he could be alone with his disciple, Victor Neuberg. Then he would recite the nineteenth Key with the name of the Aether he sought to invoke inserted in the text at the proper place. It is not clear to me whether he used the English or the Enochian version of the Key. The Enochian version would be correct practice, but in his *Confessions* he speaks of "changing two names" to suit the Key to each Aether. In the English version, two words must be changed for each Aether, but in the Enochian version, only one word. So perhaps Crowley invoked the Aethers using the English version of the nineteenth Key.

After sensing the presence of the angel of that Aether, he gazed into a large topaz that was set in a decorated wooden cross. Whatever he saw in the stone, or experienced more directly, he described. Neuberg sat beside him and wrote his words down in a notebook, just as Dee had recorded the words of Kelley more than three centuries earlier. This record formed the work known as the *Vision and the Voice.*

Crowley states in his autobiography, "We walked steadily to Bou Saâda, invoking the Aethyrs one by one, at convenient times and places, or when the spirit moved me. As a rule, we did one Aethyr every day."[10] He does not seem to have employed the first eighteen Keys while invoking the Aethers. He understood the eighteen preliminary Keys in the way they had been taught him by the Golden Dawn. Describing them, he says that the first two Keys relate to the quintessence, or elemental Spirit, while the next sixteen relate to the four elements in subdivisions of four. This is the Golden Dawn teaching.

Crowley demonstrated a sound intuitive comprehension of the Keys and the Watchtowers. He had trouble reconciling the various interpretations of the Aethers—whether they are concentric angelic spheres that lie beyond the bounds of the four Watchtowers, or angels whose names are written on the Watchtowers, or merely names for different geographical regions on the surface of the earth. This confusion is understandable, since nowhere does Dee write anything to clarify the matter.

Crowley chose to consider the Aethers in the first, most mystical sense. He describes the Watchtowers as "composing a cube of infinite magnitude."[11] This is above the usual understanding.

The Great Beast Unlocks the Gates

If, as I postulate earlier, Enochian magic was delivered by the angels to act as the catalyst for the apocalypse, it is interesting to note that the primary practitioner of that magic firmly considered himself to be the Great Beast of *Revelation*. After leaving the Golden Dawn, Crowley went on to create his own occult mythos. He saw himself as the herald for the dawning Aeon of Horus, which he believed began in April 1904, with his inspired reception of the *Book of the Law*, dictated to him by his guardian angel, Aiwass.

Crowley's guardian angel cast Crowley into a role similar to that forced upon John Dee by the Enochian angels. Crowley was both the sacred scribe and the prophet of the god Ra-Hoor-Khuit (Horus). His instruction was to record the sayings of the god and to spread his message across the world via the *Book of the Law*. "Now ye shall know that the chosen priest & apostle of infinite space is the prince-priest the Beast and in his woman; called the Scarlet Woman, is all power given. They shall gather my children into their fold: they shall bring the glory of the stars into the hearts of men."[12]

The Aeon of Horus may be understood in a general sense as similar to the astrological Age of Aquarius. Many ancient cultures divide time into a repeating series of ages, each age with its unique defining characteristics. For example, in the system of the Kabbalah, we are presently living in the Age of Geburah, which is characterized by severity and warfare. The next age will be the Age of Tiphareth, a time of harmony and peace. In Crowley's personal mythos, the dawning Aeon of Horus has supplanted the old Aeon of Osiris, the Egyptian god of death and rebirth that Crowley related to Jesus Christ.

There are some parallels between Crowley's angel-inspired *Book of the Law* and Dee's *Key of the Thirty Aethers*. In the *Book of the Law* is written: "We have nothing with the outcast and the unfit: let them die in their misery: For they feel not. Compassion is the vice of kings: stamp down the wretched & the weak: this is the law of the strong: this is our law and the joy of the world."[13] In the Key of the Thirty Aethers appear the words: "Govern those that govern; cast down such as fall; bring forth with those that increase, and destroy the rotten."[14] Both these passages refer to the effects of karma, the cause and effect of the natural world. Elsewhere in the *Book of the Law* is written: "Yea! deem not of change: ye shall be as ye are, & not other. Therefore the kings of the earth shall be Kings for ever: the slaves shall serve. There is none that shall be cast down or lifted up: all is ever as it was."[15]

The Aeon of Horus is one of strife and warfare, even as the time of the apocalypse is a time of destruction. Horus states in the *Book of the Law:* "Now let it be first understood that I am a god of War and of Vengeance."[16] And elsewhere: "Mercy let be off: damn them who pity. Kill and torture; spare not; be upon them."[17] In the Key of the Thirty Aethers is written: "the reasonable creatures of Earth (or men), let them vex and weed out one another; and the dwelling places, let them forget their names; the work of man and his pomp, let them be defaced...."[18]

Crowley embraced the symbolism in *Revelation*, applied it to himself, and understood it with reference to his prophetic *Book of the Law*. He called himself the Great Beast, his wife (and later his various mistresses) the Scarlet Woman and the Whore of Babalon (in Enochian the word *babalon* means "wicked" and the word *babalond* means "whore"—thus the change in spelling of this word, although Crowley justified in on numerical grounds). He also interpreted the text of the *Book of the Law* to mean that his son would become the Antichrist. Concerning the Scarlet Woman, the *Book of the Law* states: "then will I breed from her a child mightier than all the kings of the earth."[19] This interpretation was an error: the Antichrist has yet to show himself.

There are no direct references in the *Book of the Law* to the Enochian Keys, although two places are suggestive. Part of the *Book of the Law* reads: "There are four gates to one palace; the floor of that palace is of silver and gold, lapis lazuli & jasper are there, and all rare scents jasmine & rose, and the emblems of death. Let him enter in turn or at once the four gates; let him stand on the floor of the palace."[20] This might be interpreted as a reference to the Great Table of the Watchtowers, which is four-sided and has four parts. Elsewhere is written: "in these are mysteries that no Beast shall divine. Let him not seek to try: but one cometh after him, whence I say not, who shall discover the key of it all."[21] If there really is a hidden connection between the *Book of the Law* and Enochian magic, perhaps this refers to the Enochian Keys.

ENOCHIAN MAGIC IN THE MODERN WORLD

Many modern groups that practice the form of ritual magic descended from the Golden Dawn (directly or via Crowley) use Enochian magic extensively. Particular notice might be taken of the Aurum Solis, an organization dedicated to Hermetic philosophy and magic founded in England in 1897, which claims to be completely independent of the Golden Dawn. The Aurum Solis teachings include the Great Table of the Watchtowers, the Keys, and the spirits of the thirty Aethers.[22] The late Anton LaVey, leader of the California-based Church of Satan, employed an edited version of the Keys that was derived from the writings of Aleister Crowley.

In the last few decades Enochian magic has undergone another period of rebirth. Increasingly, Dee's writings are finding their way into popular books of ceremonial magic. This process is slow, and it is unfortunate that no single text exists that contains the complete Enochian communications with the numerous Latin passages translated into English. However, enough of the material has emerged to present an overview of Enochian magic that is fairly complete, and to allow the magic to be used for practical ends.

CHAPTER SIX

The Tools of Enochian Magic

GIFTS FROM THE ANGELS

The articles of furniture for the scrying sessions were all added at the direction of the Enochian angels. At first, it appears than no special instruments were used. Dee placed one of his scrying crystals in a "frame" on the edge of his desk in his private study at Mortlake. This frame (given to him by a friend) is nowhere clearly described, but a small drawing of it made by Dee appears in the margin of the manuscript page dated December 22, 1581 (Sloane MS 3188, folio 8), beside the words "I thereupon, set by him, the stone in the frame."[1] The picture shows a frame with four outward-curved legs resting on a flat circular ring. The crystal itself is surrounded by a vertical band of the frame that leaves its front (and presumably its back) exposed. On the top of this band is a small cross. It may have been made of gold, since a gold frame is mentioned elsewhere.

On the first scrying with Kelley, which took place on March 10, 1582, the alchemist knelt on the floor in front of Dee's desk. He peered into the stone, which may have been placed in the sunlight beaming through the west-facing window of the study, in obedience to orders the angel Annael had delivered to Barnabas Saul on

December 21, 1581. Kelley prayed aloud and invoked the angel Annael into the stone. Meanwhile, Dee retreated to his Oratory (a small room attached to his study) and entreated the appearance of the angels with prayers of his own. Within fifteen minutes, Kelley saw the angel Uriel in the stone.

The angels had informed Saul on December 21 that he and Dee might "deal both kneeling and sitting."[2] It is likely that Kelley soon began to use the green chair in the study, with the crystal in its stand on the edge of the desk. Dee sat on the other side of the desk, recording in his journals the events described by Kelley. Prayer was frequently used to encourage the angels to appear in the stone when they were slow to come. Dee fell into the habit of using prayer to both open and close the scrying sessions. These prayers appear to have been spontaneous compositions, not predetermined elements of a formal ritual. The appearance of the angels in the stone was often preceded by the withdrawing of a "golden curtain" from the depths of the stone.

Almost immediately, the angels began to describe to Kelley the essential ritual furniture the two would require for future communications. This consisted of the sacred stone, the Table of Practice, the seven Ensigns of Creation, the Sigillum Aemeth and four lesser sigils of the same pattern to be placed under the legs of the table, various silk cloths to be spread under and over the table, circular seals to be placed under the scryer's feet, a seal ring, and a lamen which contained a "token" of Dee's name hidden amongst its letters.

Dee continued to employ the Table of Practice, the Sigillum Aemeth, and the angelic stone throughout his association with Kelley. It is probable that he also continued to use the other ritual objects, although they are not mentioned in the later transcript. Dee considered these things essential to the success of the communications because they had been explicitly prescribed by the angels themselves. However, it should be noted that Kelley first established communication quite easily without them.

THE SEAL RING

The seal ring was delivered on March 14 by the angel Michael. Charlotte Fell Smith states that this was a physical ring,[3] presumably going on the assumption that it was a plant by Kelley to impress Dee. This may be a misreading of the transcript on her part. The angel Michael makes the seal ring appear out of the flames of his sword, then says to Dee through Kelley: "After this sort must be the ring. Note it. I will reveal thee this ring, which was never revealed since the death of Solomon, with whom I was present."[4] The implication is that the ring is the same as Solomon's fabled seal ring. Then Michael sets the ring down on the table of practice and has Dee note it with care. "After that he threw the ring down upon the table and it seemed to fall through the table."[5]

The transcript of the conversations can sometimes be misleading. The passage quoted above probably means that Kelley described Michael setting down the

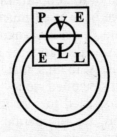

Enochian Ring of Solomon

ring, described the ring in detail to Dee, then told how the angel threw the ring through the tabletop. The ring is apparently important, since Michael tells Dee: "Without this ring thou shalt do nothing."[6]

The ring bears the name of an angel, Pele (P-E-L-E), which means "Worker of Wonders." Dee recognized the name from Reuchlin's *De Verbo Mirifico*.[7] The name of this angel also appears in Agrippa's *Occult Philosophy*,[8] presumably drawn from Reuchlin. In addition to these four letters, there is a large circle in the center of the square bezel with a horizontal bar through its center, and above the bar the letter V while below the bar the letter L appears. Note that these two letters appear in the upper right corner of the Ensign of Sol. It is possible that the circle and bar are intended for the letters O and I. The angel Carmara mentions that the ring is to be made "in perfect gold."[9]

THE ANGELIC STONE

Dee owned at least three scrying speculums, and probably more. One was a flat, circular obsidian mirror with a small handle on one side that had a hole drilled through it for hanging the mirror up on a thong or peg. This is commonly said to be of "Aztec origin"[10] although I have never seen any proof to support this assertion. It does not appear to have been used much, if at all, to communicate with the Enochian angels. Another was a crystal globe that was probably the size and shape of a small egg. It is likely to this that he refers when he speaks of his "first sanctified stone." This was the stone into which Dee first tried to scry. It was also used by Barnabas Saul and, for the period from March 10 to April 28 of 1582, by Edward Kelley.

The third magic mirror, Dee's "principal stone" and "holy stone" and "usual shew-stone," was delivered to Dee in an apparently miraculous manner on April 28, 1582. While scrying at Dee's desk, Kelley looked toward the west window of the study and saw a bright object lying on the mat that covered the earthen floor beside one of Dee's stacks of books. An angel the size of a small child, with a flaming sword in his hand, picked up the object "as big as an egg" and extended it to Dee. The angel Michael told Dee through Kelley, "Go toward it and take it up." Dee writes:

> I went toward the place, which E K pointed to: and till I came within a foot of it, I saw nothing, and then I saw like a shadow on the ground or mats hard by my books under the west window. The shadow was round, and less than the palm of my hand. I put my hand down upon it, and felt a thing cold and hard. Which (taking up) I perceived to be the Stone before mentioned.[11]

For the rest of his life, Dee remained convinced that this crystal had been given to him by angelic means. It immediately became the main scrying instrument. When Dee went to Europe, the stone went with him. He valued it above all his other material possessions, with the possible exception of his library at Mortlake. Speaking of the angels to the Emperor Rudolph II, he said, "yea they have brought me a Stone of that value, that no earthly Kingdom is of that worthinesse as to be compared to the vertue or dignity thereof."[12]

What are we to make of this crystal? It seems likely that it was placed on the floor by Kelley before the scrying began—perhaps unconsciously while Kelley was possessed by the angels. Kelley was susceptible to possession. At one point he complains to Dee that he does not like the spirits "moving in his head." Elsewhere, he tells Dee of "a great stir and moving in his brains, very sensible and distinct, as of a creature of humane shape and lineaments going up and down to and fro in his brains, and within his skull: sometimes seeming to sit down, sometimes to put his head out at his ear."[13]

If so, where would Kelley have obtained such a stone? Large, near perfect spheres of rock crystal were no more common, and no cheaper, in the sixteenth century than they are today. Kelley was not a rich man. Perhaps the crystal really was an apport—the appearance of a physical object out of thin air. It is a mystery that is never likely to be solved. In any case, Dee had the stone set in a gold frame with a cross on the top, a depiction of which is shown below.

Modern students of Enochian magic cannot count on the angels materializing a crystal for them. A sensible alternative is to buy a crystal ball of good quality, either of glass or rock crystal, and a stand to set it on.

THE TABLE OF PRACTICE

On April 29, the day after the delivery of the holy stone, the Table of Practice was finished. It was two cubits high. By two cubits, an English yard (thirty-six inches) was

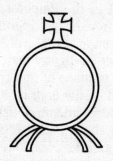

Frame of Dee's Showstone

meant.[14] The top was square, also a yard in both dimensions, so that the overall shape of the table was cubic. It stood on four narrow wooden legs. The angels specified that it be made of "sweet wood," which is another name for laurel. The laurel tree has powerful associations in magic and scrying dating back to ancient Greece.

The distinguishing feature of this table is the design painted on its top. This is clearly illustrated at the beginning of Casaubon's *True and Faithful Relation* by a brasscut engraving that was taken from the original table in the Cottonian library. Around the edge is a border of

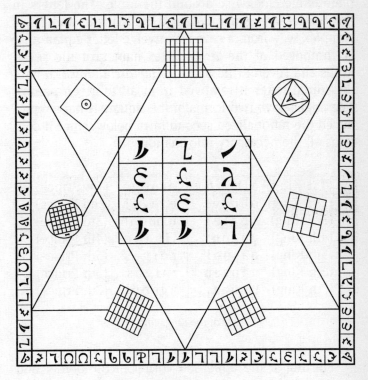

Table of Practice

Enochian letters. Each side of this border contains twenty-one letters—the number of letters in the Enochian alphabet. An Enochian B is inscribed in each corner of the border. Robert Turner speculates that the Enochian B is equivalent to the number seven.[15] This is a reasonable speculation, in view of the importance of seven in Enochian magic and the prevalence of the Enochian B.

The letters in this border are read right to left, after the normal manner of Enochian writing, and are oriented to be read from outside the edge of the table, so that a person reading the border would walk in a complete circle clockwise around the table. The letters in the border are generated in a Kabbalistic and fairly complex way from a seven-by-twelve-letter square that is composed of the seven-letter names of the seven Kings and seven Princes of the *Heptarchia Mystica* with the initial letter B removed from all fourteen names. The angels give two forms of this square. I have reproduced the rationalized second form below, since it contains all the necessary information.

(1st King) aligon	ornogo	(1st Prince)
(2nd King) obogel	efafes	(2nd Prince)
(3rd King) abalel	utmono	(3rd Prince)
(4th King) ynepor	lisdon	(4th Prince)
(5th King) naspol	rorges	(5th Prince)
(6th King) napsen	ralges	(6th Prince)
(7th King) lumaza	agenol	(7th Prince)

Table of the Kings and Princes

Starting at the upper-left corner of the border and moving clockwise, each side of the Holy Table contains the letters in three adjacent columns from the table of the Kings and Princes. The columns are read right to left and top to bottom from the first to the seventh Prince or King. Thus, the upper edge of the Holy Table begins o-s-o-n-s-s-l whereas the bottom edge begins n-l-l-r-l-n-a.

It is not really necessary to understand this table of the Kings and Princes to practice Enochian magic, but it is interesting to know where the letters in the border of the Table of Practice come from. Also, it illustrates very clearly that the Enochian magic of the seven Kings (which is linked to the seven traditional wandering bodies of astrology) is an essential component of the Enochian magic of the Watchtowers and Keys as it was received by Kelley using the Holy Table. In Enochian magic based on the Golden Dawn system, the importance of the Kings is not understood.

The smaller table at the center of the Table of Practice consists of twelve Enochian letters. Its pattern is the same as that of the twelve stones on the breastplate of the high priest of ancient Israel: four rows and three columns. These twelve letters relate to the twelve tribes, the twelve gates of New Jerusalem, the twelve overt permutations of Tetragrammaton, the twelve signs of the zodiac, and the twelve Enochian names of God that appear on the middle rows of the Watchtowers. Unfortunately, this relationship is not always clear in Dee's manuscripts.

The letters on the central table (3 x 4) of the Holy Table of Practice are extracted from the middle of the 7 x 12 table of the Kings and Princes. I have highlighted them in boldface type to make them easier to locate.

Robert Turner makes the emphatic assertion that the Holy Table as it appears in Casaubon's brass cut plate is transposed left to right from the way it should appear. He bases this on the single extant diagram of the Table design which appears in *Liber Mysteriorum Quinta Appendix*, saying "Casaubon's rendering is quite plainly in error. The letters that border the top and bottom edges of the table are obviously written backwards, while those that make up the left and right hand borders are transposed. In addition to these errors the 4 x 3 square that takes up the centre is also given in a reversed order."[16]

Turner blames this inversion in Casaubon's plate on an error by the engraver. He suggests that such errors are common, and are due to the process of engraving itself. He cannot understand why so many Enochian scholars have failed to pick up on what is, to him, an obvious error, and blames it on the habit of occultists to blindly accept traditions in magic without examining their source material (which is certainly true).

After carefully considering the question, I have come to the conclusion that the plate in Casaubon is probably a correct representation of Dee's Table of Practice. The artist who executed the plate was working from Dee's actual Table, and in other respects he seems to have done a fairly accurate job. Why should he make the glaring mistake of inverting everything left to right? It does not seem reasonable, especially when the seven smaller tables, the Ensigns of Creation (which, in my opinion were actually painted onto the surface of Dee's Table of Practice) are not inverted, but occupy their correct position. If the engraver was going to invert the rest of the Table left to right, it is fair to assume he would also have inverted the Ensigns of Creation.

Turner may have failed to consider that the design for the Table of Practice that appears in *Liber Mysteriorum Quinta Appendix* is executed in Latin letters. Latin is read left to right. Enochian is read right to left. When an Enochian word is transposed into English, it must be mirror-inverted as we do with Hebrew words, which are also written and read right to left.

We may presume that the Enochian letters in the border of the Holy Table form words of power (even though these words are not known) or at least that their order is significant to the angels. Dee must have understood the need to invert everything when transposing the Latin letters in his manuscript design into the Enochian letters on the actual physical Table. Thus, it seems likely that Casaubon's engraver made no mistake, and the representation of the Table in the brass cut is correct.

The angels tell Dee concerning the Sigillum Aemeth: "We have no respect of cullours."[17] However, of the Table they say the Enochian letters written around the edges must be painted in yellow oil paint, and that the oil used to mix the pigment should be "perfect oil, used in the church." [18] Yellow must be significant in connection with Enochian letters. This color for the letters agrees with the color in which they first appeared to Kelley in a vision:

> ... it is to be Noted, that, when E.K. could not aptly imitate the forme of the Characters, or letters, as they were shewed: that they appeared drawn on his paper with a light yelow culor, which he drew the blak vppon, and so the yellow cullor disapearing, there remayned onely the shape of the letter in blak ...[19]

As a substitute for oil used in a church, which the modern Enochian magician will find hard to obtain, premixed oil paints should be consecrated before they are applied to the Table, which was apparently painted in several colors: "The table was painted in brilliant colours, primarily yellow, blue and red ...."[20]

Beneath the Table on the floor of the scrying chamber a red silk carpet "two yards square" was laid. The four smaller seals of Aemeth (see below) within their protective containers of laurel were set upon the carpet, and the Table legs positioned on top of them, probably in depressions cut into the lids for added stability. These containers were probably disk-shaped, although they may have been spherical or hemispherical.

On top of the Table a simple white linen cloth was spread that hung down almost to the floor. Upon this was placed the wax Sigillum Aemeth and (if they were made of tin rather than painted directly on the tabletop) the seven Ensigns of Creation. Over the Sigillum Aemeth (and the tin Ensigns), a silk cloth with tassels at the corners was spread. This was colored an iridescent red and green, so that it changed from one color to the other when viewed from different angles. On top of this red-green silk cover, the scrying stone in its golden frame was placed directly upon the Sigillum Aemeth in the middle of the Table.

These are the explicit directions of the angels. However, there is some evidence that Dee did not adhere in every respect to these instructions. Casaubon in his preface speaks of a cushion and a candlestick with a taper. His reference is based on the June 25, 1584, entry in Dee's diary:

> A voyce said, bring up the shew-stone.
> *Dee:* I had set it down on the Table, behinde the Cushion with the Crosses, for I had furnished the Table with the Cloath, Candles, etc. as of late I was wont: Hereupon I set up the stone on the Cushion.[21]

There appear to have been at least two candlesticks involved. The "Cushion with the Crosses" may have been placed upon the Sigillum Aemeth, and may have been a substitute for the red-green cloth with the tassels.

The cushion seems to have served as a support for the stone. The candles were probably placed on either side of the stone on the Table of Practice.

THE ENSIGNS OF CREATION

The seven complex talismans known as the "Arms" or "Ensigns of Creation" may either be painted directly onto the top of the Holy Table of Practice, or engraved on tablets of purified tin, which are then placed in a circle around the Sigillum Aemeth. It is evident from the reproduction of Dee's Table that appears in Casaubon that Dee painted these talismans directly onto the surface as an integrated part of the design.

Their placement is shown by the outlines on the illustration of the Holy Table, above (see p. 67). They are arranged radially so that they may be read from the point of view of the center of the table. Turner notes that they are to be placed seven inches from the edge of the Holy Table[22] although they are shown nearer the edge in the Casaubon engraving.

Precisely what these talismans are remains mysterious. A note in the appendix of *Liber Mysteriorum Quintus* states that the Arms are "proper to every King and Prince in their order."[23] This implies that they relate directly to the Kings and Princes of the planets on the Table of the forty-nine Good Angels, which appears in Dee's *De Heptarchia Mystica*.

The only occultist who appears to have made a serious attempt to understand these Ensigns is Thomas Rudd. He assigned the Ensigns in a circle clockwise according to the ascending kabbalistic order of the seven "planets"—Moon, Mercury, Venus, Sun, Mars, Jupiter, Saturn. To the letters in the Ensigns, he gave the names of various demons from the *Goetia* such as Buer, Belial, Gaap, and so on.[24]

In briefly examining Dr. Rudd's system, Turner observes "I feel that we can safely disregard Dr. Rudd's

2 ┼ b b │ 3 b b	G b b	g	B 22	24·b bbb 246	b b L b	B rog	Ⓑ
8 b b b 2	b̶b̶ 8	G b	GG b	152 b	152 b	52 BBB	B ┼ B
☽ q B q	b o o o	B 7	bbb bbb bbb 9	11 B 5	b b b b b	b b b	b 8 b̶ 3
b b b b b b	b b b15b b b	bM 166	7 △bb	Ⓑ 5	G M ┼	ꓭ	b A 1556
1 b	2 3 B 123	b	b T b	4 ꓒꓭ 9	BBB b b	b b 72 F	b

The Ensign of Venus
King: Baligon   Prince: Bornogo

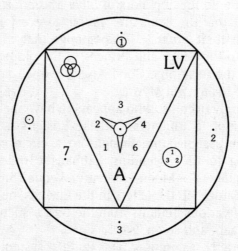

The Ensign of Sol
King: Bobogel   Prince: Befafes

G B ✝ 28	m · 30 q B·9· d · 4 ·	q·q·q Q B o·g og
♂ 30 B G 33 A	✝ B A 9 ○	L get B h go
5 b ☾	m id b d 2A	L 30 b pp
V H b 9 22	qq· qQ b og a	25 L b d

The Ensign of Mars
King: Babalel   Prince: Butmono

2 bb 2	bb ▽	537 bbb	b B G 11	T 13 bbb	b 9
V · 4 B	0 4 B B	B 14 a	bbb P·3·	b G O	b b C V
8 c b	Q·o 7 b b	♋ 5	q q b 3	q · 9 B	L b·8
go·30 B	9·3 b b	q q 5 ·b·b·	d │ b ┼ b A	7·2 b·B	BB Λ 8 3

The Ensign of Jupiter
King: Bynepor   Prince: Blisdon

g D2 g	B l 1 /30	B B 8	B 2	B Ω·22	B·o p d 30	L o B·q q·29	B 8 2	9̶ 6 B
o p B 9 8	+9 ∩ B	b b 2. 8·G	b b 9 F	b 2 Q	bbb 2 Q	b ii Q		B B 1 2 T
B B b 8	M 2 bb	M 5 b	M bb b 20	M 6·89 F	d B 17	A 6 3		B B B 2
M b 99 L	b 6 ✝ 4 b	b 9 b	b b 1 9	6 6 2	B 4	H N B 38 B 9		b b 4 b

The Ensign of Mercury
King: Bnaspol   Prince: Brorges

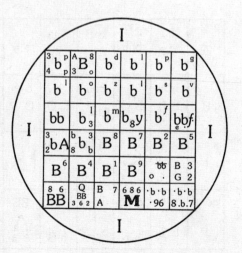

The Ensign of Saturn
King: Bnapsen   Prince: Bralges

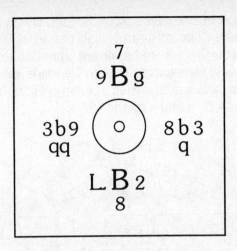

The Ensign of Luna
King: Blumaza   Prince: Bagenol

hypotheses with regard to these matters."[25] I am in complete agreement with Turner here. Rudd's notion that all the numerous occurrences of the letter B in the Ensigns indicates the names of goetic demons whose names all start with B is, to put it mildly, absurd. The reasoning behind the complex structure of these seven talismans is unknown, and will likely remain unknown into the foreseeable future, since it is nowhere explained in the surviving record of the angelic conversations.

SIGILLUM AEMETH

The Sigillum Aemeth, or more properly Emeth (seal of truth), also called by the angels the Sigillum Dei (seal of God), is a wax disk that is placed in the center of the Holy Table. The crystal in its gold holder rests on top of the disk during scrying. Its making is described in the second book of Dee's *Liber Mysteriorum*, which is as yet unpublished. Concerning this sigil, the angel Uriel tells Dee: "This seal is not to be looked upon without great reverence and devotion."[26] It is to be made of "perfect wax," nine inches in diameter, and between an inch and a half and an inch and a quarter thick.

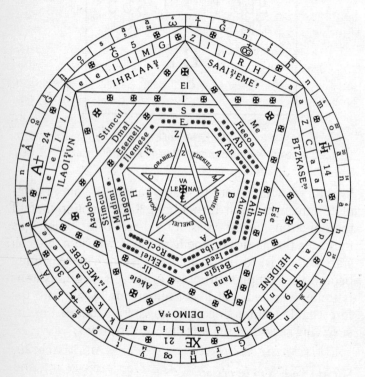

Sigillum Aemeth (front)

In March, 1582, Dee was instructed by the angel Michael to draw a circle and divide its edge into forty equal parts. There appeared to Kelley forty "white creatures, all in white silk long robes, and they were like children."[27] Each of these spirits opened its silk robe at the breast to reveal a letter and number, or sometimes a letter alone. Dee was instructed to write these in the spaces at the edge of the seal clockwise in order beginning at the top.

Within the outer circle of forty letters and numbers, Dee inscribed concentrically a heptagon, an interlocking heptagram, a smaller heptagon, and at the center an interlocking pentagram.

The larger heptagon is divided into forty-nine parts, and filled up with forty-eight letters (the final space contains a cross). There is probably a direct connection between these forty-nine spaces containing forty-eight letters and the forty-nine gates of understanding, of which only forty-eight may be opened. Each side of the larger heptagon contains one of the seven sacred names of God, which Dee derived from a forty-nine letter square.[28]

```
Z  l  l  R  H  i  a
a  Z  C  a  a  c  b
p  a  u  p  n  h  r
h  d  m  h  i  a  i
k  k  a  a  e  e  e
i  i  e  e  l  l  l
e  e  l  l  M  G  +
```

This square was delivered to Kelley on March 20, 1582. The angels instructed Dee to read downward, and when he did so he discovered that the square consists of the names of seven familiar angels of the planets in the Kabbalah: Zaphkiel (Saturn), Zadkiel (Jupiter), Cumael (Mars), Raphael (Sun), Haniel (Venus), Michael (Mercury) and Gabriel (Moon). This same list appears in Cornelius Agrippa's *Three Books of Occult Philosophy*,[29] a work in Dee's library with which Kelley was familiar. Agrippa was also used by the angels as the source for the ninety-one geographical regions of the earth later in the angelic communications. When the rows of this square of planetary angels are read across from left to right, they yield the seven sacred names of God in the larger heptagon.

Just inside the larger heptagon appear seven names that are characterized by the angels as "names not known to the angels, neither can they be spoken or read of man. These names bring forth seven angels, the governors of the heavens next unto us. Every letter of the angels' names bringeth forth seven daughters. Every daughter bringeth forth her daughter, every daughter her daughter bringeth forth a son. Every son hath his son."[30]

This seems confusing but is actually fairly simple. The seven names of God that not even the angels can pronounce are arranged in the form of a letter square that was scryed by Kelley on March 21, 1582:[31]

S	A	A	$^{21}/_8$	E	M	E₈
B	T	Z	K	A	S	E₃₀
H	E	I	D	E	N	E
D	E	I	M	O	L₃₀	A
I₂₆	M	E	G	C	B	E
I	L	A	O	I$^{21}/_8$	V	N
I	H	R	L	A	A	L$^{21}/_8$

This square is structured upon another set of seven planetary angels found in the literature of the Kabbalah:

Sabathiel (Saturn), Zedekiel (Jupiter), Madimiel (Mars), Semeliel (Sun), Nogahel (Venus), Cochabiel (Mercury), Levanael (Moon). Like the first square, it also is given in the *Occult Philosophy of Agrippa.*[32] The names are based on the Hebrew names of the planets, with the suffix "el" added to make them the names of angels.

To extract the names of the seven new angels of the "heavens next unto to us" (that is, the spheres of the planets), read the letters down diagonally from the upper right to the lower left, starting with the letter S in the upper left corner of the square (thus, for Zabathiel: S, ab, ath, 21/8 = iel). To extract the names of the Seven Sons of Light, read the letters diagonally from upper left to lower right starting at the lower left corner of the square, but separated into individual names by each diagonal line (thus, I, Ih, Ilr, etc.). To extract the names of the Sons of the Sons, read diagonally up from the lower left to the upper right starting with the lower right corner of the square (thus, E, An, Ave, etc.). To extract the names of the Daughters of Light, read diagonally from upper left to lower right starting at the upper right corner of the square (thus, E(l), Me, Ese, etc.). To extract the names of the Daughters of the Daughters of Light, read diagonally from the upper right to the lower left starting at the upper left corner of the square (thus, S, Ab, Ath, etc.).

You will notice that some compromise and adjustment must be made in fitting the letters of the names to the letters in the square. The S in the upper left corner becomes the similar sounding Z in the name of the planetary angel Zabathiel. The fraction 21/8 signifies variously El, E or L separately, I, or Iel. When 8 appears alone, it stands for L. The numbers 26 and 30 also appear to stand for L. The Enochian spelling of the planetary angel of Mercury (Corabiel) differs from the spelling that appears in Agrippa (Cochabiel).

The names of the "governors of the heavens" are written between the points and in the center of the pentagram: Zabathi(el), Zedekiel, Madimiel, Semeliel, Nogahel, Corabiel and Levanael.

The seven names written upon the the interlocking heptagram are the Seven Sons of Light, who are subject to Prince Hagonel.[33] Reading clockwise, they are: I, Ih, Ilr, Dmal, Heeoa, Beigia and Stimcul. The names on the smaller heptagon are the Seven Sons of the Sons and derived from the Sons of Light: E(l), An, Ave, Liba, Rocle, Hagon(el) and Ilemese. It is intended that these names have from one to seven letters. To accomplish this, it is sometimes necessary to double the "el" into a single compound character.

The names inside the points of the interlocking heptagram are those of the Daughters of Light: E(l), Me, Ese, Iana, Akele, Azdobn and Stimcul. Similarly, the names just outside the smaller heptagon are the names of the Daughters of the Daughters: S, Ab, Ath, Ized, Ekiei, Madimi and Esemeli.

On the back of the Sigil of Emeth, Uriel ordered Dee to inscribe a large circle-cross with double beams on the end of each arm. In the angles of the cross are written the four letters A, G, L, A clockwise from the upper left corner. AGLA is a Kabbalistic name of God compounded from the first letters in the Hebrew phrase "Ateh Gebor Le-Olahm Amen" (Thou art mighty forever, O Lord).

The angels ordered that four smaller wax seals be made that were identical to the Sigillum Aemeth. These were to be set under the legs of the Holy Table inside hollow wooden cavities. It is unclear whether these wooden containers, which were to be made of "sweet

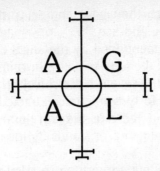

Sigillum Aemeth (back)

wood" (laurel) were attached to the legs of the Table, or were disk-shaped wooden boxes upon which the legs rested. "The four feet of the table must have 4 hollow things of sweet wood, whereupon they must stand. Within the hollow spheres thy seals may be kept unperished. One month is all for the use thereof."[34]

Dee considered the Sigillum Aemeth his most sacred possession, with the possible exception of the holy stone which he believed had been supernaturally materialized by the angels. He carried it with him on his travels through Europe, and brought it back intact to Mortlake. It has survived to the present, and may be seen in the British Museum along with the other relics of Dee's scrying.

SEALS OF THE ANGELIC MINISTERS

Dee is told by Carmara on November 17, 1582: "when thou invokest, thy feet must be placed upon these tables ... comprehending 42 letters and names. But with this consideration: that the character (which is the first of the 7 in the former book) be placed upon the top of the table, which thou wast and art and shall be commanded to have and use."[35]

The tables mentioned by the angel Carmara are the circular seals of the forty-two angelic ministers that serve under each of the seven heptarchical Princes. Each seal is formed from forty-two letters extracted by Kabbalistic means from the Table of the forty-nine Good Angels. Each letter is the name, or stands for the name, of a ministering angel.

First, the letters are written in a letter square of six rows and seven columns. Then this square of forty-two is transformed into a ring, with each of the six rows written out in its own compartment, proceeding clockwise around the ring. Turner interprets the second part of Carmara's instructions quoted above to mean that Dee must place the seal or character of the Prince who rules the forty-two ministers on top of the circular table of the ministers. Accepting this interpretation for the moment, it is not perfectly clear whether the seal of the Prince must be a separate seal that fits within the ring of the forty-two ministers, or whether it may be inscribed within the ring upon the circular table of the forty-two ministers itself. The latter practice would be more convenient.

I am inclined to interpret the second part of Carmara's instructions to mean that the seal of the Prince who rules the day the scrying is performed should be placed on top of the Holy Table of Practice, beside the showstone in its golden frame. However, the wording is ambiguous, and may be taken either way.

No dimensions for the seals of the forty-two angelic ministers are given, but they probably should be large enough to place both feet together upon them. It may be that they are intended to be small, and that the feet should be set over the seals to cover them; or it may be that the feet should fit inside the ring of forty-two letters. If the feet are to fit inside the central space on the seals, a diameter of at least twelve inches is required. If the feet are merely to be set on top of the seals, a diameter of four inches will suffice. This is left to the discretion of the Enochian magician. (See Chapter Nine, where the seals of the Princes and the tables of their Ministers are shown.)

THE HOLY LAMEN

On March 10, 1582, Dee received from an angel who called himself Uriel an irregular triangular figure filled with obscure characters. This was to be his personal symbol of authority, called a Lamen in ritual magic (Dee spelled it "Lamyne"). It was out of keeping with the rest of the Enochian symbols, being unbalanced and seemingly not based on a letter-number system of derivation. Indeed, it had a very goetic look.

At a later date the angel Il declared to Dee that this first Lamen was "false and divilish" and that the angel who had represented himself as Uriel was an impostor. Another Lamen was revealed to Dee, and is represented in Dee's *Liber Mysteriorum Quinta Appendix*.

This true Lamen is composed of eighty-four Enochian letters inscribed upon a symbol that consists of a square tilted up on its corner, within another square which it touches at the corners, which in turn is set inside a third square. It is to be drawn on a piece of paper four inches by four inches. The Enochian letters should be done in yellow oil paint. I suggest that the background be alternate colors of red and blue, to harmonize the Lamen with the Holy Table.

Ideally, this Lamen should be placed in a gold frame so that it may be hung around the neck on a gold chain,

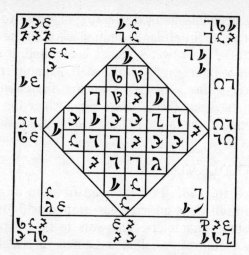

John Dee's Second Lamen

with the letters clearly visible. A frame similar to a small picture frame with a glass front would reveal the letters while at the same time protecting the Lamen from damage. However, none of this is specified by the angels, so the exact form of the frame and its material is at the discretion of the maker.

The angel Carmara tells Dee that the Lamen comprehends "the form of thy own name."[36] Dee, who was skilled in ciphers, was unable to locate any trace of his name in the form of letters on the Lamen.

Dee: The character or lamen for me was noted that it should contain some token of my name. And now in this accounted the true character of dignification, I perceive no peculiar mark or letters of my name.
Uriel: The form in every corner considereth your name.
Dee: You mean there to be a certain shadow of Delta?
Uriel: Well.[37]

By "Delta" Dee means the Greek letter Delta, which he was in the habit of substituting for his name in his magical diaries. It is not clear to me how a Delta may be extracted from the corners of the Lamen, unless it is the triangular spaces created between the central and middle squares. Also, there are three Enochian letters in each corner of the middle square. These form a triangle and might be considered a "shadow of Delta."

Since there seems to be no specific occurrence of Dee's name in the letters of the Lamen, it may be used as a general Lamen in all Enochian magic. To make it personal, the magician should write his or her magical name on the back of the square of paper where the Lamen is drawn and colored. The magical name is the name given to the magician during group initiation, or received psychically during solo practice, and represents the magical self of the magician.

If there are any Enochian magicians foolish enough to deliberately seek to evoke the evil spirits or demons of the Great Table, it would be appropriate for them to use the first goetic version of Dee's lamen, and to write their magical name on the back to personalize it. Since the sole function of this first lamen is in goetic theurgy, it did not seem necessary to reproduce it in this book. Those determined to go to the Devil in their own fashion will find the goetic lamen in Turner's *Heptarchia Mystica of John Dee.*

THE TABLES OF THE KINGS

The Tables of the Kings are to be painted on flat disks of laurel ("sweet wood") small enough that they can be held in the hand during ritual work. Each consists of the seal of the King (a geometric sigil with the name of a related Son of the Sons of Light written upon it in Latin characters) surrounded by a ring containing the name of the King, which in turn is surrounded by an outer ring containing seven letters (or numbers), some of which are reversed left to right. The letters of the outer ring appear to be related by some unknown cipher system to the letters in the name of the King.

Unfortunately, Dee does not describe the method by which the letters on the outermost ring are derived. He refers to them only as the "characters and words annexed to the Kings' names in the outer circumference of the great circle or globe."[38] This would not have mattered had he drawn all seven of the tables of the Kings, but he left only a single example in the margin of his manuscript.

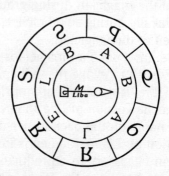

Round Table of King Babalel

It seems fairly obvious that the letters in the outermost ring of the table relate directly to the letters in the name of the King. Babalel's name contains two *B*s, two *A*s, two *L*s and one *E*. The outer ring contains two *S*s, two *R*s, two odd characters that look like reclining 6s, and one inverted *P*. However, I have not been able to determine the method of this cipher. For this reason, it is not possible to perfectly re-create the other six tables of the Kings. They may be made with the outer rings blank so that, if in the future the method for deriving the outer characters is discovered, they may be filled in on the tables.

The Use of the Furniture

Most, if not all, of the furniture and tools described above were used by Dee and Kelley at each scrying session. They certainly employed the Holy Table of Practice, the angelic showstone, the Ensigns of Creation, the single large Sigillum Aemeth and its four smaller replicas under the legs of the table. Dee probably wore the Lamen and ring at each communication with the angels. He and Kelley may have worked with their feet upon the circular seals of the forty-two angelic Ministers of the Princes. If these seals of the Ministers were employed, they would probably have been used in turn on the days ruled by the Princes. However, I have seen no evidence that these seals of the Ministers were ever employed by Dee.

In the Golden Dawn system of Enochian magic, which is the most prevalent form of Enochian magic worked in modern times, all of the above instruments are completely ignored. This simplified the Enochian system of the Golden Dawn, but was a serious oversight on the part of its creator (probably MacGregor Mathers).

I strongly recommend that anyone who is serious about the practice of Enochian magic construct the Holy Table, the Sigillum Aemeth with its four lesser counterparts, the seven Ensigns of Creation (if these are not painted on the surface of the Table itself), the ring, the Lamen, the seven seals of the forty-two Ministers (to be placed under the feet during scrying in the crystal on the corresponding days of the week), and the seven round tables of the Kings. This is the basic minimum requirement for Enochian magic as it was delivered by the angels to Dee through Kelley.

CHAPTER SEVEN

The Enochian Language

THE TONGUE OF THE ANGELS

The force that empowers Enochian magic is the
Enochian language. The angels claimed that this was the
actual language spoken in heaven before the expulsion
of Adam from Paradise. When Adam entered the world
and time began, said the angel Gabriel, he could not
speak. He had forgotten the angelic tongue spoken by
him in his innocence. He "began to learn of necessity"
the primal form of Hebrew, which is not the same form
that Hebrew takes in historical times, although it did
share the same basic division of letters into groups of
three, seven and twelve.

The true pronunciation of this primal Hebrew has
been lost, which is why Hebrew does not carry the same
occult force it originally possessed. However, even the
primal Hebrew spoken by Adam could not begin to compare with the authority and might of the tongue of the
angels: "for as this Work and Gift is of God, which is all
power, so doth he open it in a tongue of power, to the
intent that the proportions may agree in themselves."[1]

According to the angels, the Enochian language is
able to express the primal essence of things directly.

In this language, every letter signifieth the member of the
substance whereof it speaketh. Every word signifieth the
essence of the substance. The letters are separated, and in

91

confusion: and therefore, are by numbers gathered together, which also signify a number. For as every greater containeth his lesser, so are secret and unknown forms of things knit up in their parents. Being known in number, they are easily distinguished, so that herein we teach places to be numbered, letters to be elected from the numbered, and proper words from the letters, which signify substantially the thing that is spoken of in the center of the Creator.[2]

When the patriarch Enoch was taken up into heaven alive, he was instructed in the primal language of the angels, and learned to speak it. For this reason it is called Enochian, being the tongue taught to Enoch. In order to work the magic of the Watchtowers, it is necessary to be able to sound Enochian letters and speak the Keys in the original Enochian. The Keys are of little power when voiced in English.

THE ENOCHIAN ALPHABET

The Enochian alphabet is written from right to left and has twenty-one letters, rather than the twenty-two of Hebrew. This allows the letters to be divided into three groups of seven. Three and seven are magically potent numbers. Three is the number of the holy trinity in its numerous forms in different religions. Seven is the number of the traditional planets of astrology (which include the Sun and Moon). These are the seven "lights" that rule the twelve names of God that rule the ninety-one geographical spirits on the Great Table of the Watchtowers.

The Germanic rune alphabet known as the *futhark* is divided into three families or clans of eight runes each. This threefold division is so ancient, it may be coeval with the invention of runes. Each clan, or *aett*, takes its name from the first rune in the clan, which is regarded as its patriarch. The structure of the Enochian alphabet appears to be very similar, except that each family of Enochian letters contains seven members. We know the Enochian alphabet has a threefold division because the names of the letters were revealed to Kelley in three groups of seven.[3]

Donald Laycock points out that all the letters in the Enochian names for the Enochian letters total sixty-four, a number that may have significance as a magic square. Enochian appears to be an alphanumeric cipher system rather than a normally evolved language. It is possible that the names for the letters were generated by letter squares similar to those so common throughout Enochian magic, although no one has proposed how this may have been accomplished.

The names, shapes and ordering of the letters of the alphabet we can be fairly confident about, because the letters were revealed to Kelley in a vision on May 6, 1583, as recorded in his own manuscript diary *Liber Logaeth*.[4] They appeared on the page before him in a "light yellow cullor" and Kelley traced their outlines exactly before this supernatural color faded. Despite the fact that Kelley traced out each letter to ensure absolute accuracy, the common Enochian typeface used today contains several serious inaccuracies. For the table of the Enochian alphabet given here, and the other illustrations in this work, I have created a completely new Enochian typeface in both print and script characters that I call Madimi. It more accurately represents the shapes of the letters that Kelley received from the angels.

Particular notice should be taken of the small dot in the corner of the letter Pal, which is transliterated into English as x. This dot, which seems to be similar to the dot in the lowercase Latin letter i, is invariably overlooked

🐝 THE ENOCHIAN ALPHABET 🐝

Family of Pn			Family of Tal			Family of Pal		
name	print	script	name	print	script	name	print	script
1. Pn b			8. Tal m			15. Pal x		
2. Veh c/k			9. Gon i/y			16. Med o		
3. Ged g/j			10. Na h			17. Don r		
4. Gal d			11. Ur l			18. Ceph z		
5. Or f			12. Mals p			19. Van u/v/w		
6. Un a			13. Ger q			20. Fam s		
7. Graph e			14. Drux n			21. Gisg t		

Table of Enochian Letters, Print, and Script

when the Enochian alphabet is reproduced. Yet it cannot be a mere blemish in the manuscript, because it appears in both the set of letters transmitted to Kelley on May 6, which may be called formal or print letters, and in the less detailed set of letters recorded by Dee in pen, which may be called Enochian cursive or script.

In the standard Enochian typeface used in Regardie's *Golden Dawn* and elsewhere, the letter Veh (c/k) is shown as two completely separate parts. This is wrong. Also, the letter Med (o) appears as two strokes that curve in opposite directions. The strokes should curve in the same direction. In the standard typeface the letter Gal (d) has two appendages that curve in opposite directions. The bottom appendage should be straight. By the same token, the letter Or (f) has two straight appendages in the standard typeface, whereas the lower appendage should be crescent. The letter Pal (x) is shown as a simple right angle in the standard typeface, but the horizontal bar should project beyond the vertical bar on the left side. The letter Fam (s) appears as two separate crescent strokes in the *Golden Dawn*, but it is shown in both the print and script versions, as well as in the engraving of the Table of Practice in Casaubon, as a single connected figure. Finally, the letter Ceph (z) is almost identical in the standard typeface to the Latin letter P, but the upper point of the crescent should project well past the vertical bar on the left.

I point out these serious errors in the shapes of the Enochian letters that appear in books (including my own books, in those cases where I allowed the *Golden Dawn* typeface to be used) because this is a matter that is never questioned. Although I have stylized the letters for my Madimi font, you may be certain that the significant features of the letters are accurately presented.

ENOCHIAN NUMEROLOGY

What is uncertain is the numerical value of each letter. Robert Turner suggests that the initial letter Pa (B) has a value of seven, because seven is the most important number in the early Enochian communications, and Pa is the most common and most important letter.[5] Why else would it be set in the corners of the Table of Practice, except to stand for the sevenfold magic of the angelic heptarch? Why else would it head the names of the 49 good angels of the heptarch?

We may speculate that the reason the Enochian alphabet is headed by the letter B is because this is the first letter in the first word of the first book of the Bible. The Hebrew Genesis begins with the word "BeReshit," which translates "In the beginning." If the first Enochian letter does have a value of seven, the values of the remaining letters do not seem to follow any logical order, as do the letters of Hebrew. A system of numerical values can easily be imposed on the Enochian alphabet, but this would not be a natural part of Enochian magic.

Laycock postulated the letters that stand for the numbers from one to nine, based on their occurrence in the Enochian Keys.[6] When we add in Turner's B, we get this list:

L = 1	S = 4	B = 7
V = 2	O = 5	P = 8
D = 3	N = 6	M = 9

It is simple to produce higher numbers by combining these letters if some positioning system is used to indicate powers of ten, but this is not the system employed by the Enochian angels. For example, the number 12 is not, as we might expect, LV—it is OS. The number 33 is PD. The number 456 is CLA. No one has yet been able to make sense of this strange numeration. Therefore, numbers can be used in Enochian magic where these have previously been generated by the angels, but it is dangerous for the modern Enochian magician to generate new numbers, since it is impossible to be certain of their meaning.

PRONUNCIATION OF ENOCHIAN WORDS

Enochian names are uncommonly difficult to pronounce, and also very hard to remember, because the arrangement of their letters appears almost random. This results in strange little consonant clusters that never occur in English or any other European language. For example, the name of the demon *Tplabc* would puzzle most speakers, as would that of the angel *Rxnl*. Enochian names are generated by various systems of magic squares. Their significance, and thus their power, arises from the placement of the letters in the name upon those squares.

This is not the case with actually Enochian words, which usually may be vocalized in the normal way without tripping up the tongue. Enochian words appear to constitute a true language with its own odd rules of syntax, although there are numerous exceptions to the rules. The verb conjugations are often irregular. For example, the present tense of the verb "to be":

> I am .... *zir, zirdo*
> we are .... *gea* (?)
> you are .... *geh*
> he/she/it is ... *i*
> they are .... *chiis, chis, chi*

There is no form for "we are" in the Enochian text transmitted to Dee and Kelley. None of the verb declensions are complete. I have conjectured *gea*, but Enochian is so irregular there is only a slight chance that this is the correct form. This limitation of the language led Crowley to coin a number of Enochian words for use in his personal system of magic. Crowley's new words have, through decades of use, acquired a certain respectability.

Eventually, if Enochian is ever to attain the usefulness of a true language, someone with extensive linguistic training will have to radically expand its vocabulary.

Concerning the structure of the language, Laycock states, "there is nothing strikingly un-English about the grammar: no trace of the construct case or irregular plurals of Hebrew or Arabic, no clear indication of multiple cases or complex verb forms, as in Latin and Greek."[7] He goes on to say that the order of the words is similar to English. This is what we might expect if Enochian were drawn from the unconscious mind of Edward Kelley, who knew little Latin and no Greek or Hebrew (although he was able to transmit Greek dictated to him by the angels, who used it as a means to communicate privately with Dee through his scryer without Kelley knowing what was discussed).

The more I study Enochian, the more I am inclined to believe that the angels were autonomous residents of the unconscious, not of Kelley, but of Dee himself. They were able to draw upon Dee's extensive knowledge of ciphers, his vast literary scholarship, and his language skills, to construct the system of Enochian magic and the Enochian language. In my opinion they used Kelley merely as an instrument for communicating with Dee's conscious mind. This radical hypothesis explains how Kelley was able to deliver the Enochian teachings, so many of which are completely beyond his conscious intellectual capability. It presupposes that the angels were able to link Dee's unconscious mind with that of Kelley in some mysterious way. It also explains how Dee was able to make sense out of the convoluted angelic teachings (they were based on his own thoughts and studies), and shows why on several occasions the angels referred to Dee and Kelley as two parts of a single whole.

However, if the Enochian language was the product of Dee's unconscious, we would expect it to be more consistent. Dee's abilities as a linguist were extensive. Perhaps the irregularities in the grammar can be explained by the complex method of transmission and the source. Dee's conscious mind was uncommonly well ordered, but his unconscious may have been less linear.

THE GOLDEN DAWN METHOD

The technique used by the members of the Hermetic Order of the Golden Dawn to pronounce Enochian names was straightforward. Regardie sums it up succinctly in his introduction to the Enochian teachings in the Order papers: "for practical purposes, the language is pronounced by taking each letter separately, whenever a lack of vowels renders it necessary. But, with a little practice, the pronunciation will come instinctively when the student wants it. 'Z' is always pronounced 'Zod' with a long 'o.'"[8]

The leader of the Golden Dawn, S. L. MacGregor Mathers, wrote concerning the pronunciation of Enochian:

> Briefly, regarding the pronunciation of the Angelical Language, thou shalt pronounce the consonants with the vowel following in the nomenclature of the same letter in the Hebrew Alphabet. For example, in [the Hebrew letter] Beth, the vowel following "B" is "e" pronounced AY. Therefore, if "B" in an Angelic Name precede another as in "Sobha" [whose, or whom], thou mayest pronounce it "Sobeh-hah." "G" may be either Gimel or Jimel (as the Arabs do call it) following whether it be hard or soft. This is the ancient Egyptian use, whereof the Hebrew is but a copy, and that many times a faulty copy, save in the Divine and Mystical Names, and some other things.

Also "Y" and "I" are similar, also "V" and "U," depending whether the use intended be vowel or consonant. "X" is the ancient Egyptian power of Samekh; but there be some ordinary Hebrew Names wherein "X" is made Tzaddi.[9]

One of the three original founders of the Golden Dawn, Wynn Westcott, inserted the following note into one of his rituals:

In pronouncing the Names, take each letter separately. M is pronounced Em; N is pronounced En (also Nu, since in Hebrew the vowel following the equivalent letter Nun is "u"); A is Ah; P is Peh; S is Ess; D is Deh.

NRFM is pronounced En-Ra-Ef-Em or En-Ar-Ef-Em. ZIZA is pronounced Zod-ee-zod-ah. ADRE is Ah-deh-reh or Ah-deh-er-reh. TAASD is Teh-ah-ah-ess-deh. AIAOAI is Ah-ee-ah-oh-ah-ee. BDOPA is Beh-deh-oh-peh-ah. BANAA is Beh-ah-en-ah-ah. BITOM is Beh-ee-to-em or Beh-ee-teh-oo-em. NANTA is En-ah-en-tah. HCOMA is Heh-co-em-ah. EXARP is Eh-ex-ar-peh.[10]

In another place Westcott mentions that the name OOMDI should be pronounced "Oh-Oh-Meh-Deh-ee."[11]

Following these directions literally, beginners in Enochian magic sometimes attempt to pronounce each individual Enochian letter, even where there is no need. The advice of Regardie that the letters be pronounced separately "wherever a lack of vowels renders it necessary" should be borne firmly in mind.

THE METHOD OF DEE AND KELLEY

The members of the Golden Dawn overlooked the directions in Dee's diaries concerning the correct pronunciation of the Enochian language. As a rule of thumb, wherever possible, Enochian should be pronounced as you would pronounce English. Only where unnatural consonant clusters in the names make this impossible should individual letters be sounded. Effectively, the names are made pronounceable by the addition of vowels in somewhat the same way that written Hebrew, which consists solely of consonants, is voiced by the insertion of vowel marks.

Dee left scattered phonetic keys in the section of the diaries dealing with the Enochian language. He used "dg" to indicate soft "g" and "s" to indicate soft "c." In several places he indicates that "ch" is to be pronounced "k." The word *ds* (who, which, that) is pronounced "di-es." The letter "z," as Regardie observed, is to be pronounced "zod" where it cannot be merged with the rest of the word, but not always.

For example, the name of the angel Zaxanin would be vocalized as it is in English, but the word *znurza* (swear; swore) should be pronounced "zod-nur-za." By way of contrast, Aleister Crowley, who learned the pronunciation of Enochian in the Golden Dawn and sounded every letter, voiced this word "zod-en-ur-re-zod-a." Besides being awkward, this is clearly contrary to Dee's practice.

Donald Laycock, who provides the most complete directions on the pronunciation of Enochian[12] gives the general rule "consonants as in English, vowels as in Italian." Unfortunately, this is likely to be of limited use to those who do not speak Italian. He goes on to explain that this means "u" should be pronounced as in "put," not as in "but," and also states that in Dee's time the "r" would always be pronounced wherever it occurs.

It should be noted that in Elizabethan times it was a common fashion to substitute "v" and "u," and also "i" and "j." In places I have exchanged the "v" that occurs in Dee's original spelling for a "u" to render pronunciation easier. In the Enochian alphabet "v" and "u" are both indicated by the letter Van. When this letter occurs at the beginning of a word, it is written "v" when followed by a vowel, but "u" when followed by a consonant.

THE TRUE FORM OF ENOCHIAN

The bottom line on the pronunciation of Enochian is that no one really knows what pronunciation Dee and Kelley used, let alone how the angels intended the language to be pronounced. Kelley undoubtedly heard it spoken correctly by the angels, and probably transmitted an accurate version to Dee. But Dee's phonetic notations are makeshift and haphazard. One thing we know for certain is that the members of the Golden Dawn and Aleister Crowley spoke Enochian incorrectly.

An expert linguist with a knowledge of how Elizabeth English sounded, and what accents were current near London and in the county of Worcestershire (where Kelley grew up), who studied Dee's phonetic guides carefully, could probably make a fairly close approximation of the Enochian language spoken by Dee. The rest of us will have to content ourselves with a less accurate version. We can take some comfort in the knowledge that, no matter how badly we mispronounce Enochian words, we are almost certain to be closer to the original than MacGregor Mathers or Aleister Crowley, who both used Enochian magic with good results.

CHAPTER EIGHT

The Heptarchia Mystica

THE ANGELIC HEPTARCHY

In 1582, Edward Kelley scried the complete system of angel magic that is recorded in Dee's manuscript *De Heptarchia Mystica*. This was one of the works found in the secret drawer of Dee's chest fifty-four years after Dee's death, and for this reason it escaped inclusion in Casaubon's *A True and Faithful Relation*. Its neglect has continued down to the present. Although the magic of the angelic heptarchy is an integral part of Enochian magic, it was completely ignored by the Golden Dawn, and consequently by Aleister Crowley, who learned his Enochian magic from the Golden Dawn. Most modern Enochian magicians rely on these three sources, and seem at a loss to know what to do with the heptarch.

A heptarchy is a government of seven rulers. The word had particular meaning for Dee as an Englishman and historian. Anglo-Saxon England was composed of seven kingdoms between A.D. 449 and 828. This group of seven kingdoms was called the Heptarchy. Seven has great occult significance because there are seven wandering bodies that rule the heavens in ancient astrology. The seven astrological planets also rule the Earth through the seven days of the week.

The divine authority of the seven planets is recognized in Christian mythology. They are the seven stars held in the right hand of Christ (*Revelation* 1:16) and the seven lamps of fire that burn before the throne of God, who are also called the seven Spirits of God (*Revelation* 4:5). Each planet is thus a ruling angel. The imagery in *Revelation* plays a large role in the Enochian teachings, as I have tried to show in my book *Tetragrammaton*.[1]

THE TABLE OF THE FORTY-NINE GOOD ANGELS

In the Enochian heptarchy, the seven spheres of the planets are ruled by seven angelic Kings. Each King has a Prince, who is the active power of the King. Under each Prince are five Nobles. The names of these forty-nine angels begin with the letter B, which may represent the number seven. The names were revealed to Kelley letter by letter upon a complex table in the shape of a cross with seven separate parts.[2]

Kelley received this sevenfold cross on April 29, 1582. Seven angels approached holding seven square tables. Each square table was composed of forty-nine cells, and each cell had a letter and a number written in it. The ordering of these letters and numbers appears to be random. The first table was filled with the letter B. The angels used this as the center of the cross, and joined the other six tables to its sides. Moving around the central table clockwise, tables two and three were compressed together and joined to the top, table four was joined to the right, tables five and six were compressed and attached to the bottom, and table seven was joined to the left edge of the central table.

It was then a simple matter to extract the names for the forty-nine good angels of the planets. Starting with the cell in the central table of the cross that contained B1, Dee looked to the cell in the second table that also contained the number one, and found there the letter A.

In the third table of the cross, the cell with the number one contained the letter L. In the fourth table the cell with the number one contained the letter I. In the fifth, the letter G. In the sixth, the letter O. In the seventh, the letter N. These seven letters composed the name of the first of the heptarchical Kings, BALIGON.

In this way, Dee extracted in order forty-nine angels, which he arranged in the form of a ring that was divided into seven parts, each containing seven names. These parts of the ring were associated with the seven planets in an apparently random order. Dee called this table the Tabula Angelorum Bonorum 49.

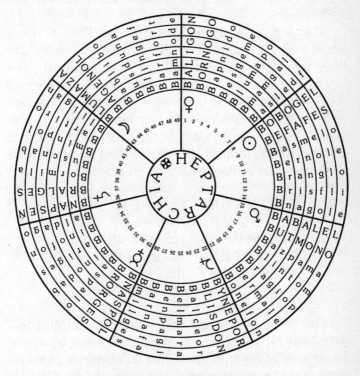

Tabula Angelorum Bonorum 49

THE MINISTERS OF THE PRINCES

Each Prince also has a hierarchy of forty-two Ministers who rule the hours of the day in six groups of seven Ministers, each group ruling four hours of the twenty-four. Every one of these forty-two Ministers is represented by a single letter, so that each of the six groups collectively has a single name that is composed of seven letters. The names of the forty-two Ministers under each Prince are "extracted by a laboriously complex method from the Table of the forty-nine Good Angels."[3] In this way they are composed of the names of the angels. Fortunately, it is not necessary to know this method to use the Ministers.

The angels informed Dee that the King of each planet and his subordinate Prince rule the entire day associated with the planet of the King. Curiously, the serving Prince of each King is associated with a different planet on the Tabula Angelorum Bonorum. The six ranks of seven Ministers rule four-hour periods in succession, beginning at midnight.[4] To take the Ministers of Prince Blisdon (Jupiter) who serves King Bnaspol (Mercury), the ruler of Wednesday, as an example:

E L G N S E B	(hours 1–4)
N L I N Z V B	(hours 5–8)
S F A M L L B	(hours 9–12)
O O G O S R S	(hours 13–16)
N R P C R R B	(hours 17–20)
e r g d b a b	(hours 21–24)

The individual letters that represent the Ministers were each expanded into a seven-letter name by a simple process of permutation.[5] This technique is common throughout Enochian magic. The letter of each Minister is moved to the front of its rank, and the remaining six letters written behind it. To take as an example the Ministers of Prince Blisdon, shown above:

ELGNSEB:
Elgnseb, Lgnsebe, Gnsebel, Nsebelg, Sebelgn, Ebelgns, Belgnse

NLINZVB:
Nlinzub, Linzubn, Inzubnl, Nzubnli, Zubnlin, Ubnlinz, Bnlinzu

SFAMLLB:
Sfamllb, Famllbs, Amllbsf, Mllbsfa, Llbsfam, Lbsfaml, Bsfamll

OOGOSRS:
Oogosrs, Ogosrso, Gosrsoo, Osrsoog, Srsoogo, Rsoogos, Soogosr

NRPCRRB:
Nrpcrrb, Rpcrrbn, Pcrrbnr, Crrbnrp, Rrbnrpc, Rbnrpcr, Bnrpcrr

ergdbab:
Ergdbab, Rgdbabe, Gdbaber, Dbaberg, Babergd, Abergdb, Bergdba

Seven and Twenty-Four

It should be noted that each group of seven Ministers rules 240 minutes. These numbers have significance with respect to the throne of God described in *Revelation* 4:4-5:

> And round about the throne were four and twenty seats: and upon the seats I saw four and twenty elders sitting, clothed in white raiment; and they had on their heads crowns of gold.
> And out of the throne proceeded lightnings and thunderings and voices: and there were seven lamps of fire burning before the throne, which are the seven Spirits of God.

The twenty-four Elders rule over time: specifically the twelve hours of the day and the twelve hours of the night. They are measured, or governed, by the seven lamps before the throne, which are the seven planets. In the heavens, the planets govern the time divisions of the twelve houses by moving through them. On earth, the planets are represented by the days of the week, and in magic are assigned the twenty-four hours of the day to rule in a week-long cycle. The planets repeat themselves in twenty-four sets of seven over the 168 hours of the week. The assignment of the forty-two Ministers to the hours in groups of seven, each of which rules 240 minutes, is another expression of this ancient temporal relationship between twenty-four and seven.

The Grimoire

The grimoire portion of *De Heptarchia Mystica* is somewhat confused in the manuscript. It seems to have been deliberately scrambled by the angels during its transmission. However, it can be reassembled with a fair degree of confidence. It is divided into seven sections. Each part concerns a day of the week, the angelic King who rules that day, and the planet of that day. Serving each King is the Prince of a different (but presumably related) planet, and the forty-two Ministers of that Prince. The single-letter names of the Ministers are arranged in a square of six rows, each row containing the seven letters that rule the 240-minute segment of the day of the King whom their Prince serves.

In addition to these angelic names, each part of the grimoire contains the circular seal of the forty-two Ministers of the Prince, the seal or character of the Prince himself, and a seal containing the name of one of the seven Sons of the seven Sons of Light. These seals that contain the names of the Sons are probably the seals of the Kings.

You will recall from Chapter Six that the names of Sons of the Sons were derived by reading diagonally on a letter table received by Kelley on March 21, 1582. You will also recall that the character of the Prince is to be placed on the Table of Practice (or perhaps on the circular seal of the Ministers, depending on the interpretation), and the circular seal of the Ministers is to be put under the feet of the magician during the invocation of the angels into the stone.

THE FIRST TABLE OF THE KINGS AND PRINCES

The relationship between the Kings and the Princes has a basis elsewhere in the angelic communications. It results from the first form of the letter square from which the Enochian letters on the Holy Table of Practice were derived. This letter square is composed of the names of the Kings and Princes (minus the initial B in each name) written side by side in a square of seven rows and twelve columns. I gave the second, rationalized form of this table in Chapter Six while explaining how the Enochian letters on the Table of Practice were derived. Shown here is an earlier form in which each King was not aligned with its own Prince.[6]

(7th Prince)	lonega	nogila	(1st King)
(1st Prince)	ogonro	legobo	(2nd King)
(2nd Prince)	sefafe	lelaba	(3rd King)
(3rd Prince)	onomtu	ropeny	(4th King)
(4th Prince)	nodsil	lopsan	(5th King)
(5th Prince)	segror	nespan	(6th King)
(6th Prince)	seglar	azamul	(7th King)

First Table of the Kings and Princes

The relationship between the King and Prince on each row of this table is the same relationship that exists in Dee's heptarchical grimoire. The letters in the names of this earlier table are read from right to left. For example, Bnaspol, the King of Mercury who rules Wednesday and is the fifth King on Dee's circular Tabula Angelorum Bonorum 49, is mated with the fourth Prince, Blisdon, who is the Prince of Jupiter. Why this odd relationship between the Kings and Princes exists is not clear, but at least there is a letter square to show that it was not a mistake.

PREPARATIONS FOR THE USE OF THE HEPTARCHY

In general preparation for the work, the magician should fast moderately and maintain a scrupulous cleanliness, both of the body and the clothing. The ritual place must also be kept clean and tidy. Alcohol, tobacco, drugs and sex should be avoided for at least a day before the ritual. Avoid all extremes of behavior. If a series of related rituals is undertaken, abstinence and chastity on the part of the magician will greatly increase the likelihood of success.

A general prayer for the success of the work should be spoken three times each day during the entire period of the ritual working: at dawn, at midday, and at sunset. Dee used the following prayer, which I have simplified somewhat, but the magician may compose an original prayer that perfectly expresses his or her attitude toward the work.

> O Almighty, eternal, true and living God; O King of Glory; O Lord of Hosts; O Creator of Heaven and Earth, and of all things visible and invisible: grant unto your simple servant (N.) your manifold mercies.

I most humbly beseech you to have mercy upon me, to have pity upon me, to have compassion upon me, one who long since has faithfully and sincerely sought to obtain a portion of true knowledge and understanding of your laws and ordinances established in the natures and properties of your creatures.

And since it has pleased you, O God, of your infinite goodness, by your faithful and holy spiritual messengers, to deliver to me a true understanding and comprehension of the orderly form and manner of heptarchical magic, that I may have the use, counsel and help of your many good angels according to their functions and offices, I do most humbly beseech your divine Majesty to favor and forward my present endeavor in this work.

For the sake of your dearly beloved Son, Jesus Christ (O Heavenly Father) I ask that you grant to me this blessing and portion of your heavenly grace. Henceforth enable me and make me apt and acceptable in body, soul and spirit, so that I may always enjoy the friendly conversation and plain, sensible and perfect help, in both word and deed, of your mighty, wise and good spiritual messengers; especially blessed Michael, blessed Gabriel, blessed Raphael and blessed Uriel. Also, especially of those Ministers of the heptarchical mysteries, under the method of the seven mighty Kings and their seven faithful and princely ministers, with their subjects and servants to them belonging.

In your great mercy and grace, O Almighty God, confirm that you are the true and Almighty God, creator of heaven and Earth, upon whom I call and in whom I put my trust. And that your Ministers are true and faithful angels of light, with whom I deal by this heptarchical art.

Grant this prayer, O Heavenly Father, that I may be enabled to better serve you to your greater honor and glory. Grant this for the sake of your only begotten son, Jesus Christ.

Amen. Amen. Amen.[7]

ERECTING THE RITUAL CHAMBER

The magician lays the red silk carpet or its substitute on the floor of the ritual chamber, positions the four hemispherical cases of laurel that contain the four lesser duplicates of the Sigillum Aemeth, and sets the legs of the Table of Practice upon the disks holding the wax seals. The Table is oriented so that its top edge is in the east. Over the surface of the Table a plain linen undercloth is laid that hangs down almost to the carpet. The Sigillum Aemeth is placed on this cloth, in the exact center of the table. If tin plates are used for the seven Ensigns of Creation, these are spaced around the great wax seal of Aemeth as shown in the diagram of the tabletop. Otherwise, the Ensigns are painted directly upon the Table.

A smaller cloth of iridescent red-green silk with golden tassels at its corners is now laid over the Sigillum Aemeth and the Ensigns. The tassels should hang about midway down the legs of the Table. On top of this in the middle of the Sigillum Aemeth is set the scrying stone in its gold frame of four legs (in my opinion this frame should have three legs, but Dee illustrates it with four legs). A consecrated white candle in a single candlestick should be put in the middle of the eastern quarter of the Table to burn during the ritual.

On the edge of the red carpet to the west of the Table of Practice, the magician places the circular table of the forty-two Ministers who serve on the day of the ritual. He stands on this circle of letters during the invocations, and, when seated in the green wooden chair while scrying, rests his feet on it.

The seal of the Prince of the day, who rules the Ministers, is set in the middle of the western quadrant of the Table of Practice. (By another interpretation of Dee's text, this seal is placed on top of the circular table of the Ministers, and then the magician stands on both the seal and the table.)

During the invocations and scrying, the magician holds in his hand (probably the left hand) a circular disk of laurel on which is painted the seal of the King associated with the day. The seal is surrounded by a ring containing the seven letters in the name of the King of the day. A second outer ring contains corresponding cipher letters related to the letters in the name of the King.

Around the neck on a gold chain or silk thread the holy Lamen hangs so that it lies over the heart of the magician. The seal ring of Solomon is worn on the finger (probably the right index finger). Although no robe is mentioned in the manuscript, a simple robe of white linen would be appropriate for ritual work. The feet are best left bare, but this is not specified.

EXORDIUMS TO THE KINGS AND PRINCES

Standing on the circular table of the Ministers of the Prince who serves the King of the day, with the round table of the King in the left hand and the seal of the Prince on the Table of Practice, the magician speaks the Exordium to the Heptarchical King:

> O noble King (N.), in this name and by whatever other names you are called or may truly be called (recite his other names, if known), and by your government, charge, disposition and kingly office, which is (briefly describe the office of the King), in the name of the King of Kings, the Lord of Hosts, the Almighty God, creator of heaven and earth and of all things visible and invisible, I invoke and summon you into this holy crystal stone. Amen.

O right noble King (N.), come now and appear with your Prince and his Ministers, and your subjects, clearly to my sight in a good and friendly manner to my comfort and help, to advance the honor and glory of Almighty God by my service. That by the wisdom and power of your kingly office and government I may be helped and enabled to attain my purpose, which is (state your purpose). Amen.

Come, O right noble King (N.), I say, come! Amen.[8]

After reciting the Exordium to the King, the magician speaks the Exordium to the Prince:

O noble Prince (N.), in this name and by whatever other names you are called or may truly be called (recite his other names, if known), and by your government, charge, disposition, office and princely dignity, which is (briefly describe the office of the Prince), in the name of Almighty God, the King of Kings, and for his honor and glory to be advanced by my faithful service, I invoke and summon you into this holy crystal stone. Amen.

I require you, O noble Prince (N.) to come now, and to show yourself visibly in a good and friendly manner, along with your Ministers, servants and subjects, to my comfort and help, that my purpose shall be well and truly fulfilled, which is (state your purpose) in Wisdom and Power according to the properties of your noble office. Amen.

Come, O noble Prince (N.), I say, come! Amen.[9]

These exordiums to the Kings and Princes have been modernized and edited to clarify their purpose. The spaces in the exordiums should be filled in using the information provided in the descriptions given in Chapter Nine. In a separate section of his manuscript, Dee listed specific characteristics and qualities of the individual Kings and Princes that are intended to be used in their invocation into the stone.

A portion of this material is composed of statements actually uttered by the spirits to Dee through Kelley.

These statements express essential aspects of the spirits. By repeating these statements, prefaced by the words "you have said," the magician demonstrates a true knowledge of the spirit. It is an ancient belief in magic that by reciting the acts and nature of a spirit, as well as voicing its name and describing its appearance, power is gained to command that spirit. Dee relied on this technique in his invocations.

Where several statements made by a spirit were recorded by Dee, I have selected only the most potent and characteristic. In a few instances no statements are given by Dee. I have supplied them from the descriptions of the spirits. These descriptions of the spirits, their functions, their alternative names and their statements must be incorporated into the appropriate places of the exordiums. It is this explicitly expressed knowledge of the names, descriptions, statements, and offices of the spirits that gives the magician power over them.

CLOSING THE RITUAL

After communicating with the angels through the medium of the scrying crystal and directing them according to the ritual desire, the magician speaks a general prayer of thanks to God, the King, and the Prince, then dismisses the angels from the stone in the name of the King of Kings, Almighty God. The candle is extinguished and the stone put away. The tasseled silk cloth is removed and the Sigillum Aemeth stored in a safe place, along with the seals and other instruments. If the Table of Practice is erected in a ritual temple where it will not be disturbed, it may be left covered by the white linen cloth and standing on its four wax seals and red carpet.

CHAPTER NINE

The Heptarchical Angels

THE KING OF KINGS

There is some confusion about the names and offices of the seven Kings. King Carmara, the first King to appear to Kelley, is related by Dee to both Monday (Moon) and Friday (Venus). The same is true of Prince Hagonel, the Prince who serves Carmara. Yet both Monday and Friday have Kings and Princes of their own whose names begin with B, in accordance with the system used for all the other names of the forty-nine good angels.

Dee states quite clearly concerning Baligon, the King of Friday and Venus, "he is the same mighty King, who is here first described by the name of Carmara."[1] Nevertheless, I am inclined to place Carmara in a position of superior authority over the other seven Kings, and similarly to place Hagonel in authority over the other seven Princes whose names start with B.

Carmara is pre-eminently a King of the Moon, which enjoys a special position in Enochian magic. Monday is the Enochian Sabbath, or holy day, on which Dee and Kelley received the majority of important angelic communications. Thus, in my opinion, Carmara is a kind of King of Kings (although this title, strictly speaking, is reserved for Jesus Christ), and Hagonel is a Prince of Princes.

Carmara tells Dee:

> First cast thine eyes unto the general Prince, Governor or Angel that is principal in this world. Then place my name that thou hast already. Then the name of him that was showed thee yesterday (with the short coat). Then his power, with the rest of his six perfect ministers. With these three thou shalt work to a good end. All the rest thou may use to God's glory for every one of them shall minister to thy necessities.[2]

The principal Governor of the world is probably Jesus Christ. After him in authority follows Carmara, followed by Hagonel, his Prince. Then come the six ranks of Ministers who serve Hagonel, with each rank containing seven members. "All the rest" would seem to be the seven Kings whose names begin with B, along with their Princes and Ministers.

I find it useful to think of Carmara acting as the general leader of the Kings under the name of King Blumaza, a name he assumes for his function as King of the Moon. Similarly, I regard Prince Hagonel as assuming the name of Prince Bagenol for his position of authority as the Prince of the Moon.

The cause of the confusion is Dee's identification of Carmara and Hagonel with the King Baligon (Venus) and Prince Bagenol (Moon), who rule Friday, but also with King Blumaza (Moon) and Prince Bralges (Saturn), who rule Monday. This dual identity, and indeed the very existence of Carmara and Hagonel, has never been satisfactorily explained. They would seem to be unnecessary to the system of heptarchical magic. Yet clearly the angels placed them in the position of highest importance.

THE COMING OF KING CARMARA

Carmara was called into the showstone by the archangel Uriel. He came with the appearance of a gracefully proportioned man dressed in a long purple robe (purple was the regal color of the Roman emperors) wearing a triple crown upon his head. Seven other spirits who took the form of men and subsequently declared themselves to be the seven heptarchical Princes waited on him. Uriel gave Carmara a rod divided into three parts, two of which were black (probably the ends) and one red. Concerning Carmara, Dee writes:

> This King only was the orderer, or disposer of all the doctrines which I term Heptarchical, and first by calling the 7 Princes, and after that the 7 Kings: and by giving instructions for use and practice of the whole doctrine Heptarchical: for the first purpose and fruit thereof to be enjoyed by me ...[3]

We may assume that the Princes were summoned first because they are the active agents of the heptarchical magic. The Kings sit in authority over the Princes and command their actions, but do nothing directly. The Kings are the seats of power, and the Princes are their instruments.

Carmara revealed to Dee a flag on a pole. The pole had three points, similar to a crown, at its top. The obverse or front of the flag bore, on the right side, the image of a woman without arms standing in a dress. On the left side, it bore the large capital letters C and B, one above the other, inverted as in a mirror left to right. On the reverse of the flag were the Royal Arms of England, called by Dee "the flag old," which was the English flag from 1400–1603. It consists of four quarters, with two quarters diagonally opposite each containing three fleurs-de-lis (symbol of France), and the other two quarters each holding three reclining lions (lions passant guardant—symbol of England).

Carmara called this flag "the Sign of the Work." We can only speculate about its meaning, since it was never explained by the angels. The fact that the figure on it is female is significant, since all the other heptarchical angels are male (or, in some cases, male and female combined). Queen Elizabeth was the symbol of supreme authority in England in Dee's day. This image may represent her heavenly counterpart, the mysterious Mother of the angel Madimi, who is the same as the Queen of Heaven of *Revelation* 12:1. Perhaps she is shown without arms because she acts through her angelic agents, not directly. The C on the flag may signify the name Carmara, while the B may stand for the forty-nine good angels whose names all begin with B.

PRINCE HAGONEL AND HIS GREAT SEAL

After Carmara, Prince Hagonel appeared in the form of a man in a red robe. Dee notes that all the Princes have red robes, but the robe of Hagonel was shorter than the robes of the other Princes. Likewise, all the Princes have circlets of gold upon their heads rather than crowns. Hagonel held in the palm of his right hand "a round ring with a prick in the midst," which may mean a disk since Dee describes it as "hanging also over his middle fingers." Hagonel told Dee that this ring or disk was Hagonel's seal. It bore the name Barees. Dee drew it in the form of the symbol of the Sun ($\odot$) in his manuscript.

All of the Princes together held up a great star with seven points which Dee called the "Heptagon Stellar." It seemed to Kelley to be made of copper, the metal of Venus. Dee drew this star in his manuscript. The seal of

Hagonel was placed in its uppermost point. The name of the first Prince, Bornogo (Venus), who is Prince under King Bobogel (Sun) on Sunday, was written to the right of the uppermost point. The name of the second Prince, Befafes (Sun), who is Prince under King Babalil (Mars) on Tuesday, was written to the right of the second point, moving clockwise.

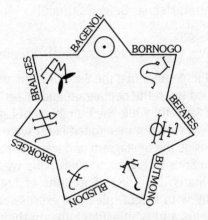

The Heptagon Stellar

This copper star appears to be the great seal of the heptarchical grimoire. It illustrates the correct order of the days for the material that follows. The days are to be ordered according to the order of the Princes on the ring of the forty-nine good angels: Bornogo (Sunday), Befafes (Tuesday), Butmono (Thursday), Blisdon (Wednesday), Brorges (Saturday), Bralges (Monday) and Bagenol (Friday). Dee adheres to this order in his presentation, with the exception of placing the angels of Friday (seventh Prince) ahead of the angels of Monday (sixth Prince). I believe this to be an error, and I have corrected it in the present chapter.

The Sons of Light and Their Sons

After the Princes present this great copper symbol, the servants of Prince Hagonel are presented. These are the "Sons of men and their Sons." The "Sons of men," Dee noted, are the same as the Sons of Light.

Sons of Light
I, Ih, Isr, Dmal, Heeoa, Beigia, Stimcul

Sons of the Sons
E(l), An, Ave, Liba, Rocle, Hagon(el), Ilemese

You will remember that the Sons of Light and their Sons were inscribed upon the heptagram and lesser heptagon of the Sigillum Aemeth, while the Daughters of Light and their Daughters (who are not mentioned here) were inscribed in the spaces inside the heptagram and lesser heptagon.

Both the Sons of Light and their Sons were described to Dee on March 21, 1582. The Sons of Light came as seven youths with bright, pleasant expressions, wearing white garments and white silk cloths on their heads that hung down like twisted rope in the back to touch the ground. Every one of them carried a metal ball in his hand. The first Son carried a ball of gold, the second silver, the third copper, the fourth tin, the fifth iron, the sixth quicksilver, and the seventh lead. All had round tablets of gold on their breasts that bore the letters of their names.

The Sons of the Sons came in the forms of small boys wearing purple gowns with long, hanging sleeves ("like priests' or scholars' gown-sleeves"), and purple cloths about their heads that hung in the back in twisted wreaths down to the ground. They had green triangular tablets on their breasts on which were written the letters of their names. Dee notes that the letters of the first Son of the Sons, El, were combined together into a single character. Sometimes only the E is used to represent this spirit. It should be noted that the "el" in the name Hagonel is also combined into a single character to produce six letters in this name.

THE KEY TO THE SEALS OF THE KINGS

The metal balls in the hands of the Sons of Light may be extremely important. I am inclined to believe that they are the key to the correct placement of the seals of the Kings (each of which contains a name of the Sons of the Sons) with the proper day and King. The planetary metal associated with the Son of Light who corresponds with the Son of the Sons on the seal of each King should be the same as the planetary metal of the Prince serving the King. If my speculation is correct, the relationship between the seals of the Kings and the Princes of the Kings would be as follows:

Sunday
1st Prince: Bornogo (Venus)
2nd King: Bobogel (seal of 3rd S. of S. Ave: copper)

Tuesday
2nd Prince: Befafes (Sun)
3rd King: Babalel (seal of 1st S. of S. E(l): gold)*

Thursday
3rd Prince: Butmono (Mars)
4th King: Bynepor (seal of the 5th S. of S. Rocle: iron)

Wednesday
4th Prince: Blisdon (Jupiter)
5th King: Bnaspol (seal of the 4th S. of S. Liba: tin)*

Saturday
5th Prince: Brorges (Mercury)
6th King: Bnapsen (seal of the 6th S. of S. Hagonel: quicksilver)

Monday
6th Prince: Bralges (Saturn)
7th King: Blumaza (seal of the 7th S. of S. Ilemese: lead)

Friday
7th Prince: Bagenol (Moon)
1st King: Baligon (seal of the 2nd S. of S. An: silver)*

The asterisks after the metals of the Sons of the Sons in the seals of the Kings are those that have been changed from the ones given in Dee's manuscript. The placement of the other four seals in the *Heptarchia Mystica* is in accord with this system I have proposed.

Below, I have allowed the seals of the Kings to remain in the days and with the Kings to which Dee assigned them in his *Heptarchia Mystica*. The key I have suggested above may be in error. Since so much of the structural basis for Enochian magic remains hidden, it is always dangerous to make changes, or to state emphatically that some portion of the system is incorrect.

THE ANGELS OF THE SEVEN DAYS

In the descriptions that follow, it should be noted that although I use the words of Dee's manuscript in many places, this is not a transcription of the *Heptarchia Mystica*, but my attempt to interpret and expand Dee's often cryptic comments, and to rationalize the structure of the grimoire.

Sunday

Second King: Bobogel (Sun)
He appeared in a black velvet coat, close round hose with velvet upperstocks overlaid with gold lace, wearing on his head a velvet hat-cap with a black feather in it. His cape hung rakishly from one shoulder. He wore

Seal of King Bobogel: 3rd S. of the Sons – Ave

his purse on a long thong around his neck that was tucked inside his girdle, and on the other side of his girdle an ornamental gilded rapier. Platform overshoes raised his silk slippers above the mud of the street. His beard was long, his manner ostentatious.

His office is the granting and distribution of all wisdom and science. He teaches philosophy, natural history, and a true understanding of the mysteries of the universe.

"It is not too late to learn."

First Prince: Bornogo (Venus)

He appeared in a red robe wearing a gold circlet upon his head, and showed his seal.

His is the art of transforming the corruption of nature into perfection. He teaches the knowledge of metals, and ministers under his king Bobogel the bestowing of all true learning that is grounded in wisdom.

"What thou desirest in me shall be fulfilled."

Seal of Prince Bornogo

The 42 Ministers of Bornogo

The first group of seven ministers appeared in costly formal clothing similar to that worn by King Bobogel. The other ranks were dressed as ruffians. The last group of seven appeared to be women from the front but men from the rear. They danced, leapt into the air, and kissed one another.

All came forward into a circle. The seven sages stood together. The first sage raised his right foot to reveal an L, the letter of his name. The rest did the same, each in his turn.

```
L E E N A R B
L N A N A E B
R O E M N A B
L E A O R I B
N E I C I A B
A O I D I A B
```

Seal of the Ministers of Bornogo

The first seven merged together into a flame and sank down into the transparent fiery globe of the new world. The second seven fell through the earth like drops of molten metal. The third seven clasped their hands together and dropped down in a dense smoke. The fourth seven joined together and fell like drops of water. The fifth seven fell down like hailstones. The last seven vanished away.

On another occasion when summoned by King Carmara these ministers came carrying a large round table over their heads. They laid it on the ground and stood around it. On the table before each minister was the letter of his name.

Tuesday

Third King: Babalel (Mars)

He appeared wearing a long white robe. The left sleeve was white and the right sleeve black. He seemed to stand upon the surface of water. A crown of gold adorned his head. On his forehead the letters of his name were written.

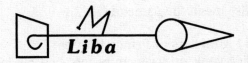

Seal of King Babalel: 4th S. of the Sons – Liba

The power of this king arises from the depths of waters. He is the mighty and wonderful ruler of waters.

"Glorify, praise and honor God."

Second Prince: Befafes (Sun)

He appeared in a long red feathered robe with a circlet of gold upon his head. Written on his golden girdle were the letters of his name. He opened the front of his robe, and appeared to be lame when he walked. His manner was noble and courteous.

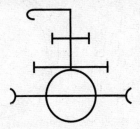

Seal of Prince Befafes

He is the prince of the seas whose power is on the waters. He served Moses to punish Pharaoh of Egypt by closing up the Red Sea on the Egyptian army, and also was a servant of Solomon and the magician Michael Scot, who named this prince Mares. It may have been Dee's belief that it was this spirit who saved him and Kelley from drowning in the English Channel during a gale.[4] The Egyptians named him Obelison, that is, a pleasant deliverer.

"Use me in the name of God."

The 42 Ministers of Prince Befafes

The first rank of seven ministers had circlets of gold around their heads to indicate that they are Princes of the Waters. All of the ministers had the letters of their names written on their foreheads. The letters of the first seven fell down between their feet and were covered over with moving water.

The first seven took the water in their hands and threw it into the air. It became clouds. The second seven threw up the water, and it turned into hail and snow. Each rank in turn threw the water into the air. Then all dived into the water and vanished away.

E I L O M F O
N E O T P T A
S A G A C I Y
O N E D P O N
N O O N M A N
E T E V L G L

Seal of the Ministers of Befafes

These noble ministers are of great power, dignity and authority. Some measure the motions of waters and regulate the saltiness of the seas. Some give success in sea battles. Some rule the fishes and monsters of the deep. Some deliver up treasures and unknown substances from beneath the waves. In general they distribute God's judgments upon the waters that cover the globe.

Thursday

Fourth King: Bynepor (Jupiter)

He appeared in royal robes with a golden crown on his head. The power of this king is distributed throughout and sustains the general state and condition of things. He is in all, and all have their being by him. Although he had a beginning, he can never have an end. He is the workmanship of the word of God, only a single degree lower than the *Vita Suprema* (Highest Life). He is the *Vita Superior* (Higher Life), of whom it may be said: the *Vita Infima* (Lowest Life) is measured by your hands. He begins new worlds, new peoples, new royal dynasties, and new forms of government. Yet none of his power is of himself, but all comes from the name of God.

"Thou shalt work marvels by my workmanship in the Highest."

Seal of King Bynepor: 5th S. of the Sons – Rocle

Third Prince: Butmono (Mars)
He appeared in a red robe with a golden circlet on his head.

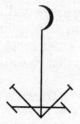

Seal of Prince Butmono

All the beasts of the earth are embrued with the vital essence of this spirit, and take their living pattern from him, excepting only humankind, which is formed in the image of God. He knows the origin, the living, and the end of all beasts, and regulates them with the measure of time. His seal is their glory.

"O God, thou art sanctified: and thou rejoicest."

The 42 Ministers of Prince Butmono
They appeared as formless, smoky ghosts, each with a glittering fiery spark in his midst. The first seven in the foremost rank were red as blood, the second rank were

```
B B A R N F L
B B A I G A O
B B A L P A E
B B A N I F G
B B O S N I A
B B A S N O D
```

Seal of the Ministers of Butmono

orange, the third were whitish. These three had sparks larger and brighter than the rest. The fourth, fifth and sixth ranks were of mingled colors, with smaller sparks in their middle sections. Each spark had the letter of the name of a minister written within it.

Wednesday

Fifth King: Bnaspol (Mercury)
He appeared in a red robe wearing a golden crown on his head.

Seal of King Bnaspol: 2nd S. of the Sons – An

The bowels of the Earth and all her secrets are delivered into the hands of this king. He has knowledge of the mysteries of the past.

"He in whom thou art is greater than thou."

Fourth Prince: Blisdon (Jupiter)
He came dressed in a robe of many colors, but predominantly red, and wore on his head a circlet of gold.

Seal of Prince Blisdon

It is his function to conceal or reveal the secrets hidden within the earth, according to the commands of his king. He finds treasures that are buried and rich veins of metals to be mined. All caverns and subterranean rivers are known to him.

"To me the keys of the mysteries of the earth are delivered."

The 42 Ministers of Prince Blisdon

They seemed to stand in a ring around a little hill of clay. Behind them in the distance stood a multitude of ugly dwarfs, who are spirits of perdition that guard the treasures of the earth for the Devil. The ministers had in their hands the letters of their names.

E L G N S E B
N L I N Z V B
S F A M L L B
O O G O S R S
N R P C R R B
e r g d b a b

Seal of the Ministers of Blisdon

Saturday

Sixth King: Bnapsen (Saturn)

He appeared in the form of a king wearing a long robe with a golden crown on his head.

Seal of King Bnapsen: 6th S. of the Sons – Hagon(el)

The office of this king is to banish and exorcise evil spirits, and to reveal the wicked thoughts and deeds of bad men. He has dominion over the gates of death.

"By me you shall cast out wicked spirits."

Fifth Prince: Brorges (Mercury)

He appeared dressed all in red. When he opened his clothes, ghastly and terrible flames of fire issued out of his sides, which no mortal eye could look upon for more than an instant. Within the flames the letters of his name were tossed to and fro.

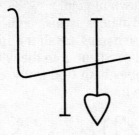

Seal of Prince Brorges

He carries out the commands of his king upon evil spirits and wicked men.

"I know the door of death."

The 42 Ministers of Prince Brorges

The ministers appeared carrying a round table. On the table were written the letters of their names. They cast this table into the midst of flames.

```
B A N S S Z E
B Y A P A R E
B N A M G E N
B N V A G E S
B L B O P O O
B A B E P E N
```

Seal of the Ministers of Brorges

Monday

Seventh King: Blumaza (Moon)

He appeared as a man with a regal manner, wearing a red robe and a crown of gold.

The power of names is his, both to know and to bequeath. By these names are all the spirits of the earth made subject and obedient unto the will of man.

"These mysteries hath God lastly, of his great mercies, granted unto thee."

Seal of King Blumaza: 7th S. of the Sons – Ilemese

Sixth Prince: Bralges

He appeared in a red robe with a circlet of gold on his head. He is the last of the seven Princes who hold up the points of the Stellar Heptagon. He set down his burden and extended his hands to the others to form a ring around the copper star. The seven Princes danced playfully in a circle around the star.

Seal of Prince Bralges

At the command of his King he teaches the secret names of the invisible spirits by which they are summoned and ruled.

"The creatures subject unto me shall be known to you."

The 42 Ministers of Prince Bralges

The ministers are invisible, but appear as little puffs of white smoke without any form. All around them the world shone with brightness.

O E S N G L E
A V Z N I L N
Y L L M A F S
N R S O G O O
N R R C P R N
L A B D G R E

Seal of the Ministers of Bralges

FRIDAY

First King: Baligon (Venus)

He came in the form of a well-proportioned man wearing a long purple gown and a triple crown of gold on his head, and carried a measuring rod of gold in his hand that was divided into three equal parts. The central part of the rod was red, the two outer parts black. His greater name is Carmara, which is voiced among the angels Marmara (but the first M is silent).

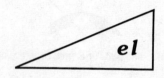

Seal of King Baligon: 1st S. of the Sons – E(l)

From the angel Uriel he had received the golden rod of governing and measuring, as well as the chair of dignity and doctrine. He was the first to appear. He is the teacher, the orderer or disposer of all the doctrines termed heptarchical.

"Come, let us seek the works of God."

Seventh Prince: Bagenol (Moon)

He came wearing a short red robe with a circlet of gold upon his head. In the palm of his right hand he carried a ring or disk with a small hole in the center. This is his seal, which is named Barees.

The Sons of Light and their Sons, and the Daughters of Light and their Daughters, are all his servants. To his power the operation of the earth is subject. He is the first of the twelve, and commands the kings, princes and noblemen of nature. By the seven of the seven Sons

Seal of Prince Bagenol

he works marvels among the people of the earth. He is also called Hagonel.

"By me you shall work marvels."

The 42 Ministers of Prince Bagenol
They appear like bright people. About them the air swarms with creatures. Their letters are on their foreheads.

A O A Y N N L
L B B N A A V
I O A E S P M
G G L P P S A
O E E O O E Z
N L L R L N A

Seal of the Ministers of Bagenol

CHAPTER TEN

The Great Table of the Watchtowers

THE FORTY-EIGHT GATES TO THE CITIES OF WISDOM

On April 12, 1584, at Cracow, the angel Nalvage (through Kelley) said, concerning Enochian magic:

Raphael that brought up the prayers descended: and he was full with the power, & spirit of God: and it became a Doctrine, such was never from the beginning: Not painted, or carved: filed, or imagined by man, or according to their imaginations, which are of flesh: but simple, plain, full of strength, and the power of the holy Ghost: which Doctrine began, as man did, nakedly from the earth: but yet, the image of perfection. This selfsame Art is it, which is delivered unto you an infallible Doctrine, containing in it the waters, which runne through many Gates: even above the Gate of Innocency, wherein you are taught to finde out the Dignity and Corruption of nature: also made partakers of the secret Judgements of the Almighty to be made manifest, and to be put into execution.... I am therefore to instruct and inform you, according to your Doctrine delivered, which is contained in 49 Tables. In 49 voyces, or callings: which are the Natural Keyes, to open those, not 49 but 48 (for One is not to be opened) Gates of understanding, whereby you shall have knowledge to move every Gate, and to call out as many as you please, or shall be thought necessary, which can very well, righteously, and

wisely, open unto you the secrets of their Cities, & make
you understand perfectly the [mysteries] contained in the
Tables. Through which knowledge you shall easily be able
to judge, not as the world doth, but perfectly of the world,
and of all things contained within the Compasse of Nature,
and of all things which are subject to an end.[1]

On May 21 of the same year, after delivering to Dee
the names of the parts of the earth that are ruled by the
first fourteen Aethers, the angel Mapsama spoke more
specifically about the Gates:

> *Mapsama:* These Calls touch all the parts of the World.
> The world may be dealt withall, with her parts; Therefore
> you may do anything. These Calls are the keyes into the
> Gates and Cities of wisdom. Which [Gates] are not able to
> be opened, but with visible apparition.
> *Dee:* And how shall that be come unto?
> *Mapsama:* Which is according to the former instruc-
> tions: and to be had, by calling of every Table.[2]

When Nalvage says that the doctrine of Enoch is not
"painted, or carved: filed, or imagined by man, according to their imaginations, which are of flesh: but simple,
plain, full of strength," he means that it is mathematical
and geometrical in nature. The forty-nine tables are the
large number-letter squares in Dee's *Book of Enoch*,
each of which has forty-nine rows by forty-nine
columns. From these were extracted, at the directions of
the angels, the Enochian Keys.

The forty-eight gates of the cities, or astral residences,
that may be open by the forty-eight Calls or Keys, are
symbolically represented by a large letter square that is
divided into four parts by a central cross called the Black
Cross (it is colored black in Dee's manuscript). This large
letter square is known as the Great Table. Each of the four
quadrants on this Table is called a Watchtower. Twelve of

the celestial cities are accessed through each Watchtower. The gates of the Watchtowers must be opened to allow the passage of the Enochian angels from their own cities into the universe of human consciousness. Each city is represented, or keyed, by a set of letters in a geometric and numerical pattern.

```
r Z i l a f A  y t l p a e  b O a Z a R  o p h a R a
a r d Z a i d  p a L a m    u N n a x o   P S o n d n
c z o n s a r  o Y a u b x  a i g r a n   o o m a g g
T o i T t z o  P a c o C a  o r p m n i·  n g b e a l
S i g a s o m  r b z n h r  r s O n i z   i r l e m u
f m o n d a T  d i a r i p  i z i n r C   z i a M h l

o r o i b A    h a o z p i  M O r d i a   l h C t G a
t N a b r V    i x g a s d  h O C a n c   h i a s o m t
O i i i t T    p a l O a i  A r b i z m   i i l p i z
A b a m o o    o a C u c a  C O p a n a   L a m S m a P
N a o c O T    t n p r n T  o d O l o P   i n i a n b a
o c a n m a    g o t r o i  m r x p a o   c s i z i x p
S h i a l r    a p m z o x  a a x t i r   V a s t r i m

m o t i b      a T n a n    n a n T a    b i t o m

T a O A d u    p t D n i m  a d o n p a   T d a n V a a
a a b c o o    r o m e b b  o l o a G e   o o b a u a
T o g c o n    x m a l G m m O P a m n    o V G m d n m
n h o d D i    a l e a o c  o a p l s T   e d e c a o p
p a t A x i    o V s P s N* C s c m i o   o n A m l o x
S a a i x a    a r V r o i  h V a r s G   d L b r i a p

m p h a r s    l g a i o l  o i P t e a   a p D o c e

M a m g l o    i n L i r x  p p s u a c   n r Z i r Z a
o l a a D n    g a T a p a  S i o d a o   i n r z f m
p a L c o i    d x P a c n  r d a l t T   d n a d i r e
n d a z N z    i V a a s a  a d i x o m   o n s i o s p
i i d P o n    s d A s p i  x O o D p z   i A p a n l i
x r i n h t    a r n d i L* e r g o a n   n P*A*C r a r
```

Tyson's Restored Great Table

THE GREAT TABLE AND THE CITY OF GOD

There seems to be an implicit similarity between the structure of the Great Table and the structure of New Jerusalem described in *Revelation* 21 and 22. New Jerusalem is laid out in a square. Each wall has three gates, for a total of twelve, "and at the gates twelve

Four Rivers of New Jerusalem

angels, and names written thereon, which are the names of the twelve tribes of the children of Israel." The walls of the city have twelve foundations, or foundation stones, each a semiprecious stone upon which is written the name of one of the twelve apostles of Jesus. These stones are probably intended to be the same that were in the breastplate of the High Priest of Israel.[3]

In the center of New Jerusalem, the Lamb of God (Christ) is seated upon a throne from which flows the river of the water of life. This is usually depicted as having four streams that flow outward in the four cardinal directions.

John Dee was aware of this similarity in structure between the Great Table and New Jerusalem. He drew two square diagrams showing the assignment of the twelve tribes to the four directions of space based on *Numbers* 2 and 7, and *Revelation* 21, in his magical journal that deals with the assignment and evocation of spirits on the Great Table.[4]

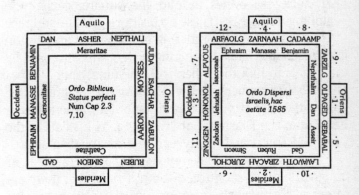

Order of the Twelve Tribes of Israel

The diagram on the left places the tribes of Israel in the quarters of the world they are assigned in the second chapter of the biblical book of *Numbers*, where the ordering of the tents of the tribes around the Tabernacle is described. This same ordering of the tribes to the directions occurs in the seventh chapter of *Numbers*, which sets forth the order in which the tribes made sacrifice at the altar. The order unfolds in a single cycle east, south, west and north, proceeding clockwise. As will be seen later on, this ordering of the directions is crucial to a true comprehension of the placement of the Watchtowers on the Great Table. In the center of the diagram, Dee has written in Latin that this is the biblical order and perfect condition of the tribes.

In the diagram on the right, the tribes are ordered to the directions as they were delivered to Dee by the Enochian angels. Next to the name of each tribe is the name of its guardian or tutelary angel. Notice particularly the numbers Dee has inserted into this diagram. The ordering of the tribes and the angels proceeds in three of four clockwise cycles around the square, each cycle beginning in the east. These cycles have great importance in connection with the ordering of the Enochian Keys on the Great Table. This numbering system was also used by the angels to link the tribes with the ninety-one Princes of the Thirty Aethers. In the center of this diagram, Dee has written in Latin that this is the order of the tribes of Israel after the Diaspora, or scattering, as it exists in the year 1585 (presumably the year he drew the diagram).

These diagrams may represent New Jerusalem or the great altar of sacrifice, or both. Notice that there are three levels in each diagram, or (regarding them as altars) three steps. It is not clear in the diagrams whether the tabs containing the directions should be considered as a separate level, or placed on the same level as the first step. The altar for burnt offerings was square and three cubits high, which may have signified three steps or levels.[5]

THE ARCHITECTURE OF THE GREAT TABLE

The Great Table as a whole reflects this imitation of the pattern of New Jerusalem. Ignore for the moment the letters written on it and consider it as the ground plan for a walled city or fortress that contains within it lesser walled compounds. Each of the long columns and rows would then represent a street. At the ends of these streets are gates. The city has three primary avenues leading into it from each of its four sides, and four lesser avenues. When the four lesser avenues are considered, each side of the Great Table has seven gates, for a total of twenty-eight; a significant number, because it is the number of the Mansions of the Moon. The Great Black Cross that runs through the center of the Table may be assumed to represent the four streams of the river of life that flows out from the throne of Christ, situated at the intersection of the cross.

There are forty-two of these avenues on the Great Table, and since each avenue has two gates, eighty-four gates in all (twenty-one gates, the number of Enochian letters, for each Watchtower). The Great Table may be considered as a whole entity which is divided into four quarters by the Black Cross running through its center. Each quarter, or Watchtower, is in some respects a smaller version of the Great Table. It also has a cross running through its center that divides it into four quarters. Each Watchtower has one main gate in each side and two lesser gates, for a total of twelve exterior gates. By the same token, each quarter of a Watchtower has a cross running through it that divides it into four parts.

Quarters of the Watchtower have only one external gate in each wall, for a total of four.

The central row of each Watchtower, called the "line of God," contains three divine names of power. Reading left to right, these names are composed of three, four and five letters each. For example, the line of God in the Watchtower that occupies the upper left corner of the Great Table contains the divine names ORO, IBAH and AOZPI. There is a direct correlation between these twelve divine names, the twelve permutations of the Hebrew name of God, IHVH, and the twelve tribes of Israel, as I will demonstrate later. It should be noted that each line of God contains a total of twelve letters, and that all four contain forty-eight letters, the number of the gates to the angelic cities.

There may be an important distinction between the spirits represented by the letters in the avenues upon the Great Table, and the spirits represented by the letters contained within the sixty-four walled enclosures. I am inclined to think of the spirits whose names lie within the enclosed spaces as female, and the spirits whose names lie on the avenues, or arms of the crosses, as male, although there is no explicit evidence in Dee's diaries that this sexual division exists. The enclosed spaces call to my mind the walled-off seraglios of Eastern monarchs where their brides and concubines were kept isolated.

This diagrammatic aspect of the Great Table and the Watchtowers is almost never mentioned in descriptions of Enochian magic. Dee makes no reference to it directly in his Enochian diaries and workbooks, but it may be inferred from comments made by the angels. I do not wish to mislead you. This city architecture of the Great Table is my personal speculation, and is not an established aspect of modern Enochian magic.

The Square and the Circle

It is more certain that the Great Table is intended to be surrounded by a larger circle. The square of the Table represents our own earthly realm below the sphere of the Moon. The angels inhabit it in their manifest, earthly forms—that is, their names. The greater circle stands for the totality and unity of creation, embracing the three realms of heaven, earth and hell. The Great Table is thus the central portion of the plan of the universe, foursquare because it is manifest and imperfect.

The image of the Great Table as a square within a circle appears a number of times in the Enochian books. Perhaps the most important occurrence is a diagram in the unpublished manuscript *Liber Scientiae* that was drawn by Dee. It represents the Great Table surrounded

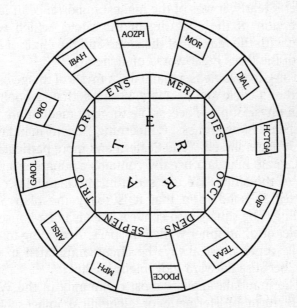

Order of the Twelve Enochian Banners

by flags bearing the twelve divine names that occur in the middle rows of its Watchtowers. This image is vitally important because it established the orientation of the quarters of the Great Table to the four directions. The upper left quadrant lies in the east, the upper right quadrant in the south, the lower right quadrant in the west, and the lower left quadrant in the north.

The square or cross surrounded by a circle also occurs on the golden medallion that shows the various elements of Kelley's Vision of the Four Watchtowers (see the next chapter). It appears in the illustration of the thirty Aethers, where the innermost of thirty concentric circles is divided into four, whereas all the other circles are divided into three. It is a part of Kelley's Vision of the Round House which (in my opinion) describes the flow of dynamic forces upon the Great Tablet. Clearly, it was of the highest importance. It is an expression of the squaring of the circle, which was, along with the making of the stone and the elixir of life, one of the three great works of alchemy.

The Great Table is a mandala, a mystical image composed of a circle and a square, or cross, that symbolizes a non-physical place accessible through meditation and transcendent awareness. Concerning Eastern mandalas, Carl Jung remarked: "The Eastern and more particularly the Lamaic mandala usually contains a square groundplan of the stupa. We can see from the mandalas constructed in solid form that it is really the plan of a building. The square also conveys the idea of a house or temple, or of an inner walled-in space. According to the ritual, stupas must always be circumambulated to the right, because leftward movement is evil."[6]

The mandala appears most commonly in the West in the form of Hermetic or alchemical images. The accompanying mandala of Solomon's Temple is particularly interesting, because it shows seven gates in each side, which are explicitly linked to the twenty-eight Mansions of the Moon. The inner cross, lying within the circle of the Moon, has three gates in each arm, and these are explicitly linked to the twelve months of the year. Notice that the central eye of God has seven points, which stand for the seven planets.

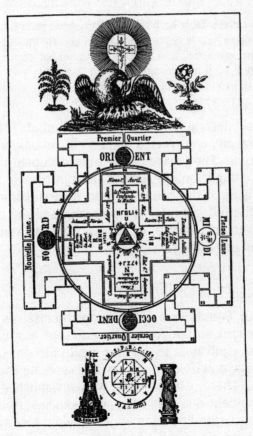

Solomon's Temple

THE THREE LEVELS

The Great Table has three levels or hierarchies of angels that are reflected in its structure. The first level concerns the entire Table. When this is divided into four parts by the Great Black Cross, the second level of the four Watchtowers is indicated. Similarly, when each Watchtower is divided into four parts, the third level of the sixteen lesser quarters appears. The angels tell Dee:

> For every Table hath his key, every key openeth his gate, and every gate being opened, giveth knowledge of himself, of the entrance, and of the mysteries of those things whereof he is an enclosure. Within these Palaces you shall find things that are of power. For every Palace is above his City and every City above his entrance.[7]

This description evokes the ground plan of a medieval city constructed upon a hill, a familiar sight in Dee's time. The palace of the ruler occupied the crest. Surrounding it on the sloping sides of the hill huddled the houses of the common folk. At a still lower level down the hill, a protective wall enclosed the city. The wall contained a gate, or gates, to permit travel both into and out from the city.

THE KEEPERS OF TIME

The four Watchtowers, which are themselves angels, stand guard at the four extremities of our universe. They are equivalent to the four great pillars of Egyptian mythology that hold up the sky and separate Earth from heaven. These Watchtowers were established at the same moment Adam and Eve were expelled from Eden, or so testify the Enochian angels: "Adam received punishment for his offense, in that he was turned out into the earth, and so did Adam, accursed, bring all misery and wretchedness into the world. But in the same instant when Adam was expelled, the Lord gave unto the world her time, and placed over her Angelic Keepers, Watchmen, and Princes."[8]

There are several important points to be noticed in the quotation above. One of the most important is that because of Adam's sin of disobedience, God laid a curse upon the entire world. This curse is what we know as karma, or cause and effect. Karma exists in time. Time began the moment Adam was driven out of Paradise. At the same moment, it was necessary to establish angelic Keepers and Watchmen to ensure the continuance of the Earth in time. The Princes mentioned are presumably the aerial spirits known as the "princes of the air," who are said to be present throughout the entire world.

Access through the gates of the four Watchtowers is access outside the realm of time and karma. It is access to the angels who dwell in Paradise, and indeed to all spiritual creatures who have been barred by God's curse from walking the paths of the Earth. The high angels in the palaces and cities behind the gates of the Watchtowers have the authority to rule over the lesser spirits who inhabit the aerial terrestrial realms of our universe. By some Kabbalistic accounts, these earth-bound spirits are the offspring from the union between the fallen angels described by Enoch and mortal women.

The Ninety-One Regions of the Thirty Aethers

Among these earth-bound spirits are those that rule over the various geographical regions of the world. Each of these geographical spirits (which is identified with the region it rules because it is the tutelary spirit or genius of that region) has its own sigil on the Great Table.

In my opinion, it was the prospect of obtaining command of these tutelary spirits of the kingdoms of the world that was the basis of John Dee's attraction to Enochian magic. Dee received this system of magic in the years just prior to the launch of the Spanish Armada against England. It was a time of exploration and colonization for his native country. This expansion of influence was threatened by the might of Spain. Dee earnestly sought control of the geographical spirits on the Great Table so that through them he could control the fates of the kings of Europe, and remove the dark cloud of foreign domination from England's horizons.

About these geographical genii the angel Nalvage states:

> There are 30 Calls yet to come. Those 30 are the Calls of Ninety-one Princes and spiritual Governours, unto whom the Earth is delivered as a portion. These bring in and again dispose Kings and all the Governments upon the Earth, and vary the Natures of things with the variation of every moment; Unto whom, the providence of the eternal Judgement, is already opened. These are generally governed by the twelve Angels of the 12 Tribes: which are also governed by the 7 which stand before the presence of God [see *Revelation* 4:5].⁹

It was no doubt in reference to the power of these spirits of nations that Casaubon makes mention in his subtitle to his book *A True and Faithful Relation*, which reads in part "Tending (had it Succeeded) to a General Alteration of most States and Kingdomes in the World."

THE POWERS OF THE WATCHTOWERS

In addition to controlling the tutelary spirits of the nations of the Earth, the Watchtowers offer the promise of all human knowledge, including the perfect knowledge of medicine, the arts, and the sciences. They give command of the elemental spirits of the world, movement from place to place (presumably by supernatural means), the transformation of the forms of things, and enable the discovery of hidden things, including the location of treasures and rich mines. No human secret is unknown to them.

The promise of limitless knowledge, even of an abstract kind, was alluring to Dee, who had dedicated his life to study. Later, in his private meeting with Rudolph II, Dee would confide this lifelong passion to the Emperor:

> Hereupon I began to declare that All my life time I had spent in learning: but for this forty years continually, in sundry manners, and in divers Countries, with great pain, care, and cost, I had from degree to degree, sought to come by the best knowledge that man might attain unto in the world: And I found (at length) that neither any man living, nor any Book I could yet meet withal, was able to teach me those truths I desired, and longed for: And therefore I concluded with my self, to make intercession and prayer to the giver of wisdom and all good things, to send me such wisdom, as I might know the natures of his creatures; and also enjoy means to use them to his honour and glory.[10]

Even more attractive must have been the prospect of peering into the veiled intrigues of the courts of Europe, and gaining information concerning the political plots and maneuverings of great men. As a secret agent of the English crown, his mouth must have watered at the intelligence-gathering possibilities of the Watchtowers.

Perhaps sensing this lust for forbidden knowledge, both heavenly and earthly, the angel Ave cautions Dee and Kelley about the limitations of the Watchtowers. At the same time, he cannot resist boasting of their powers:

Ave: Notwithstanding, to know the world before the waters, To be privy to the doings of men, from the waters to Christ; from Christ unto the rewarding of the wicked: The wicked doings of the flesh, or the fond and devilish imaginations of man, or to see what the blessed Kingdom shall be, and how the earth shall be dignified, purged, and made clean, is a meat too sweet for your mouths.

Dee: Curiosity is far from our intents.

Ave: But there is neither Patriarch nor Prophet sanctified, Martyr, or Confessor, King, or Governour of the people upon earth, that his name, continuance, and end, is not (like the Moon at midnight) in these Tables.[10]

[Dee's marginal note: Ergo, these are here to be learned out.][11]

This is quite a boast. It is easy to see why Ave said to Kelley concerning lesser systems of magic, "Nay, they all played at this." Other forms of magic deal with the angels and spirits already present in our universe—the spiritual offspring that arose from sexual union between the fallen angels who taught sciences and arts to humankind and mortal women. Enochian magic holds out the promise to reach beyond the sealed gates of the four Watchtowers and gain the authority and power of the higher angels who have never fallen from grace or walked the byways of the earth. Conversely, it also allows communion with the dark angels who have been cast down into the Abyss for their sin of rebellion. The gates of the Watchtowers are the gates to both heaven and hell.

CHAPTER ELEVEN

The Vision of the Watchtowers

DRAMA IN THE CRYSTAL

The four Watchtowers were not delivered to Kelley merely in the form of abstract letter squares, but were also presented as visionary dramas in which the crystal became the stage and the angels and lesser spirits assumed the roles of characters. The most important and complete playlet is the one I have named the Great Vision. It is remarkable for its beauty, complexity, and mystery.

The Great Vision represents the different classes of angels whose names appear on the tables of the Watchtowers and their hierarchical relationship. Because this vision is so central to Enochian magic, I have given it here in its entirety, along with my commentary.

> Wednesday, June 20, 1584
> *Dee:* It is first to be noted, that this morning (early) to E.K. lying in his bed, and awake, appeared a Vision, in manner as followeth: One standing by his beds head, who patted him on the head gently, to make him the more vigilant. He seemed to be cloathed with feathers, strangely wreathed about him all over, etc.
>
> There appeared to him [E.K.] four very fair Castles, standing in the four parts of the world: out of which he heard the sound of a Trumpet. Then seemed out of every Castle a cloath to be thrown on the ground, of more then the breadth of a Table-cloth.

155

Out of that in the East, the cloath seemed to be red, which was cast.

Out of that in the South, the cloath seemed white.

Out of that in the West, the cloath seemed green, with great knops on it.

Out of that in the North, spread, or thrown out from the gate under foot, the cloath seemed to be very black.

Out of every Gate then issued one Trumpeter, whose Trumpets were of strange form, wreathed, and growing bigger and bigger toward the end.

After the Trumpeter followed three Ensign bearers.

After them six ancient men, with white beards and staves in their hands.

Then followed a comely man, with very much Apparel on his back, his Robe having a long train.

After him came five men, carrying up of his train.

Then followed one great Crosse, and about that four lesser Crosses.

These Crosses had on them, each of them ten, like men, their faces distinctly appearing on the four parts of the Crosse, all over.

[Marginal note: These Crosses seemed not to be on the ground, but in the aire in a white Cloud. The great Crosse seemed to be of a Cloud, like the Rain-bow.]

After the Crosses followed 16 white Creatures.

And after them, an infinite number seemed to issue, and to spread themselves orderly in a compasse, almost before the four foresaid Castles.

Upon which Vision declared unto me, I straight way set down a Note of it; trusting in God that it did signifie good.

After noon, as E.K. sat by me, he felt on his head some strange moving: whereby he deemed that some spiritual Creature did visit him; and as we were continuing together, and I had red to E.K. some rare matter out of Ignatius' Epistles, Policarpus, and Martialis; some of the Sacrament, and some of the Crosse, a voyce answered, and said, That it is true, that the sign of the Crosse is of great force and vertue.

After this, the spiritual Creature seemed to E.K. to be very heavy on his right shoulder, as he sat by me in my study: and as E.K. considered the numbers of such as he had numbered to passe out of the four Gates (it is to wit, 1.3.6.1.5) The spiritual Creature said, the number 16 is a perfect number, consisting of 1.3.6.1.5. He said further more, God the father is a standing Pillar.

Dee: Upon which word I asked him, if I should write such matter as he was to speak. And he answered to E.K. at his right ear.

Spirit: If thou wilt.

Dee: His voyce was much like unto a man's voyce, not base, nor hollow.

Spirit: Divided with a straight line, is one and two.

Dee: What is to be divided with a straight line?

Spirit: The Pillar.[1]

This spirit identified itself as Ave, the second of the Sons of the Sons of Light, who were revealed to Dee and Kelley during the reception of the heptarchical magic. His name appears on the smaller heptagon on the Sigillum Aemeth. He declared himself to be the feathered spirit who had patted Kelley on the head in the early morning hours, and said that it was he who had delivered the vision of the Watchtowers to Kelley. Ave commented at length on Kelley's vision.

Ave: Now therefore hearken unto me: for I will open unto you the secret knowledge of the Earth, that you may deal with her, by such as govern her, at your pleasure; and call her to a reckoning, as a Steward doth the servants of his Lord.

I expound the Vision.

The 4 houses, are the 4 Angels of the Earth, which are the 4 Overseers, and Watch-towers, that the eternal God in his providence hath placed, against the usurping blasphemy, misuse, and stealth of the wicked and great enemy, the Devil. To the intent that being put out to the Earth, his envious will might be bridled, the determinations of God fulfilled, and his creatures kept and preserved, within the compass and measure of order.

What Satan doth, they suffer; And what they wink at, he wrasteth: But when he thinketh himself most assured, then feeleth he the bit.

In each of these Houses, the Chief Watchman, is a mighty Prince, a mighty Angel of the Lord: which hath under him 5 Princes (these names I must use for your instruction.) The seals and authorities of these Houses, are confirmed in the beginning of the World. Unto every one of them, be 4 characters, (Tokens of the presence of the son of God: by whom all things were made in Creation.)

Ensignes, upon the Image whereof, is death: whereon the Redemption of mankind is established, and with the which he shall come to judge the Earth.

These are the Characters, and natural marks of holinesse. Unto these, belong four Angels severally.

The 24 old men, are the 24 Seniors, that St. John remembereth.

These judge the government of the Castles, and fullfil the will of God, as it is written.

The 12 Banners are the 12 names of God, that govern all the creatures upon the Earth, visible and invisible, comprehending 3, 4, and 5.

Out of these Crosses, come the Angels of all the Aires: which presently give obedience to the will of men, when they see them.

Hereby may you subvert whole Countries without Armies: which you must, and shall do, for the glory of God.

By these you shall get the favour of all the Princes, whom you take pity of, or wish well unto.

Hereby shall you know the secret Treasures of the waters, and unknown Caves of the Earth.

And it shall be a Doctrine, for you onely, the instrument of the World.

For, the rest of your Instructions, are touching the Heavens, and the time to come: of the which, this is the last and extream knowledge.

This will I deliver unto you, (because I have yeilded you before the Lord.)

Upon Monday next, I will appear unto you: and shall be a Lesson of a few dayes.

Kelley: The will of God be done.

Dee: Amen.

Ave: In the mean season, desire you of God, such things, as are necessary for you.

He that filleth all things, and from whom all things live, and in, and through whom, they are sanctified, blesse you, and confirm you in peace.

Dee: Amen.

I beseech you, to Notifie this morning's Vision, by words: as all other holy Prophets have recorded theirs.

Ave: A Vision.

The sign of the love of God toward his faithful. Four sumptuous and belligerant Castles, out of the which sounded Trumpets thrice.

The sign of Majesty, the Cloth of passage, was cast forth.

In the East, the cloth red; after the new smitten blood.

In the South, the cloth white, Lilly-colour.

In the West a cloth, the skins of many Dragons, green: garlick-bladed.

In the North, the cloth, Hair-coloured, Bilbery juyce.

The Trumpets sound once. The Gates open. The four Castles are moved. There issueth 4 Trumpeters, whose Trumpets are a Pyramis, six cones, wreathed. There followeth out of every Castle 3, holding up their Banners displayed, with ensigne, the names of God. There follow Seniors six, alike from the 4 Gates: After them cometh from every part a King: whose Princes are five, gardant, and holding up his train. Next issueth the Crosse of 4 Angles, of the Majesty of Creation in God attended upon every one, with 4: a white Cloud, 4 Crosses, bearing the witnesses of the Covenant of God, with the *Prince [*King] gone out before: which were confirmed, every one, with ten Angels, visible in countenance: After every Crosse, attendeth 16 Angels, dispositors of the will of those, that govern the Castles. They proceed. And, in, and about the middle of the Court, the Ensigns keep their standings,

opposite to the middle of the Gate: The rest pause. The 24
Senators meet: They seem to consult.
I, AVE, STOOD BY THE SEER:
It vanisheth.
So I leave you.[2]

Dee thought the Great Vision so important that he
had a medallion made of solid gold upon which the
vision was depicted (see the illustration of the Golden
Talisman, opposite). This relic has survived the centuries and is now in the keeping of the British Museum.

ANALYSIS OF THE GREAT VISION

Kelley sees four castles standing in the four quarters of the
world. Ave informs Dee that these castles, which he calls
"houses," are the four angels of the Earth, who are also
the four Overseers and Watchtowers—it is not uncommon
in magic for a place or thing to also be a spirit.

On Dee's golden talisman, these castles are depicted
as medieval stone towers each with seven battlement
stones (the northern tower has eight stones), one small
square window containing four panes, and a large, open
semi-circular gate. The seven battlement stones stand
for the traditional planets of astrology, the square window represents the letter square of the Watchtower on
the Great Table, and the arch of the gate is the crescent
of the Moon, through whose sphere all heavenly beings
must pass on their journey to the Earth.

This symbolism was probably unconscious, which
would account for the eight battlement stones on the
northern tower (unless this number has some hidden
significance). The four Watchtowers are depicted similarly on the medallion, with only minor variations, so
Dee probably intended them to be perceived as identical.

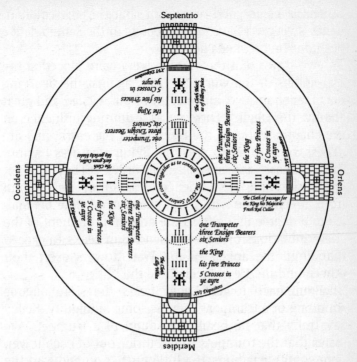

The Golden Talisman

It should be noted that in the engraving of the medallion in Casaubon the colors of the four cloths are inverted top to bottom and left to right. The engraver shows green in the east, red in the west, black in the south and white in the north. I have restored the colors to the arrangement described in Kelley's vision. This inversion was not an error by the engraver—it also appears on the original golden medallion in the British Museum. Dee may well have had some reason for inverting the colors, and it may be the same reason the Enochian letters were inverted on the actual Table of Practice from the arrangement in Dee's manuscript drawing of the Table. However, since I can think of no good reason for changing the colors in Kelley's vision, I have put the colors in the same relative positions on the medallion.

Ave states that the Watchtowers were placed at the extremities of the world by God "against the usurping blasphemy, misuse, and stealth of the wicked and great enemy, the Devil." They act as a limiting influence on the chaotic works of the Devil upon the earth, and are necessary in order to preserve living creatures "within the compass and measure of order." They do not entirely exclude the influence of Satan, or prevent him from affecting the world, but check and bridle his malice to a degree that allows the orderly fulfillment of the "determinations of God." When Satan seeks to exceed that limit, the angels of the Watchtowers exert their power, and the Devil "feeleth he the bit."

From each tower, Kelley hears the simultaneous sounding of a trumpet. There is some ambiguity. Kelley says only that he hears the sound of a trumpet. Ave states that the trumpets sound thrice out of each tower, then contradicts himself a little further on and says the trumpets sound once. It may be that the trumpets sound one time, but sound three distinct notes.

Ave adds the detail that the gates open, and the "four Castles are moved," that is, show signs of movement within. Four cloths, each as wide as a tablecloth, are thrown out from the mouths of the towers toward the center, which Ave refers to as the "Court." Ave calls these the "sign of Majesty, the Cloth of passage." They are equivalent to the red carpets that are unrolled for the passage of dignitaries in our own day. The colors are important because they are linked to the four directions. The color of the east is red, that of the south is white, that of the west is green, that of the north is black.

Ave is more descriptive of these colors. The cloth of the east is the scarlet of new-spilled blood. The cloth of the south is the soft white of the lily petal. The cloth of the west is textured with the scales of a dragon and is serpent-green. The cloth of the north is the color of very dark human hair, or of bilberry juice (a deep blue-black berry that grows in England).

From each open gate a Trumpeter walks along the carpet toward the center court. The trumpets are of a very strange shape, with six bells. Ave describes them as a "Pyramis, six cones, wreathed." Kelley says that they are "of strange form, wreathed, and growing bigger and bigger toward the end." This would seem to mean that viewed from the front the six branching bells of each trumpet spread in the shape of a triangle. They were probably wreathed with flowers.

The beings who proceed out of each Watchtower after its Trumpeter are the angels ruling in that quarter of the Earth.

The three Ensign Bearers carry upon their flags the divine names that are written on the middle rows of the Watchtowers of the Great Table. The first flag bears a name of three letters, the second of four letters, the last of five letters, for a total of twelve. Ave calls these twelve ensigns (three from each tower) "the 12 names of God, that govern all the creatures upon the Earth, visible and invisible, comprehending 3, 4, and 5." These names have a direct correspondence with the twelve overt permutations of the Hebrew name of God, IHVH, which is known as the Tetragrammaton because it contains four letters.

After the twelve ensigns bearing the names of God come twenty-four Seniors who walk six abreast from each gate. Ave says of these old men that they are "the 24

Seniors, that St. John remembreth." St. John the Divine
was the supposed author of the New Testament book *Revelation*. The reference is to *Revelation* 4:4—"And round
about the throne were four and twenty seats: and upon
the seats I saw four and twenty elders sitting, clothed in
white raiment; and they had on their heads crowns of
gold." The Seniors are the lords of the hours of the day.
They establish and regulate linear time: the time-space
continuum that we are familiar with as incarnated souls.

Ave explains: "These judge the government of the
Castles, and fullfil the will of God, as it is written." The
"government of the Castles" is what is known in the
East as karma. Cause and effect is a function of time.
Without time, karma would cease, and chaos would
reign. There would be no divine law, no cosmic justice,
no rational order. Satan (or Coronzon as the Enochian
angels call him[3]) seeks to overthrow the regulation of
the Seniors, but is held in check by the four Overseers.

Behind each rank of six Seniors walks a richly robed
King. Five Princes who serve him carry the hem of his
long train. They are guardant, meaning that they walk
with their faces turned toward Kelley. Of the King, Ave
says: "the Chief Watchman, is a mighty Prince, a
mighty Angel of the Lord." Twice, Ave calls the King of
each Watchtower a Prince, causing Dee to write a cor-
rection in the margin of his manuscript (indicated with
asterisks on page 159). The name of each King appears
in its corresponding Watchtower on the Great Table,
written in the form of a spiral about the intersection of
the great cross of that Watchtower.

Connected with each King, and the Watchtower of
which he is the animate expression, is a seal composed
of four characters. Ave calls these "the authorities of
these Houses" and says that they were "confirmed in

the beginning of the World." About the four characters connected with each, he states that they are "Tokens of the presence of the son of God: by whom all things were made in Creation."

It is not clear what is meant here, unless it is the four graphic seals that were subsequently linked by the angels to the four Watchtowers on the Great Table. Three of these have four divisions, but one does not. The reference to four parts may be to the four letters of Tetragrammaton. At least, this is how this passage was interpreted by the founders of the Golden Dawn, who assigned the letters of Tetragrammaton in a complex relationship to the different parts of the Watchtowers on the Great Table.

After the Princes, a large cross with four lesser crosses in its quarters emerges from each tower. These seem to Kelley to float in the sky on white clouds, with each cross shimmering like a rainbow of many colors. Their pattern is reflected in the Watchtowers on the Great Table—each Watchtower has a large cross dividing it into four quarters, and a smaller cross in each quarter. On the smaller crosses, Kelley reports ten male faces. Ave refers to these as "ten Angels, visible in countenance." The lesser crosses on the Watchtowers of the Great Table each contain ten letters. Each letter is the name of one of these angels, who, as Ave says, bear "the witness of the Covenant of God."

Following the cloud with its five crosses, sixteen "white Creatures" issue from the gate of each Watchtower. Ave calls these "angels, dispositors of the will of those, that govern the Castles." The names of these angels occur in the lesser quarters of each Watchtower on the Great Table.

Finally, an "infinite number" of lesser angels issue forth and arrange themselves in a large circle, standing close to the towers. The wording of Kelley's vision suggests that they come out of the gates after the sixteen Dispositors, but Ave indicates that this multitude is made up of the angels of the thirty Airs, or Aethers, and that they come out from the rainbow crosses. These angels "presently give obedience to the will of men, when they see them." This is extremely important, because it explains why Enochian magic can only be worked with "visible apparition." The obedience of the angels of the Aethers to the magician requires that the magician see the angels in the crystal, or by some similar means.

This echoes the Irish folk tale that a leprechaun can only be commanded by a human being to reveal his treasure while he is held captive. Once he slips beyond the reach of his captor, he regains his freedom. Similarly, the jinn imprisoned by Solomon in brass bottles could be compelled to grant wishes to the persons who discovered them. These tales express a fundamental principle of spirit magic. To be controlled, a spirit must be embodied in some form. This form may be an image or a name. The manifest form of the spirit acts as a kind of psychic bottle that constrains the spirit and binds it to the human mind that conceives the form.

The Ensign Bearers stop at the ends of their ground cloths and maintain their ranks opposite their respective gates. The twenty-four Seniors approach each other in the middle of the Court, while the rest stand waiting in their places. The Seniors form a ring facing inward and seem to hold a consultation with each other. That is the end of Kelley's vision.

Ave points out to Kelley the importance of the numbers of each rank in this procession ($1 + 3 + 6 + 1 + 5 = 16$). This is the number of the Dispositors, or Disposers—those who arrange and set in right order the things of the manifest world, and who ensure that everything happens in its proper season and due sequence.

The communication between Dee and Ave following the initial description of Kelley's vision seems enigmatic, but is really quite simple. Ave merely points out to Dee that the vertical pillar of the central cross on each Watchtower of the Great Table will contain two columns of letters, and therefore it may either be regarded as one pillar, or two if the columns of letters are divided. At this point Dee has not received the Great Table, so the directions mean nothing to him.

CHAPTER TWELVE

The Transmission of the Great Table

THE TABLE OF THE EARTH

As he had promised during his exposition of the Great Vision, the angel Ave appeared to Kelley on the following Monday (June 25, 1584) and delivered the letter squares of the Watchtowers that compose the quadrants of the Great Table. These were presented in the form of visual images within the crystal.

First, Kelley saw the interior of the stone obscured by a white curtain. The curtain was then withdrawn and discarded in a heap in the background to reveal a standing figure in a white smock with a white circlet around his head. Although Kelley did not recognize the angel, Dee knew him to be Ave because the angel had promised to appear on Monday. As Kelley watched, fire consumed the angel to ashes. From the ashes he rose up renewed and brighter than before, saying: "So doth the glory of God comfort the just, and they rise again with a threefold glorie."[1]

The angel extended his hands and seemed to spread or part the air in front of him. A square table appeared before the angel. This table represented the Great Table of the Watchtowers. Dee wrote in the margin of his manuscript "The Table of the Earth." This is also true, since the Great Table applies to the earthly (manifest) realm.

From the table Ave removed a black "Carpet" or cloth. From Kelley's earlier vision of the Watchtowers, we know that this corresponds to the north. Beneath the black cloth was a green cloth, which the angel next removed. The green cloth stands for the west. Beneath the green cloth was a white cloth, representing the south. After Ave pulled off the white cloth, a red cloth was revealed, corresponding with the east. The removal of the red cloth revealed the tabletop itself, which to Kelley appeared to be made of "earth, as Potter's Clay, very raw earth." The table was square, with four legs made of clay or earth. Two of the legs touched the ground, but two did not.

It should be noted that the removal of the different colored cloths symbolically traced a complete circle around the world counterclockwise. This is the direction of motion (as Carl Jung observed) from the conscious mind to the unconscious.[2] The motion is from the circumference in to the center, which is symbolized by the bare clay top of the table. It is the ground of creation and the clay of Adam. The direction of travel around the compass is opposite to that which usually occurs in the Enochian manuscripts, but this is because Ave is traveling from the outward manifest world of Dee and Kelley into the secret center of the Earth, where all mysteries lie concealed.

Why the table should have two legs that touch the ground and two that do not is puzzling. Perhaps it refers to the four elements, two of which (Fire and Air) are light and rise up, and two of which (Water, Earth) are heavy and fall down. However, this is only speculation.

THE FIRST SEAL

On the upper-left corner of the table (the far left from Kelley's point of view) appeared the figure of a T with four bright beams of clear light rising from its top. This is the seal of the Watchtower of the east. The direction is not given, but we know it must be the eastern quarter of the table because it is the first revealed, and the east is the first quarter in Enochian magic. Ave, as he reveals the seals and after them the Watchtowers themselves, is now progressing from the center outward to the circumference.

To make doubly certain that Kelley noticed the position of this seal on the table, Ave pointed at the T with the four beams, saying:

> *Ave:* That part of the Table of the earth of those that govern the earth: that is are governed by the seven Angels that are governed by the seven that stand before God, that are governed by the living God, which is found in the Seal of the living God, (Tau with the four) which signifie the four powers of God principal in earth, etc.
>
> *A voice:* Move not, for the place is holy, and become holy.
>
> *Ave:* I said not so, he said it, that beareth witnesse of himself. Unto this, obey the other three Angels of the Table.[3]

The "Seal of the living God" is the Sigillum Aemeth. "Tau with the four" indicates the capital letter T with the small number 4 written above it that is at the top of the outer ring of letters on the Sigillum Aemeth. This ring consists of forty letters, which are to be understood as four groups of ten. Tau is the Greek name for T. In Casaubon the last letter "u" in Tau is inverted (which often happened in old books) so that the text reads "Tan with the four," an obvious absurdity that has undoubtedly confused many students of Enochian magic.

The seven angels that "govern the earth" mentioned by Ave are the seven angels whose names appear in the larger hexagon on the Sigillum Aemeth (ZllRHia, etc.). These curious names are extracted from a magic square composed of the seven more common names for the angels of the seven planets (Zaphkiel, etc.). These latter are "the seven that stand before God" (see *Revelation* 4:5).

The common names for the angels of the planets are written down continuously in columns from left to right to form a letter square, and the uncommon Enochian names are extracted by reading the rows across the square from left to right. You will remember this square from the earlier examination of the Sigillum Aemeth. It was revealed on March 20, 1582, and is recorded in the second book of Dee's *Liber Mysteriorum:*

Z	l	l	R	H	i	a
a	Z	C	a	a	c	b
p	a	u	p	n	h	r
h	d	m	h	i	a	i
k	k	a	a	e	e	e
i	i	e	e	l	l	l
e	e	l	l	M	G	+

The voice that spoke and commanded Dee and Kelley not to move was the voice of the King of the Watchtower of the east, which the T with the four beams represents. Ave cautioned the men to also remain still while receiving the seals of the other three Watchtowers.

THE SECOND SEAL

On the upper right corner of the table (the far right from Kelley's perspective) appeared a cross which Kelley described as "like an Alphabet Crosse." This symbol, because it is the second to appear, relates to the Watchtower of the south and reveals the placement of that Watchtower on the Great Table. Kelley remarks: "This Crosse, and the other T do seem to lye upon the Table, in a dim dunnish, or a sky colour. All the Table over seemeth to be scribled and rased with new lines."

> *Ave:* The earth is the last, which is with the Angels, but not as the Angels, and therefore it standeth in the Table of the seven Angels, which stand before the presence of God in the last place, without a Letter, or number, but figured by a Crosse.
>
> It is expressed in the Angle of that Table, wherein the names of the Angels are gathered, and do appear, as of Michael and Gabriel.
>
> *Dee:* I remember, there is an Alphabetary Crosse.[4]

This is a clear reference to the small cross that marks the empty final square in the table of the seven planetary angels.

THE THIRD SEAL

The third seal of the Watchtowers appeared, as might be expected, on the lower-right corner of the table (the near right corner from Kelley's perspective). Moving around the points of the compass, this quarter of the table belongs to the Watchtower of the west. On it Kelley observed another cross with letters and numbers in its angles, as appears in the illustration of the four seals. The angel Ave makes the cryptic comment, "It is in that

Table, which consisteth of 4 and 8." This refers to the fifth Ensign of Creation, one of the tin tablets to be placed on the Table of Practice during scrying. This Ensign, which is connected with Mercury on the Tabula Angelorum Bonorum 49, consists of four rows and eight columns. The seal of the Watchtower of the west occupies the second square in the bottom row on this Ensign.

THE FOURTH SEAL

Finally, on the lower left corner of the table of earth (the near left corner from Kelley's perspective), Kelley saw "a little round smoke, as big as a pin's head." This quarter of the table is related to the Watchtower of the north, which is the final point of the compass, moving clockwise around the Earth beginning in the east. The seal of the north is usually represented as a point or tiny circle with lines radiating from it.

Original Four Seals of the Watchtowers

In my judgment, the way these seals were revealed establishes the correct placement of the Watchtowers on the Great Table, and the relationship between the seals and the Watchtowers. Dee never recognized that the table of earth was intended by the angels to represent the Great Table, or that the order in which the seals were placed was to be followed in placing the Watchtowers themselves. Consequently, he remained in doubt about the positions of the Watchtowers on the Great Table for the rest of his life.

"GOD HIS SPIRITUAL CREATURES"

After the fourth seal was revealed, the crystal was obscured by a mist and Kelley heard "a great voyce of thumbling and rumbling" in the showstone. This cleared to reveal an infinite number of bright wormlike things going up and down in the air. Higher than these he saw a cloud of little black specks. They also floated up and down, and sometimes mingled with the worms.

Ave then delivered the monologue on Enoch that I have already quoted in Chapter One ("The Lord appeared unto Enoch," etc.). This is significant because its placement here links the Watchtowers strongly with the wisdom of Enoch, and indicates how central they are to Enochian magic. The Watchtowers are the very heart of the doctrine delivered by the angels.

Dark smoke boiled up from the table of earth, leaving behind it a golden slime. The worms and motes in the air touched down on the surface and ascended up again. Ave took the smoke and "tied it up," saying "I tie her not up from all men, but from the good." Another dark cloud covered everything. This cleared to reveal a grid. Ave told Kelley to note the number, and Kelley informed Dee that he counted thirteen columns and twelve rows. Apparently Kelley was viewing this grid at a right angle, because the grid of each Watchtower has twelve columns and thirteen rows.

Within the squares of the grid appeared characters or sigils. Ave remarked to Kelley, "They be the true Images of God his spiritual Creatures." He ordered Kelley to write down what he saw. Kelley protested that he could not. Dee urged Kelley to try his best. Kelley struggled along for a time, then "fire flashed in his face, and shortly after he said, I perceive they be easie to make, so that I tell the squares, by which the lines do passe, and draw from middle prick to middle prick." He finished drawing the sigils on the grid of the first Watchtower, then proceeded to fill in the grids of the other quarters of the Great Table.

These sigils are not illustrated in Casaubon, but it is obvious that they were the sigils of the ninety-one geographical spirits of the 30 Aethers (see Chapter Fifteen). It is interesting to note that the sigils of the genii of the parts of the Earth were conveyed by the angels before the actual Watchtowers themselves. It would therefore have been impossible for Kelley to consciously connect the graphic sigils with the letters of the spirit names upon which they are based.

THE FOUR WATCHTOWERS

Again the stone grew dark. Ave ordered Dee and Kelley to rest for an hour. No doubt the strain of concentration had been almost unendurable, particularly for Kelley. When the men resumed the scrying session, Ave immediately began to deliver the letters of the Watchtower of the east:

Ave: In the name of God, be diligent, and move not for the place is holy.

Take the first square: write from the left hand toward the right, you shall write small letters and great.

Say what you see [to E.K.]

Kelley: r Z i l a f A u t l p a

Dee: I finde here one square among these Characters that hath nothing in it.

Ave: It must be filled.

Kelley: a r d Z a i d p a L a m[5]

Dee had not yet realized that the grid first seen by Kelley was tipped on its side, and had to be rotated a quarter turn. He was trying to insert the twelve letters of the first row into one of the columns, which have thirteen squares. It did not take him long to understand his error. Some of the letters in the Watchtowers are capitals because they begin the names of the ninety-one spirits of the regions of the Earth, which correspond with the sigils previously drawn on the grids (at a right angle, apparently!) by Kelley.

A few of the letters are mirror inverted left to right. These indicate that the names of the geographical genii that contain them may be written forward or backward. When written backward, they are the names of evil spirits, but when written forward, of good spirits.

Kelley scried the Watchtowers in the following order. Using their middle "lines of God" as identifiers, they are: 1) ORO, IBAH, AOZPI; 2) MOR, DIAL, HCTGA; 3) OIP, TEAA, PDOCE; 4) MPH, ARSL, GAIOL. After delivering the Watchtowers, Ave commented on the significance of the middle line and the pillar of God in each Watchtower.

Ave: Thou hast in the middle line o r o i b A h a o z p i. There are 6 lines above, and six below. That line is called linea Spiritus Sancti: and out of that line cometh the three names of God, from the East gate, being 3, 4, and 5 letters, which were the armes of the Ensignes that were spoken of before. Oro, ibah, aozpi, I said before, that God the Father a mighty pillar divided with a right line.

The Father himself, without the line.

The Father and Son by addition of the line.

These two lines beginning: f A
                                       i d
                                       a r
                                       etc.

That is the great Crosse that came out of the East gate.[6]

The meaning is that the double vertical pillar that forms the center of each Watchtower and crosses the middle row of the Holy Ghost at a right angle signifies God the Father when double, but Father and Son when the two columns are separated by a vertical line. It is not clear in Casaubon which column of the Great Cross belongs to the Father and which to the Son. However, the left column is the column of mercy, which suggest that it belongs to the Son, whereas the right column is the column of judgment, suggesting that it belongs to the Father.

Dee had no problem correctly placing the first Watchtower in the upper left quarter of the Great Table, and linking it with the east. He correctly placed the second Watchtower in the upper-right corner of the Great Table, which is associated with the south. However, for some reason he inverted the third and fourth Watchtowers. He was going to place them correctly. He noted beside the fourth Watchtower, "This is the Table that had the little round smoke," which would have enabled him to place it in the lower left quarter. But immediately below he wrote a second note, saying, "No, it was the Table before."

The result is that on the first version of the Great Table, which is known as the Original Table, Dee has (in my opinion) inverted the third and fourth Watchtowers. The seals of the Watchtowers are placed correctly at the corners of the Original Table, as they were revealed by Ave. The four inverted capital letters are indicated by asterisks. It is not immediately obvious that the capital A in the bottom row of the OIP, TEAA, PDOCE Watchtower is inverted; however, Dee has drawn the A with a hook on its right leg, and written in the margin "A is arsward."

```
r Z i l a f A u t l p a e   b O a Z a R o p h a R a
a r d Z a i d p a L a m     u N n a x o P S o n d n
c z o n s a r o Y a u b  x  a i g r a n o o m a g g
T o i T t x o P a c o C  a  o r p m n i n g b e a l
S i g a s o m r b z n h  r  r s O n i z i r l e m u
f m o n d a T d i a r i  p  i z i n r C z i a M h l

o r o i b A h a o z p i     M O r d i a l h C t G a

c N a b r V i x g a z d  h  R O c a n c h i a s o m
O i i i t T p a l O a i     A r b i z m i i l p i z
A b a m o o o a C u c a  C  O p a n a B a m S m a L
N a o c O T t n p r a T  o  d O l o P i n i a n b a
o c a n m a g o t r o i  m  r x p a o c s i z i x p
S h i a l r a p m z o x  a  a x t i r V a s t r i m

m o t i b     a T n a n     n a n T a     b i t o m

d o n p a T d a n V a a  a  T a O A d u p t D n i m
o l o a G e o o b a u a     o a l c o o r o m e b b
O P a m n o O G m d n m  m  T a g c o n x m a l G m
a p l s T e d e c a o p  o  n h o d D i a l e a o c
s c m i o o n A m l o x  C  p a t A x i o V s P s N*
V a r s G d L b r i a p  h  S a a i z a a r V r o i

o i P t e a a p D o c e     m p h a r s l g a i o l

p s u a c n r Z i r Z a  p  M a m g l o i n L i r x
S i o d a o i n r z f m     o l a a D a g a T a p a
d a l t T d n a d i r e  r  p a L c o i d x P a c n
d i x o m o n s i o s p  a  n d a z N z i V a a s a
O o D p z i A p a n l i  x  i i d P o n s d A s p i
r g o a n n P* A* C r a r e x r i n h t a r n d i L*
```

The Original Great Table of the Watchtowers

Dee numbered the Watchtowers on the Great Table in the order of their initial transmission, in two rows from left to right: 1. Upper left: ORO, etc.; 2. Upper right: MOR, etc.; 3. Lower left: OIP, etc.; 4. Lower right: MPH, etc. He was obviously uncomfortable about inverting the bottom two Watchtowers from their natural places on the points of the compass. Several times he asked the angels for confirmation.

> *Ave:* Now, what is that, that is hard to you?
> *Dee:* First, whether the Table (for the middle Crosse of uniting the four principal parts) be made perfect or no.
> *Ave:* Thou hast found out the truth of it.[7]

There is no question that this numbering of the quadrants on the Great Table was intended by the angels, at least at this stage. On January 14, 1585, Kelley received an extremely important vision which I have called the Vision of the Round House. This vision expresses, in a pictorial form, the flow of elemental energies on the Great Table. At the outset of the Vision of the Round House, the relationship between the four directions and the numbering of the quarters is clearly established.

> On that place standeth a round House, it hath four corners [within] and 4 Windows: and every Window is round, and hath 4 round partitions, round also. It hath 4 Doores, and at the East Door is one step, at the South 2 steps, and at the North 3, and at the West Door, 4 steps:[8]

The number of steps before each door is the numbering of the related quadrants on the Original Great Table.

However, accepting that this numbering of the quadrants of the Great Table is correct, it does not follow that the placement of the two lower Watchtowers on those quadrants is also correct. The seals of the Watchtowers are revealed in a circle around the points of the compass, east, south, west and north. Each class of angels also unfolds in a complete clockwise circle around the Great Table. In my opinion (and it is only that), the Watchtowers should be placed in a complete clockwise circle beginning in the east in the order in which they were first revealed.

THE TABLET OF UNION

After instructing Dee in some of the uses of the names on the Watchtowers, Ave delivered what is commonly called the Tablet of Union, because its letters appear on the central Black Cross of the Great Table. This Tablet is formed by combining the letters in the names of the three geographical spirits of the tenth Aether, ZAX: Lexarph, Comanan and Tabitom. These are written continuously left to right into the rows of a square with four rows and five columns. The initial L in the first name is omitted. Ave instructed Dee to "Look out Lexarph, with the two other that follow him, among the names of the Earth the three last: Lexarph, Comanan, Tabitom."[9]

e	x	a	r	p
h	c	o	m	a
n	a	n	t	a
b	i	t	o	m

Tablet of Union

These names for the spirits of the tenth Aether had been revealed by the angel Mapsama to Kelley more than a month earlier, on May 21, 1584, along with the names of the other spirits of the first fourteen Aethers.[10] Concerning the placing of the names of the Tablet of

Union on the Black Cross, Ave instructed Dee: "Set them down without the first Table: That shall make the crosse that bindeth the 4 Angles of the Table together. The same that stretcheth from the left to right, must also stretch from the right to the left."[11]

The meaning is that the letters in the first two rows of the Tablet of Union are written on the column of the Black Cross twice, with each set of letters progressing from the top and the bottom towards the middle so that the two sets of ten letters are reflected around the center. This type of reflection is known as a lake reflection. The letters of the last two rows of the Tablet are written on the beam of the Black Cross twice, with each set progressing from the center toward the edges so that the two sets are reflected around the center. This kind of reflection is known as a mirror reflection.

THE USES OF THE GREAT TABLE

After delivering the four Watchtowers to Dee and Kelley, Ave explicitly set out the uses to which the Great Table may be put.

> *Ave:* Now to the purpose: Rest, for the place is holy. First, generally what this Table containeth.
> 1. All humane knowledge.
> 2. Out of it springeth Physick.
> 3. The knowledge of all elemental Creatures, amongst you. How many kindes there are, and for what use they were created. Those that live in the air, by themselves. Those that live in the waters, by themselves. Those that dwell in the earth, by themselves. The property of the fire, which is the secret life of all things.
> 4. The knowledge, finding and use of Metals; the vertues of them; the congelations and vertues of Stones -- They are all of one matter.

5. The Conjoyning and knitting together of Natures. The destruction of Nature, and of things that may perish.

6. Moving from place to place [as, into this Country, or that Country at pleasure.]

7. The knowledge of all crafts Mechanical.

8. Transmutatio formalis, sed non essentialis [transmutation of forms, but not of essences].

[Dee's marginal note: The ninth Chapter may be added, and is of the secrets of men knowing; whereof there is a peculiar Table.][12]

The functions of the Great Table are set forth in greater detail in Dee's manuscript *Liber Scientiae* and will be examined in the next chapter, along with the extraction and use of the angelic names.

The Reformed Great Table of Raphael

On April 20, 1587, almost three years following the initial reception of the Watchtowers, the angel Raphael communicated a corrected version of the Great Table to Kelley. At that point, Kelley was disillusioned with the angels and wanted nothing more to do with them, but Raphael was persistent.

Dee: E.K. had this day divers apparitions unto him in his own Chamber, and instructions in divers matters which he regarded not, but remained still in his purpose of utterly discrediting those Creatures, and not to have any more to do with them. But among divers apparitions he noted this of one that said unto him.

Raphael: Joyn Enoch his Tables.

Give every place his running number.

Kelley: What mean you by places?

Raphael: The squares. Which done, refer every letter in the Table to his number, and so read what I will, for this is the last time I will admonish you.

Kelley: A man standeth in the Air in a fiery Globe of my heighth, accompanied with some hundred of Puppets: on the one side of him standeth a woman, and about her are four Clouds all white.

The man upon a white Triangle shewed these Numbers with spaces, as you see following [here follows a large numerical table, which I have omitted].

Dee: Note: When E.K. had shewed me this Note, I by and by brought forth my book of Enoch his Tables, and found the four letters r T b d to be the four first letters of the four principal squares standing about the black Cross: and that here they were to be placed otherwise than as I had set them. And in the first placing of them together, I remember that I had doubt how to joyn them; for they were given apart each by themselves.

Secondly, I found out the 4 Characters; saving they were inverted somewhat, and one of them closed: whereof I found none like, but very near. These Characters were of every square one.

Thirdly, I did take these numbers contained between the lines (some more and some fewer) to be words to be gathered out of the Table of letters: so many words as were distinct companies of numbers; it is to wit, 41.

Hereupon we began to number the squares wherein the letters stood in Enoch's Tables as I had them, but we could not exactly finde the words, but somewhat near. Hereupon being tired, and desirous to know the sense of that Cypher, we left off till after supper, and then we assayed again: but we could not bolt it out, thought we knew very near what was to be done by the instruction of a spiritual Voice, now and then helping us toward the practise.

At length, E.K. was willed to go down into his Chamber, and I did remain still at our Dineing Table till his return, which was within an hour or somewhat more. And at his return this he brought in writing [here is printed in rough form the amended Great Table of Raphael].

Raphael: The black Cross is right, and needeth no mending. But thus much I do, to let thee understand, that thou mayest consider thy self to be a man: And beneath this understanding, unless thou submit all into the hands of God, for his sake; who else leaving you, all naked, provideth in his creatures to his own glory.... I Raphael, counsel you to make a Covenant with the Highest, and to esteem his wings more then your own lives.[13]

The Reformed Great Table of Raphael, which I give here in its corrected form (see page 186), is the arrangement of the Watchtowers most often used in modern magic. The ordering of the Watchtowers on the Reformed Table was adopted by the Golden Dawn, and after the diaspora of the members of this Hermetic Order, was spread throughout English-speaking countries.

As you can see, Raphael does not allocate the Watchtowers around the quarters of the Reformed Table in the order of their initial reception any more than Dee did in the Original Table. He places the first received Watchtower (ORO, IBAH, AOZPI) on the east quarter of the Table, which is the upper left. However, he puts the fourth received Watchtower (MPH, ARSL, GAIOL) on the south quarter, the upper right. The third received Watchtower (OIP, TEAA, PDOCE) he puts on the west quarter of the Table, the lower right, but places the second received Watchtower (MOR, DIAL, HCTGA) on the north quarter of the Table, the lower left.

You must decide for yourself which version of the Great Table to use. In my opinion, neither the Original Table of Dee nor the Reformed Table of Raphael is correct in its placement of the Watchtowers on the quarters. This conviction led me to create yet a third version (see Chapter Ten), which I have named the Restored Great Table, because it restores the Watchtowers to their original sequence around the Earth. The Watchtowers are placed upon the Table in a clockwise circle beginning

r	Z	i	l	a	f	A	y	t	l	p	a	e	T	a	O	A	d	u	p	t	D	n	i	m
a	r	d	Z	a	i	d	p	a	L	a	m		a	a	b	c	o	o	r	o	m	e	b	b
c	z	o	n	s	a	r	o	Y	a	u	b	x	T	o	g	c	o	n	x	m	a	l	G	m
T	o	i	T	t	z	o	P	a	c	o	C	a	n	h	o	d	D	i	a	l	e	a	o	c
S	i	g	a	s	o	m	r	b	z	n	h	r	p	a	t	A	x	i	o	V	s	P	s	N*
f	m	o	n	d	a	T	d	i	a	r	i	p	S	a	a	i	x	a	a	r	V	r	o	i
o	r	o	i	b	A	h	a	o	z	p	i		m	p	h	a	r	s	l	g	a	i	o	l
t	N	a	b	r	V	i	x	g	a	s	d	h	M	a	m	g	l	o	i	n	L	i	r	x
O	i	i	i	T	p	a	l	O	a	i			o	l	a	a	D	n	g	a	T	a	p	a
A	b	a	m	o	o	o	a	C	u	c	a	C	p	a	L	c	o	i	d	x	P	a	c	n
N	a	o	c	O	T	t	n	p	r	n	T	o	n	d	a	z	N	z	i	V	a	a	s	a
o	c	a	n	m	a	g	o	t	r	o	i	m	i	i	d	P	o	n	s	d	A	s	p	i
S	h	i	a	l	r	a	p	m	z	o	x	a	x	r	i	n	h	t	a	r	n	d	i	L*
m	o	t	i	b		a	T	n	a	n			n	a	n	T	a			b	i	t	o	m
b	O	a	Z	a	R	o	p	h	a	R	a		a	d	o	n	p	a	T	d	a	n	V	a	a
u	N	n	a	x	o	P	S	o	n	d	n		o	l	o	a	G	e	o	o	b	a	u	a
a	i	g	r	a	n	o	o	m	a	g	g	m	O	P	a	m	n	o	V	G	m	d	n	m
o	r	p	m	n	i	n	g	b	e	a	l	o	a	p	l	s	T	e	d	e	c	a	o	p
r	s	O	n	i	z	i	r	l	e	m	u	C	s	c	m	i	o	o	n	A	m	l	o	x
i	z	i	n	r	C	z	i	a	M	h	l	h	V	a	r	s	G	d	L	b	r	i	a	p
M	O	r	d	i	a	l	h	C	t	G	a		o	i	P	t	e	a	a	p	D	o	c	e
O	C	a	n	c	h	i	a	s	o	m	t		p	p	s	u	a	c	n	r	Z	i	r	Z	a
A	r	b	i	z	m	i	i	l	p	i	z		S	i	o	d	a	o	i	n	r	z	f	m
O	p	a	n	a	L	a	m	S	m	a	P	r	d	a	l	t	T	d	n	a	d	i	r	e
d	O	l	o	P	i	n	i	a	n	b	a	a	d	i	x	o	m	o	n	s	i	o	s	p
r	x	p	a	o	c	s	i	z	i	x	p	x	O	o	D	p	z	i	A	p	a	n	l	i
a	x	t	i	r	V	a	s	t	r	i	m	e	r	g	o	a	n	n	P*	A*	C	r	a	r

The Reformed Great Table of Raphael

with the upper left quarter (east—ORO, IBAH, AOZPI), then the upper right (south—MOR, DIAL, HCTGA), then the lower right (west—OIP, TEAA, PDOCE), then the lower left (north—MPH, ARSL, GAIOL).

In this Restored Great Table, the numbering of the quadrants (as assigned to them in the Vision of the Round House) remains unchanged, but the numbers attached to the Watchtowers that occupy the two lower quadrants become inverted. The fourth Watchtower delivered by the angels (MPH, ARSL, GAIOL) is placed in the northern quadrant, which bears the number three, and the third Watchtower delivered by the angels (OIP, TEAA, PDOCE) is placed in the western quadrant, which bears the number four.

I suspect that the main reason Raphael felt compelled to deliver the Reformed Great Table to Kelley was to correct the placement of the last two Watchtowers, and that Kelley somehow got the instructions of the angel mixed up. Raphael also corrected many of the individual letters in the Watchtowers. I have adopted these letter corrections in my own Restored Great Table.

CHAPTER THIRTEEN

The Angels of the Watchtowers

"EAST AND WEST, IN RESPECT OF YOUR POLES"

Each Watchtower has distinct classes of spirits that are arranged in a hierarchy of descending authority. The structure of the hierarchy and the functions of its parts are the same for all four Watchtowers. However, those angels whose names are on the Watchtower of the East only act in the east, while those whose names are on the Watchtower of the West only act in the west, and so on.

There is some ambiguity over just where the four parts of the Earth are to be reckoned. Dee quite reasonably asked whether this meant the four directions in relation to the magician, regardless of where he might be standing, or the four regions of the Earth. Ave replied, in a somewhat ambiguous fashion, that it meant the four directions with respect to the poles of the Earth.

> *Ave:* The 24 Seniors are all of one Office: But when thou wilt work in the East, thou must take such as bear rule there; so must thou do of the rest.
> *Dee:* Do you mean the estate, in respect of any place we shall be in, or in respect of any earthly place, accounted always the East part of the world, wheresoever we be?

Ave: The East and West, in respect of your Poles. What will you else of me?[1]

It is not clear from Ave's statement which system the angel intended. Dee's first suggestion, that east should be reckoned from the location of the magician, is a much more workable solution than to try to divide up the nations of the world. To decide whether a particular place lies in the east, south, west or north is by no means an easy task. Obviously, Sweden is in the north, but is England in the north or the west? Is Russia north or east? What about South America? Or Hawaii? Or Morocco? The only certain location is Jerusalem, which was considered to be the center, or navel, of the Earth.

For the sake of simplicity, I suggest that the four directions of the world be related to the place where the Enochian magic is being worked, when the effect is to take place away from the place of working. That is to say, if the magician works a ritual in London that is to take place in Paris, he or she should use the spirits of the eastern Watchtower. Only if the magic is to take effect in the same place as the working of the ritual should the four regions of the Earth be considered. For example, if the magician works a ritual in London that is to take place in the same part of London, without a specific geographical focus, the angels of the western Watchtower would be employed (since England was, in classical times, considered part of the west).

The accompanying table (opposite) shows a Watchtower with the offices of the angels whose names are found on its quarters. It should be noted that the quarters of the Watchtowers are numbered the same way the Watchtowers themselves are numbered on the Great Table.

East 1.	South 2.
Dispositors: Knitting Together	**Dispositors:** Transportation
Good Angels: Teach Medicine and Heal the Sick	**Good Angels:** Precious Metals and Jewels
Evil Angels: Cause Sickness and Death	**Evil Angels:** Counterfeiting and Gambling
North 3.	West 4.
Dispositors: Arts and Crafts	**Dispositors:** Secrets of Men
Good Angels: Transformations of Form, not Essence	**Good Angels:** Knowledge of All Elemental Spirits
Evil Angels: Illusions and Deceptions	**Evil Angels:** Evil and Base Uses of Elementals

Offices of the Angels on Any Watchtower

THE ANGELIC HIERARCHY

The angels on the Watchtowers are those described in an emblematic way in Kelley's Great Vision. The Watchtowers also contain the names of evil spirits not mentioned in Kelley's vision. The Watchtower of the East will be used as an example, but the same classes of angels and spirits are to be found in the same places on all four Watchtowers, and the office or function of each class of angel is similar on all the Watchtowers.

THE KINGS

The King is the angel that Ave describes as the Overseer and Watchtower. This suggests that the King and the Watchtower are, to some extent, synonymous. Ave also says, "the Chief Watchman, is a mighty Prince, a mighty Angel of the Lord." Kelley describes the King as "a comely man, very much Apparel on his back, his Robe having a long train." It is the function of the King to summon the six Seniors for judgments.

The name of the King of the Watchtower of the East is either Bataiva when the King evokes the Seniors for an act of mercy, or Bataivh when the King evokes the Seniors for an act of severe judgment. Ave says, "Thou hast Bataiva or Bataivh. You must take but one of them, either the [final] A or the h. A, *comiter*, and h *in extremis Judiciis*."[2] It is a letter taken from the left column of letters on the double pillar of God in each Watchtower (presumably the column of the Son) that makes the King merciful, and a letter taken from the right pillar (presumably the column of the Father) that makes the King severe.

The name of each King is written in a clockwise spiral around the double intersection of the Great Cross on each Watchtower, beginning with the fifth letter in the line of the Holy Ghost or Spirit. The last letter in the name of the King of the east is either the A or h in the two squares that form the center of the Cross. The letters of the name Bataiva are highlighted in the accompanying diagram, which shows the center of the Watchtower of the East.

a	s	o	m	r	b
n	d	**a**	**T**	d	i
i	**b**	**A**	h	a	o
b	r	**V**	i	x	g
i	t	**T**	p	a	l

The only deviation from this pattern occurs on the OIP, TEAA, PDOCE Watchtower, which is the Watchtower of the North on the Original Table, but the Watchtower of the West on the Reformed Table of Raphael and also on my own Restored Table (remember, the quarters of the east, south, west and north do not shift on the Great Table even when the Watchtowers themselves are moved). On the OIP, TEAA, PDOCE Watchtower the letter "a" occurs twice in the intersection of the Great Cross. Dee has distinguished between the King of mercy (Eldprna) and the King of severity (Edlprna) by interchanging the second and third letters in the name of the King to indicate mercy.

The eight names of the Kings on the Original Great Table of the Watchtowers are as follows:

EAST:	Bataiva (mercy)	SOUTH:	Iczhhca (mercy)
	Bataivh (severity)		Iczhhcl (severity)
NORTH:	Eldprna (mercy)	WEST:	Raagios (mercy)
	Edlprna (severity)		Raagiol (severity)

THE BANNER NAMES OF GOD

The three names of God on the line of the Holy Ghost ("linea Spiritus Sancti") are those that were written on the three banners or ensigns carried out the gate of each Watchtower in Kelley's Great Vision. Ave called these the "names of God, that govern all the creatures upon the Earth, visible and invisible, comprehending 3, 4, 5." It is significant that there are twelve letters in the three names, and twelve names in all. This links the banner names with the twelve permutations of Tetragrammaton: a vital part of Hebrew occultism that both Dee and Kelley were familiar with from their studies.

The three banner names may be regarded as the divine authority of the King of the Watchtower, who is sometimes referred to by the angels as a prince to distinguish him from the One King, Christ. The four Kings of the Watchtowers carry out the edict of God the Son and God the Father. These two aspects of God are of one purpose, as is indicated by the pillar on the Great Cross, which is both the pillar of the Father when undivided, but also the pillar of Father and Son when divided with a line down the middle.

It is under these banners that Bataiva rules the east, Iczhhca rules the south, Raagios rules the west, and Eldprna rules the north (on the Original Table). Dee employs these twelve names in the opening "Fundamental Obesience" to God that comes before all his invocations in his personal Book of Spirits, which is recorded in his manuscript *Liber Scientiae*.[3]

The three names of God are extracted by reading across the line of Spirit from left to right. The diagram below shows the central part of the Watchtower of the East with the names of God in boldfaced type.

f	m	o	n	d	a	T	d	i	a	r	i
o	**r**	**o**	**i**	**b**	**A**	**h**	**a**	**o**	**z**	**p**	**i**
c	N	a	b	r	V	i	x	g	a	z	d

The twelve banner names of God on the Original Great Table of the Watchtowers are as follows:

EAST: Oro, Ibah, Aozpi   SOUTH: Mor, Dial, Hctga

NORTH: Oip, Teaa, Pdoce   WEST: Mph, Arsl, Gaiol

THE SENIORS

The Seniors of each Watchtower are described by Kelley as "six ancient men, with white beards and staves in their hands." Ave explicitly says of the twenty-four Seniors that they are "the 24 Seniors, that St. John remembreth." Therefore their description in the fourth chapter of *Revelation* applies: "And round about the throne were four and twenty seats: and upon the seats I saw four and twenty elders sitting, clothed in white raiment; and they had on their heads crowns of gold." Later, the elders arise from their seats and fall down upon their knees before the throne of Christ and "cast their crowns before the throne."

The Seniors (or Senators as they are also called by Ave) are the only group of angels in the Great Vision that perform two actions. They walk out of each gate in a single rank, six abreast, in company with all the other angels who surround the King. But when they reach the center of the four Watchtowers (called the "Court" by Ave, who is making a pun on the legal court of judgment), they go to the middle and form a ring. Although nothing is described in the middle of the court, this would be the location of the throne of Christ, which is always situated in the center of everything. Ave says: "They seem to consult."

In describing the manner of extracting the names of the Seniors to Dee, Ave says: "Now for your six Seniors: whose judgment is of God the Father, the Son, and the Holy Ghost."[4] The act of judicial judgement is clearly central to the role of the Seniors. The Seniors represent the twenty-four hours of the day, and thus time. They sit in judgment over the actions of the human race, which occur in time. As I have shown in my book

Tetragrammaton, the Enochian angels conceived of the Seniors as being seated around the throne of God in two rings of twelve chairs each, one ring directly above the other.[5] Each ring was in two crescents of six chairs. This is indicated quite clearly in a vision Kelley experienced on January 13, 1584:

> Now I see all those men, whose feet I saw before: And there sitteth One in a Judgement seat, with all his teeth fiery. And there sit six, on one side of him, and six on the other. And there sit twelve in a lower seat under them. All the place is like Gold, garnished with precious stones. On his head is a great stone; covering his head; a stone most bright, brighter then fire.[6]

The reason Ave says that the Seniors are "of God the Father, the Son, and the Holy Ghost" is because their names trace out the Great Cross on each Watchtower, with each name beginning from one of the two letters at the intersection of the Cross and proceeding outward. The names of the two Seniors located on the line of the Holy Spirit may be written with either six or seven letters, depending on which of the two letters at the intersection of the Cross is chosen to begin the name. For example, the name of the first Senior of the east may be either Abioro or Habioro, reading from either of the letters at the center of the Great Cross to the left along the line of Spirit.

Ave tells Dee that he should make the names of the two Seniors located on the line of Spirit to be of seven letters "when the wrath of God is to be encreased." The addition of the extra letter intensifies the power of the Seniors, which is the power of judgment. For the sake of uniformity, the names of all six of the Seniors are usually written with seven letters. In the following diagram, the names of the Seniors of the Watchtower of the East are indicated in boldfaced type.

```
                a   f   A   u
                a   i   d   p
                s   a   r   o
                t   x   o   P
                s   o   m   r
    f m o n d   a   T   d i a r i
    o r o i b   A   h   a o z p i
    c N a b r   V   i   x g a z d
                t   T   p a
                o   o   o a
                O   T   t n
                m   a   g o
                l   r   a p
```

The names of the twenty-four Seniors on the Original Great Table are:

EAST:	(H)abioro	SOUTH:	(L)aidrom
	Aaoxaif		Aczinor
	Htmorda		Lzinopo
	(A)haozpi		(A)lhctga
	Hipotga		Lhiansa
	Avtotar		Acmbicu

NORTH:	(A)aetpio	WEST:	(L)srahpm
	Adoeoet		Saiinou
	Alndood		Laoaxrp
	(A)apdoce		(S)lgaiol
	Arinnap		Ligdisa
	Anodoin		Soaiznt

THE DISPOSITORS

The sixteen Dispositors in each Watchtower are located above the arms of the four lesser crosses. Ave says: "After every Cross, attendeth 16 Angels, dispositors of the will of those, that govern the Castles." It is the Dispositors who actually carry out the will of the Kings. Kelley describes them as "16 white Creatures." Concerning these sixteen angels who are above the lesser crosses, Ave tells Dee that they "have no participation with Devils."[7]

There are four Dispositors above every lesser cross. Each is represented by a single letter. For example, the diagram below shows the subquarter of the east (upper left quarter) on the Watchtower that occupies the eastern quarter of the Original Great Table. In this diagram, the four Dispositors are highlighted in boldfaced type.

r	**Z**	i	**l**	a
a	r	d	Z	a
c	z	o	n	s
T	o	i	T	t
S	i	g	a	s
f	m	o	n	d

As was true of the single-letter names of the forty-two Ministers that serve each heptarchical Prince, these rows of single letters may be permuted to yield four names of four letters. For example, the four letters above the arm of the lesser cross in the eastern subquarter of the Watchtower of the East are r Z l a. Each letter represents an angel. By moving each letter in turn to the beginning of the row, four names of four letters are generated:

R	z	l	a
Z	l	a	r
L	a	r	z
A	r	z	l

The set of four Dispositors above the arm of each lesser cross is ruled by a specific name of God. This divine name is created by adding the letter in the Black Cross of the Great Table that stands in the same row as the four Dispositors to the head of the four letters of the Dispositors. In the example, the letter in the Black Cross that shares the same row with the Dispositors above the lesser cross in the eastern subquarter of the Watchtower of the East is e. This letter from the Black Cross is placed before the letters of the group of Dispositors to form the divine name Erzla.

By a similar process, the divine name that rules the four Dispositors above the southern lesser cross of the Watchtower of the East is Eutpa. The divine name that rules the four Dispositors of the western lesser cross of this Watchtower is Hxgzd. The divine name that rules the four Dispositors of the northern lesser cross is Hcnbr. The divine name is employed ritually to evoke the four Dispositors related to it.

Each of these four groups of Dispositors has its own function in Enochian magic.[8] Dispositors in the eastern subquarters rule the "knitting together of Natures," which means the joining together of things, as in the process of growth or healing. The opposite power also applies, which is the destruction of natures, since the creation of one thing is the destruction of another. Elsewhere, in the list of uses of the Great Table, Ave tells Dee that these angels control: "The Conjoyning and knitting together of Natures. The Destruction of Nature, and of things that may perish."[9] Those in the southern subquarters rule the "carrying from place," which probably signifies physical travel of persons and the movement of objects. In the list of uses of the Great Table Ave calls this: "Moving from place to place [as, into this Country, or that Country at pleasure]."

About those in the western subquarters, Ave tells Dee: "Herein may you find the secrets of Kings, and so unto the lowest degree," which seems generally to signify the revelation of secret things. In a marginal note, Dee shows that he understood this as "the secrets of men knowing."

Dispositors in the northern subquarters rule "All Hand-crafts, or Arts," which signifies the teaching and bringing of success in the arts and sciences. Dee understood this to mean "All humane knowledge."

The function of corresponding groups is the same on all the Watchtowers, but applies to different zones of the Earth. Ave tells Dee:

> But you must Note, That as the Angels of the first of the four Crosses in the East, which are for Medicine: so are the first of the second, the first of the third, and the first of the fourth; so that for Medicine there be sixteen, and so of all the rest in their order: but that they differ in that, some be the angels of the East, other some of the West, and so of the rest.[10]

Ave is talking about the angels beneath the arms of the lesser crosses here, but the principle applies to the Dispositors as well. For example, the office of the four angels above the lesser cross of the west on the Watchtower of the East is to reveal secrets in the eastern part of the world. The function of the similar group above the lesser cross of the west on the Watchtower of the North is also to reveal secrets, but these four angels reveal the secrets of the northern part of the world.

Listed in the accompanying table are the names of the sixty-four Dispositors who stand above the arms of the sixteen lesser crosses on the Original Great Table, along with the ruling divine names and offices of these angels. Again, it must be stressed that the quarters east, south, west and north relate to the Great Table itself, not to the individual Watchtowers. The associations of the Dispositors with the directions will be somewhat different on the Reformed Table of Raphael and my own Restored Table because the Watchtowers occupy different quarters.

Subquarter	Watchtowers				Function
	East	South	West	North	
Eastern	Rzla	Boza	Taad	Dopa	Knitting
	Zlar	Ozab	Aadt	Opad	Together
	Larz	Zabo	Adta	Pado	of
	Arzl	Aboz	Dtaa	Adop	Natures
God Names	Erzla	Eboza	Ataad	Adopa	
Southern	Utpa	Phra	Tdim	Anaa	
	Tpau	Hrap	Dimt	Naaa	Carrying
	Paut	Raph	Imtd	Aaan	from
	Autp	Aphr	Mtdi	Aana	to Place
God Names	Eutpa	Ephra	Atdim	Aanaa	
Western	Xgzd	Iaom	Nlrx	Ziza	
	Gzdx	Aomi	Lrxn	Izaz	Discovery
	Zdxg	Omia	Rxnl	Zazi	of
	Dxgz	Miao	Xnlr	Aziz	Secrets
God Names	Hxgzd	Hiaom	Pnlrx	Pziza	
Northern	Cnbr	Roan	Magl	Psac	Teaching
	Nbrc	Oanr	Aglm	Sacp	of Arts
	Brcn	Anro	Glma	Acps	and
	Rcnb	Nroa	Lmag	Cpsa	Crafts
God Names	Hcnbr	Hroan	Pmagl	Ppsac	

The Dispositors on the Original Great Table

The Angels Both Good and Evil

These are the angels in each Watchtower whose names are written on either side of the lesser crosses beneath the arms of the lesser crosses. They are obviously related to the sixteen Dispositors, but this relationship is never made completely clear by the Enochian angels. The sixteen angels above the arms of the lesser crosses are said by Ave to be wholly good, whereas the sixteen angels below the arms are of a mixed nature, neither wholly good nor wholly evil.

Only one set of sixteen angels for each Watchtower appears in Kelley's Great Vision, so it is possible that by the Dispositors Ave intends the angels below the arms of the crosses. I tend to believe that the Dispositors are the angels above the arms because all the other angels in the Great Vision are good. It might be speculated that the sixteen angels above the arms rule the sixteen below the arms, but Ave does not directly state this relationship.

There are four good angels and four sibling evil angels below the arm of each lesser cross. The letters that make up the names of the good and evil angels in the eastern subquarter of the Watchtower of the East are highlighted below in bold type.

r	Z	i	l	a
a	r	d	Z	a
c	**z**	o	**n**	**s**
T	o	i	**T**	**t**
S	i	g	**a**	**s**
f	**m**	o	**n**	**d**

When the names of the angels below the arms of the lesser crosses are written with four letters, they are good angels, but when they are written with only three letters, they are evil angels. Thus they form two distinct sets of angels, but since both good and evil angels derive from the same letters, they should be understood as related, each pair composed of a good and an evil twin.

THE GOOD ANGELS

The names of the good angels are derived by reading across each row from left to right. In the example, the good angels of the subquarter of the east on the Watchtower of the East are Czns, Tott, Sias and Fmnd. To greatly increase the effectiveness of their function, they may be made into names of five letters by including the letters in the column of the lesser cross: Czons, Toitt, Sigas, Fmond.

Each group of four good angels in the subquarter of a Watchtower has its own particular function. The function of the four angels in the example is healing. By adding the letters in the stem of the lesser cross to the names, their power of healing becomes enhanced. Ave says concerning the four good angels in the subquarter of the east on the Watchtower of the East: "If it be an incurable disease (in the judgment of man) then adde the letter that standeth against the name, and make him up five: then he cureth miraculously."[11]

Dee understood Ave's words to mean the letter in the column of the lesser cross should be added to the names, and in his *Liber Scientiae* he gives the names of the good angels with five letters based on this assumption. I should point out, however, that the directions of the angel are not altogether clear. It is possible that Ave intended that the letter in the Black Cross that occupies the same row as the name of a good angel should be added to the front of the name of the angel to intensify its power. If this is done, the four good angels whose names are of five letters would be Xczns, Atott, Rsias and Pfmnd. In giving the names of the good angels, I have adhered to Dee's understanding of Ave's directions, but I wanted to point out that another interpretation is possible.

The four good angels of each subquarter are invoked to visible appearance within the crystal, or evoked within the ritual chamber, by the name of God of six letters that lies on the column of the lesser cross in the same subquarter, reading from top to bottom. In the example, the divine name that invokes (or evokes) is Idoigo. This same group of four good angels is commanded by the name of God of five letters written on the arm of the lesser cross, reading left to right. In the example, the divine name that commands is Ardza. Speaking about the angel Czns, Ave tells Dee: "It is one of the 4 angels that serve to that crosse, which are ruled by this name Idoigo. It is the name of God, of six letters: Look in the crosse that descendeth, In that name [Idoigo] they appear, by the name [Ardza] that is in the crosse [Transversary] they do that they are commanded."

As is true of the Dispositors, each group of four good angels on a Watchtower has its own specific function. The good angels in the subquarters of the east rule over medicine. Ave tells Dee: "Those 4 be of Physick." When their names are increased to five letters, their healing power is miraculous.

The angels in the subquarters of the south are concerned with metals and mining. About them Ave says:

"They have power over Metals, to find them, to gather them together, and to use them." In enumerating the uses of the Great Table, Ave has also listed as one of their functions "The congelations, and vertues of Stones." By this, precious and semiprecious jewels should be understood.

The good angels in the subquarters of the west give knowledge and command of the elemental spirits. The first angel of the four rules the air, the second the water, the third the earth, and the fourth "the life, or fire of things that live." In his list of uses for the Great Table, Ave says concerning the power of this group of good angels: "The knowledge of all elemental Creatures, amongst you. How many kindes there are, and for what use they were created. Those that live in the air, by themselves. Those that live in the waters, by themselves. Those that dwell in the earth, by themselves. The property of the fire which is the secret life of all things."

The good angels in the subquarters of the north have the power of transformations. Ave defines this office in Latin, saying "Transmutatio formalis, sed non essentialis," which means that the change is one of outward form but not of essential nature. These angels can change a spoon into a fork, or make a beggar appear to be a king, but they cannot transform lead into gold (which must have disappointed Kelley!). They can, however, change a lump of coal into a diamond, since this is a transformation of form and not essence (both are carbon).

The four classes of good angels are the same on each of the four Watchtowers, but those on the Watchtower of the East act in the eastern part of the world, those angels who perform the same function on the Watchtower of the South act in the southern part of the world, and so for the rest.

Subquarter	Watchtowers				Function
	East	South	West	North	
Eastern	Czons	Aigra	Tagco	Opamn	Treating and Curing of Disease
	Toitt	Orpmn	Nhodd	Aplst	
	Sigas	Rsoni	Patax	Scmio	
	Fmond	Izinr	Saaiz	Varsg	
Invoking	Idoiga	Angpoi	Olgota	Noalmr	
Commanding	Ardza	Unnax	Oalco	Oloag	
Southern	Oyaub	Omagg	Malgm	Gmdnm	Knowledge, Finding and Use of Metals
	Pacoc	Gbeal	Leaoc	Ecaop	
	Rbznh	Rlemu	Vspsn	Amlox	
	Diari	Iamhl	Rvroi	Briap	
Invoking	Llacza	Anaeem	Nelapr	Vadali	
Commanding	Palam	Sondn	Omebb	Obaua	
Western	Acuca	Msmal	Xpacn	Adire	Knowledge of All Elemental Creatures
	Nprat	Ianba	Vaasa	Siosp	
	Otroi	Izixp	Daspi	Panli	
	Pmzox	Strim	Rndil	Acrar	
Invoking	Aourrz	Spmnir	Iaaasd	Rzionr	
Commnding	Aloai	Ilpiz	Atapa	Nrzfm	
Northern	Abamo	Opana	Palco	Daltt	Changes of Form, not Essence
	Naoco	Dolop	Ndazn	Dixom	
	Ocanm	Rxpao	Iidpo	Oodpz	
	Shial	Axtir	Xrinh	Rgoan	
Invoking	Aiaoai	Cbalpt	Maladi	Volxdo	
Commanding	Oiiit	Arbiz	Olaad	Sioda	

The Good Angels on the Original Great Table

On the table of the good angels, the letters extracted from the pillars of the lesser crosses to increase the number of letters in each name from four to five are indicated in boldfaced type.

THE EVIL ANGELS

If only the first two letters in the name of each good angel are taken, and to the front of them is prefixed the letter in the Black Cross that occupies the same row, the name of an evil angel is created. These evil angels always have names of three letters, as Ave tells Dee: "Every name, sounding of three letters, beginning out of that line [of the Black Cross], is the name of a Devil, or wicked Angel, as well from the right, as from the left...."

When describing to Dee the four evil angels of the subquarter of the east on the Watchtower of the East, Ave says:

> *Ave:* But if thou wilt send sicknesse, then take two of the letters, and adde the letter of the Crosse [Dee: the black crosse] to that, as in the second, a T o.
>
> [Dee: This a, is of the crosse of union, or the black crosse.]
>
> *Ave:* Then he is a wicked power, and bringeth in disease: and when thou callest him, call him by the name of god, backward: for unto him, so, he is a god: and so constrain him backward, as Ogiodi.
>
> *Dee:* I think the Constraint must be, by the name of the Transversary backward pronounced, as of Ardza, is backway, azdra: For ogiodi, should but cause him to appear by the order of Idoigo, used for the 4 good Angels.[12]

The meaning of this passage is that the evil angels are evoked or called to visable appearance by the name of God in the pillar of the lesser cross for their particular subquarter read backward, from bottom to top. They are commanded by the name of God in the arm of the cross read backward, from right to left. Because they are evil, these inverted names of God are divine to them, and have power over them.

There is some confusion in the angelic transcript over whether the sixteen evil angels native to each Watchtower should even be used in Enochian magic. Ave refers to them when he speaks about sending sickness, and also in connection with obtaining money in the form of coins:

> *Ave:* These [evil angels of the southern subquarter] can give money coined, in Gold or Silver.
> *Dee:* Which these?
> These wicked ones mean you?
> *Ave:* I.
> The other give no money coined, but the metal.
> *Dee:* You mean the good.
> *Ave:* I.

This suggests that at least some of the evil angels have a legitimate function in Enochian magic. However, a little further on in their conversation Ave strongly contradicts this assumption, much to Kelley's disgust:

> *Dee:* As concerning the wicked here, Shall I call or summon them all, as I do the good ones in the name of God?
> *Ave:* No man calleth upon the name of God in the wicked: They are servants and vile slaves.
> *Dee:* We call upon the name of Jesus in the expulsing of devils, saying in the name of Jesus, etc.
> *Ave:* That In, is against the wicked. No just man calleth upon the name of God, to allure the devil.
> *Dee:* Then they are not to be named in the first summoning or invitation.
> *Ave:* At no time to be called.
> *Kelley:* How then shall we proceed with them?
> *Ave:* When the Earth lieth opened unto your eyes, and when the Angels of Light, shall offer the passages of the Earth, unto the entrance of your senses (chiefly of seeing) Then shall you see the Treasures of the Earth, as you go: And the caves of the Hills shall not be unknown unto you: Unto these, you may say, Arise, be gone, Thou art of destruction and of the places of darknesse: These are provided for the use of man. So shalt thou use the wicked, and no otherwise.
> *Dee:* This is as concerning the natural Mines of the Earth.

Ave: Not so, for they have nothing to do with the natural Mines of the Earth, but, with that which is corrupted with man.

Dee: As concerning the coined they have power to bring it.

Ave: So they may: that they keep, and no other.

Dee: How shall we know what they keep, and what they keep not?

Ave: Read my former words; for thou dost not understand them.

Dee: I read it: beginning at the first line on this side, when the Angels of Light, etc.

I mean of coined money that they keep not; How shall we do to serve our necessities with it?

Ave: The good Angels are Ministers for that purpose. The Angels of the 4 angles shall make the Earth open unto you, and shall serve your necessities from the 4 parts of the Earth.[13]

This is not exactly a clear statement on the part of the angel. He seems to be saying that although the evil angels can be used to cause sickness and obtain coined money, they should not be named except to banish them from the clay of human flesh. Dee did not understand that Ave was speaking about the dark places of the human body, not the mines of the Earth.

The offices of the evil angels are substantially the same as those of their good brethren, but their areas of influence are perverted to evil purposes. For example, the good angels of the eastern subquarters cure disease and teach medicine, while the evil angels bring sickness and death. The good angels of the southern subquarters teach the finding and use of metals, while their evil twins teach counterfeiting and the wicked uses of money, such as gambling. The good angels of the western subquarters teach the knowledge of elemental spirits, while the evil angels teach the uses of these spirits for perverse or hurtful ends. The good angels of the northern subquarters teach transformations of form, while the evil angels teach the art of illusions and trickery of the senses.

The table of the evil angels (opposite) shows their offices and the inverted divine names of the lesser crosses by which they are summoned and commanded as they appear on the Original Great Table of the Watchtowers.

As you can see, it is possible to extract another set of sixty-four evil angels by combining the letters in the column of the Black Cross with the pairs of letters in the same row that stand on the right side of the lesser crosses. In the eastern subquarter of the Watchtower of the East, for example, the cacodemons are Xcz, Ato, Rsi and Pfm, but with this method of extraction they might just as easily be Xns, Att, Ras and Pnd. Dee makes no suggestion that this possibility ever occurred to him, nor do the Enochian angels refer to it. I merely mention it here as a point of interest.

The Questions That Went Unanswered

The explanation given by Ave concerning the parts and uses of the Great Table is incomplete. Nowhere does he mention the associations on the Table with the Trumpeters of Kelley's Great Vision. Neither does he explain the link between the Table and the five Princes in each Watchtower who hold up the train of the King. The relationship between the letters on the beam of the Black Cross (what Dee calls the "Transversary") and the Watchtowers is not set forth. About the multitude of spirits that Kelley saw, as Dee says, "standing after the sixteen Angels next the Gate," Ave says only "They be Ministers and servants."[14]

Subquarter	Watchtowers				Function
	East	South	West	North	
Eastern	Xcz	Xai	Mta	Mop	
	Ato	Aor	Onh	Oap	Bringing
	Rsi	Rrs	Cpa	Csc	Sickness
	Pfm	Piz	Hsa	Hua	and Death
Invoking	Ogiodi	Iopgna	Atoglo	Rmlaon	
Commanding	Azdra	Xannu	Oclao	Gaolo	
Southern	Xoy	Xom	Mma	Mgm	
	Apa	Agb	Ole	Oec	Obtaining
	Rrb	Rrl	Cvs	Cam	Money,
	Pdi	Pia	Hrv	Hbr	Coining,
Invoking	Azcall	Meeana	Rpalen	Iladav	Gambling
Commanding	Malap	Ndnos	Bbemo	Auabo	
Western	Cac	Cms	Rxp	Rad	
	Onp	Oia	Ava	Asi	Base and
	Mot	Miz	Xda	Xpa	Evil Uses
	Apm	Ast	Ern	Eac	of the
Invoking	Zrruoa	Rinmps	Dsaaai	Rnoizr	Elementals
Commnding	Iaola	Zipli	Apata	Mfzrn	
Northern	Cab	Cop	Rpa	Rda	
	Ona	Odo	And	Adi	Deceptive
	Moc	Mrx	Xii	Xoo	Changes of
	Ash	Aax	Exr	Erg	Form,
Invoking	Iaoaia	Tplabc	Idalam	Odxlou	Illusions
Commanding	Tiiio	Zibra	Daalo	Adois	

The Evil Angels on the Original Great Table

Dee made several pointed inquiries about these and several other more general matters, but each time he was put off by the angels, who clearly had no intention of revealing these mysteries to him. Since they did not wish Dee to actually use Enochian magic in his lifetime (despite their

212 • Enochian Magic for Beginners

intimations to the contrary), they may have withheld this essential information to prevent him from defying their order that he await permission to use the magic.

THE PRINCES

After considering the matter, it seems very likely to me that the four ranks of five Princes who hold up the trains of the Kings in Kelley's Vision are equivalent to the four rows of letters in the Tablet of Union. Each letter in the Tablet of Union stands for a Prince. The four rows in the Tablet are probably assigned to the Watchtowers in the same curious way that the Watchtowers are numbered on the Original Great Table.

1. Watchtower of the East: e x a r p
2. Watchtower of the South: h c o m a
3. Watchtower of the North: n a n t a
4. Watchtower of the West: b i t o m

By the familiar process of Enochian permutation, the single letter that stands for the name of each Prince may be extended into a five-letter name that is derived from the row of letters to which it belongs.

This arrangement of the Princes on the Great Table (opposite) is based on my personal speculation. I have not encountered it elsewhere, nor have I seen any other conjectures as to what the figures of the Princes in Kelley's Vision may signify. It does seem very suggestive that there are five Princes in each Watchtower, and that each row of the Tablet of Union has five letters.

1.	EAST	2.	SOUTH
Princes of the East	Exarp Xarpe Arpex Rpexa Pexar	Princes of the South	Hcoma Comah Omahc Mahco Ahcom
3.	NORTH	4.	WEST
Princes of the North	Nanta Antan Ntana Tanan Anant	Princes of the West	Bitom Itomb Tombi Ombit Mbito

The Princes on the Great Table

THE TRUMPETERS

Regarding the other mystery, the meaning of the single Trumpeter with his strange horn of six openings arranged in the shape of a pyramid or (seen from the front) a triangle, my guess is that this refers to the letters at the intersections of the five crosses in each Watchtower. Every lesser cross has a single letter at its intersection, but the Great Cross that runs through the middle of the Watchtower is double, and has two letters at its intersection.

These six letters, gathered together, would make a single name. One reasonable way to gather them is to take them in a clockwise circle around the Watchtower beginning with the lesser cross of the eastern subquarter, and ending at the center with the two letters of the Great Cross. This is the same pattern by which the name of the King is derived. The following four names of six letters would result:

1. Watchtower of the East: D l o i a h
2. Watchtower of the South: N n p b a l
3. Watchtower of the North: O o z o a a
4. Watchtower of the West: L e a a s l

Again, this is speculation unsupported by any statement of the angels. The letters at the intersections of the crosses are surely of significance in the scheme of Enochian magic, but what this significance may be remains unknown.

"The Letters of the Transversary"

Ave explains the use of the letters in the column of the Black Cross upon the Great Table in detail. They seem to embody the divine energy that vitalizes the lesser angels and demons, when added to their names. The rays of the Black Cross symbolize the four rivers that flow out of the throne of God in Paradise (and in New Jerusalem, which is Paradise returned to the Earth). However, Ave says nothing at all about the letters in the arm of the Black Cross.

Dee was curious as to why the three geographical regions or genii of the tenth Aether (Lexarph, Comanan, Tabitom) had been chosen to form the letters of the Black Cross. Ave refused to enlighten him.

> *Dee:* I think a mystery did depend upon the choice of the three names, Lexarph, Comanan, and Tabitom.
> *Ave:* That is not to our purpose.[15]

Dee persists, as this matter is obviously of the greatest importance. Later in the same conversation he asks:

> *Dee:* Of the Letters in the Transversary of the wicked their black Crosse, I know no use, as of motivat; nan, etc.
> *Ave:* Thou shalt know, when thou writest thy book.[16]

This was only another way of putting Dee off the question. Dee was nothing if not persistent. Five days later he got another chance to ask Ave the same question:

> *Dee:* Of the letters in the Transversary, I would know your will.
> *Ave:* They are, as the other, but for a peculiar practice.[17]

This is the only clue we get concerning the letters in the arm of the Black Cross, but it is a useful hint. It appears that the letters of the arm are to be added to the front of angel names extracted by reading the letters in the subquarters of the Great Table in columns. The names extracted from the pillars of the lesser crosses would probably be divine names by which the others are invoked, reading down the pillars in the case of good angels and up the pillars in the case of evil angels. The divine names would have seven letters, the names of the good angels six letters (five plus the intensifier in the arm of the lesser cross), and the names of the evil angels five letters.

THE GOOD ANGELS OF THE COLUMNS

For what this speculation may be worth, I have arranged the conjectured names of the good angels of the columns, along with their invoking God names, in the table below (page 216). Their functions are unknown. As is true of all the other tables in this chapter, it is based on the Original Great Table, and would be different for the Reformed Table of Raphael and my own Restored Table due to the different placements of the Watchtowers on the quarters, and minor variations in the lettering.

Subquarter	Watchtowers				Function
	East	South	West	North	
Eastern	Ractsf	Buaori	Totnps	Dooasu	Unknown
	Zrzoim	Onirsz	Aaahaa	Olppca	
	Lzntan	Zarmnn	Accdai	Pamsis	
	Aastsd	Axanir	Doodxz	Agntog	
God Names	Tidoigo	Nangpoi	Nolgota	Tnoalmr	
Southern	Upoprd	Psogri	Tomlur	Aogeab	Unknown
	Tayabi	Hombla	Dmaesu	Nbmcmr	
	Pauonr	Rdgamh	Ibgoso	Aunooa	
	Ambchi	Anglul	Mbmcni	Aampxp	
God Names	Nllacza	Tanaeem	Tnelapr	Nuadali	
Western	Xaanop	Iimiis	Naxudr	Znaspa	Unknown
	Glcptm	Alsazt	Ltpaan	Irdiac	
	Zacaoo	Oiabxi	Rpcspi	Zfrsla	
	Diatix	Mzlapm	Xanail	Amepir	
God Names	Naourrz	Tspmnir	Tiaaasd	Nrzionr	
Northern	Coanos	Raodra	Mopnix	Psddor	Unknown
	Nibach	Orpoxx	Aladir	Siaiog	
	Bimcna	Ainoai	Gaczpn	Adtopa	
	Rtooml	Nzapor	Ldonoh	Catmzn	
God Names	Taiaoai	Ncbalpt	Nmaladi	Tuolxdo	

Good Angels of the Columns on the Original Great Table

THE EVIL ANGELS OF THE COLUMNS

In the final table I have extracted the names of the conjectured evil angels of the columns from the Original Great Table, along with the inverted names of God by which they may be commanded. Their functions are unknown. Perhaps the good and evil angels of the columns, about which Ave says nothing at all, play a part in the apocalyptic transformation of the world

Subquarter	Watchtowers				Function
	East	South	West	North	
Eastern	Mctsf	Naori	Ntnps	Moasu	Unknown
	Ozoim	Airsz	Aahaa	Oppca	
	Intan	Trmnn	Tcdai	Imsis	
	Bstsd	Aanir	Aodxz	Bntog	
God Names	Togiodi	Niopgna	Natoglo	Trmlaon	
Southern	Aoprd	Bogri	Bmlur	Ageab	Unknown
	Tyabi	Imbla	Iaesu	Tmcmr	
	Auonr	Ogamh	Ogoso	Anooa	
	Nbchi	Mglul	Mmcni	Nmpxp	
God Names	Nazcall	Tmeeana	Trpalen	Niladau	
Western	Aanop	Bmiis	Bxudr	Aaspa	Unknown
	Tcptm	Isazt	Ipaan	Tdiac	
	Acaoo	Oabxi	Ocspi	Arsla	
	Natix	Mlapm	Mnail	Nepir	
God Names	Nzrruoa	Trinmps	Tdsaaai	Nrnoizr	
Northern	Manos	Nodra	Npnix	Mddor	Unknown
	Obach	Apoxx	Aadir	Oaiog	
	Imcna	Tnoai	Tczpn	Itopa	
	Booml	Aapor	Aonoh	Btmzn	
God Names	Tiaoaia	Ntplabc	Nidalam	Todxlou	

Evil Angels of the Columns on the Original Great Table

which is so often referred to by the Enochian angels in their conversations with Dee and Kelley. This might be the reason Ave refused to explain the function of the columns and the beam of the Black Cross to Dee.

CHAPTER FOURTEEN

The Enochian Keys

THE TRANSMISSION OF THE KEYS

The last word of the First Key, or Call, was transmitted to Dee through Kelley by the angel Nalvage on the morning of April 13, 1584. The Keys were revealed backward to prevent Dee from inadvertently using them as invocations when repeating them:

> *Nalvage:* Unto this Doctrine belongeth the perfect knowledge and remembrance of the mysticall Creatures. How therefore shall I inform you, which know them not?
>
> *Dee:* Mean you as Babyon, Boboyel, etc.
>
> *Nalvage:* The Characters, or Letters of the Tables.
>
> *Dee:* You mean the mystical Letters, wherein the holy book is promised to be written: and if the book be so written and laid open before us, and then you will from Letter to Letter point, and we to record your instructions: Then I trust we shall sufficiently understand, and learn your instructions.
>
> *Nalvage:* Also in receiving of the calls, this is to be noted: that they are to be uttered of me, backward: and of you, in practise, forward.
>
> *Dee:* I understand it, for the efficacy of them; else, all things called would appear: and so hinder our proceeding in learning.[1]

The Keys correspond in number to the forty-nine large letter-number squares of Dee's *Book of Enoch*, save that the first table in the book has no Key. Nalvage explains to Dee:

I finde the Soul of man hath no portion in this first Table. It is the Image of the son of God, in the bosome of his father, before all the worlds. It comprehendeth his incarnation, passion, and return to judgement: which he himself, in flesh, knoweth not; all the rest are of under-standing. The exact Center excepted.[2]

The first unexpressed Call would seem to corre-spond with the small cross at the end of the magic square of the names of the seven angels who burn as flames before the throne of heavenly Christ (*Revelation* 4:5). If this is so, then the other forty-eight Calls proba-bly correspond with the individual letters in this square, moving through the square from back to front. This is only conjecture on my part, however.

The Keys were delivered backward letter by letter (at least in the initial stage), and out of their proper sequence. This was a torturous process that must have sorely tried the patience and endurance of both Dee and Kelley:

86.

A (Two thousand and fourteen, in the sixth Table, is) D 7003. In the thirteenth Table is I.

A in the 21th Table. 11406 downward.

I in the last Table, one lesse then Number. A word, Jaida you shall understand, what that word is before the Sun go down. Jaida is the last word of the call.

85.

H 49. ascending T 49. descending, A 909. directly, O simply.

H 2029. directly, call it Hoath.

84.

225. From the low angle on the right side. Continuing in the same and next square. D 225. [The same number repeated].

A In the thirteenth Table, 740. ascending in his square.

M The 30th Table, 13025. from the low angle in the left-side.
In the square ascending.
Call it Mad.[3]

In this painful and confusing manner Nalvage revealed the last three Enochian words of the First Key of the forty-eight that are expressed. Apparently (though it is far from certain) the angel pointed to letters with a rod on a round crystal table on which he was standing. Kelley saw this in the showstone and reported the position of the pointer to Dee, who then looked up the corresponding letters on his own written tables. As Kelley worked, the crystal table of Nalvage became clearer: "His Table now appeareth very evidently to me, as that I could paint it all."[4]

THE KEYS AND THE GREAT TABLE

It is my conviction, based on the overall structure of the Great Table, that the Keys from the Third to the Eighteenth unfold themselves upon the Table in four overlapping clockwise circles (see the diagram on the next page). Each circle begins in a subquarter of the Eastern Watchtower. Each passes through the middle of the lesser cross of the corresponding subquarters on the other three Watchtowers. The circles are numbered according to the numbering of the quadrants and subquadrants—that is to say, the first circle begins in the eastern, or first, subquarter of the Watchtower of the East; the second begins in the southern, or second, subquarter; the third begins in the northern, or third, subquarter; and the fourth circle begins in the western, or fourth, subquarter.

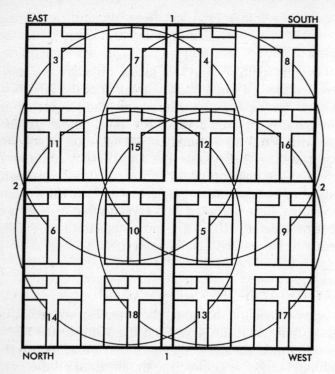

Four Cycles of the Keys on the Great Table

The first two Keys probably relate to the pillar and beam of the central Black Cross on the Great Table. The unexpressed primordial Key that corresponds with the first of the forty-nine Tables of Enoch may relate to the center of the Black Cross. It should be designated by a zero, similar to the use of zero for the first card of the Tarot (the Fool).

This relationship of the Keys to the Great Table is never clearly stated by the angels, but may be deduced from internal evidence in the Keys. On the Watchtowers, the three rays of each Great Cross are explicitly given to the Father, Son, and Holy Ghost of the Christian trinity. I suspect that the pillar, beam, and center of the Black Cross are also linked with the trinity. The Father is probably assigned the pillar of the Black Cross, and the First Key. The Son is probably assigned the beam of the Black Cross, and the Second Key. The Holy Spirit, who is the unseen Mother of many of the Enochian angels, is probably assigned the intersection of the Black Cross, which is a dimensionless point, and the unexpressed primordial Key that has nothing directly to do with the human race or the Earth.

In the biblical metaphor of New Jerusalem, which is so intimately linked with Enochian magic, the Father and Son are combined in the figure of heavenly Christ, who has the white hair of an old man (just as the hair of Moses turned white while he communed with God and received the ten Commandments). In *Revelation,* the heavenly Christ is described both as a king who sits in authority and passes judgments, and as a mounted conquering prince who wields a two-edged sword of retribution. The Holy Ghost is represented by the throne on which heavenly Christ sits at the exact center of New Jerusalem. From the throne flow the four rivers of Paradise, corresponding to the four arms of the Black Cross.

It is usual in Enochian magic to progress backwards from the end to the beginning. This was the course followed by Aleister Crowley when he worked the invocations of the thirty Aethers. He began with the thirtieth and ended with the first. It is possible that in the final apocalypse working one of the eighteen distinct Keys is to be vibrated each day, beginning with the eighteenth and working backward to the first. In this way, the magician would progress four times counterclockwise around the Great Table, beginning in the north and ending in the east (the process by which the table of clay was revealed to Dee and Kelley in the initial transmission of the Watchtowers), then would follow the two arms of the Black Cross to the center of the four Watchtowers, where lies the fountain of Holy Spirit. It is through this fountain of Spirit that the thirty Aethers are to be accessed. The intersection of the Great Cross is the doorway into the Great Table of the Watchtowers.

The Author of the Enochian Keys

The Enochian Keys are clearly ritual invocations (or evocations, depending on whether the spirits to whom they are applied are called in, or called out). Yet in discussing the Book of Spirits, the angel Ave tells Dee that he must write the invocations for the Book himself, since invocation is a function of the free will and fervent heat of the human soul, and angels have no part in it. When Dee presses Ave for more details, the angel says "I know not: for I dwell not in the soul of man."

If the angels cannot write invocations, and if the Keys are invocations, then who wrote the Keys? And why? It seems redundant that Dee should have to write a complete set of invocations to contact and bind the angels of the Watchtowers when he has already been given a complete set of invocations by the angels themselves.

The function of the Keys must be different from the function of Dee's own set of invocations, which was intended to initially call the angels of the Great Table during an eighteen-day working. It may be that Dee's invocations were also to be used in regularly summoning the angels. Ave talks about a book that is only to be used on one day, but this cannot refer to the Book of Spirits that contained Dee's invocations, which was to be used for at least eighteen days. As I have indicated, the book of one day probably is the Book of Silvered Leaves, which was (I believe) to be employed to record the seals and signatures of the invoked angels. No limit is placed on the use of Dee's own invocations.

It is usual for modern Enochian magicians to vibrate the Keys to summon the angels of the Watchtowers for everyday ritual work. This was the Golden Dawn practice. The founders of the Golden Dawn did not understand the need for the magician to compose an original set of invocations to establish initial contact with the angels. In the Golden Dawn, only the Keys were used to invoke or evoke the angels.

Perhaps the Keys have a higher and more specific purpose than everyday invocation. If they were not composed by the angels, but rather someone above the angels, they must have been written by the Father of Heaven, or by heavenly Christ the Son, or by the Mother of the angels who refers to herself only by the title I AM. They may be the text of the unrecorded apocalypse working, which I have postulated as the dark and secret heart of the Enochian communications.

Enochian magicians who employ the Keys casually for personal reasons may be unwittingly debasing them and abusing their power. Of course, if this is so, only the smallest fraction of the power of the Keys would be released during this awkward and inappropriate application. It would be akin to using a hundred-ton hydraulic press to hammer in a nail.

TEXT OF THE KEYS

The Enochian versions of the Keys were revealed before the English translations, although in some cases the

English was revealed along with the Enochian. In Casaubon the initial recording of the Keys is, to say the least, confused. Toward the end of the process, fragments of one Key are mixed with fragments of another. Fortunately, the English translations later provided by Nalvage are much clearer.

Dee recorded the text of the Keys and its translation in a much more readable form in his manuscript *48 Claves Angelicae*,[5] and it is this manuscript version and its printed transcripts that I have followed in the corrected text of the Keys that appears here. I have adhered to Dee's own practice of writing the Enochian in rows from left to right, with the English translation directly above each word.

Some of the Enochian words are written in capitals by Dee. These are the power words, the actually triggers that bring about the visual apparition of the angels. It will be noticed that two forms of the Enochian word for "move" are used, ZACAR and ZACARe. ZACAR appears much more frequently. In my opinion the lower case "e" appended to the end of the word is intended merely as an aid to pronunciation. The hyphenated Enochian words are compound words that are written as single words in Dee's manuscript. I have inserted the hyphens to make it easier to understand their composition. For the sake of clarity, I have removed the hyphens that Dee put into single words (apparently as an aid to pronunciation). The Enochian words in square brackets have been inserted by me to fill in obvious gaps in the Enochian text. Purists may prefer to ignore them.

It has been observed[6] that the Enochian language is extraordinarily compact, that one word in Enochian often signified an entire phrase in English. This fact has been used to support sceptics' claims that Enochian is not a real language. If we look at a French word in a French-English dictionary and compare its size with the size of the English definition that accompanies it, this is hardly evidence that French is not a language. Also, it should be noted that Dee was often writing the definitions or descriptions of difficult Enochian words, not merely their translations. Probably no adequate translation exists in English for many of these words.

First Key

I reign over you, saith the God of Justice,
Ol sonf vors-g, goho Iad Balt,

in power exalted above the firmaments of wrath;
lansh calz vonphu;

in whose hands the Sun is as a sword, and the Moon
sobra zol Ror I ta nazpsad, od Graa

as a through-thrusting fire, which measureth
ta malprg, ds holq

your garments in the midst of my vestures, and
qaa nothoa zimz od

trussed you together as the palms of my hands; whose
commah ta nobloh zien; soba

seats I garnished with the fire of gathering, which
thil gnonp prge aldi, ds

beautified your garments with admiration; to whom
urbs oboleh g-rsam; casarm

I made a Law to govern the Holy Ones, which
ohorela taba Pir, ds

delivered you a rod with the ark of knowledge.
zonrensg cab erm Jadnah.

Moreover, you lifted up your voices and swore obedience
Pilah, farzm znra adna

and faith to Him that liveth and triumpheth; whose
  gono   *Iadpil ds*   *hom*   *toh;*   *soba*

beginning is not, nor end cannot be; which shineth
[iaod]   *ipam,*   *ul*   *ipamis;*   *ds*   *loholo*

as a flame in the midst of your palace, and reigneth
   vep   *zomd*   *poamal, od* *bogpa*

amongst you as the balance of righteousness and truth.
      aai   *ta*   *piap*   *piamos*   *od vaoan.*

Move, therefore, and show yourselves! Open
ZACARe, ca,   *od*   *ZAMRAN!*   *Odo*

the mysteries of your creation. Be friendly unto me:
   cicle   *qaa.*   *Zorge:*

for I am the servant of the same your God,
lap zirdo   *noco*   *MAD,*
the true worshipper of the Highest.
     hoath   *Jaida.*

Second Key

Can the Wings of the Winds understand your voices
Adgt   *Upaah*   *Zong*   *om*   *faaip*

of wonder, O you, the Second of the First? Whom
  sald,   *Viu*   *L? Sobam*

the Burning Flames have framed
    Ialprg   *izazaz*

within the depths of my jaws; whom I have prepared as
                piadph;   *casarma*   *abramg ta*

cups for a wedding, or as the flowers in their beauty
talho   *paracleda*   *q-ta*   *lorslq*   *turbs*

for the chamber of righteousness. Stronger are
     oogo   *baltoh.*   *Givi*   *chis*

your feet than the barren stone, and mightier are
    lusd   *orri,*   *od micalp chis*

your voices than the manifold winds: for you are become
    bia   *ozongon: lap*   *noan*

a building such as is not, but in the mind
  trof   *cors ta*   *ge*   *oq*   *manin*

of the All-powerful. Arise, saith the First! Move,
    Iaidon.   *Torzu,*   *gohe-l!*   *ZACAR,*

therefore, unto his servants! Show yourselves in power,
  ca,   *c-noqod*   *ZAMRAN*   *micalzo,*

and make me a strong see-thing, for I am
od ozazm   *urelp,*   *lap zir*

of Him that liveth forever.
  Ioiad.

Third Key

Behold, saith your God, I am a circle
Micma, goho   *Piad, zir*   *comselh*

on whose hands stand 12 kingdoms; six are the seats
  a-zien   *biab os londoh;*   *norz chis*   *othil*

of living breath, the rest are as sharp sickles, or
     gigipah,   *undl chis ta*   *puim, Q*

the horns of death; wherein the creatures of the Earth
   mospleh teloch; quiin   *toltorg*

are and are not except by mine own hand; which also
chis i-chis-ge   *M*   *ozien;*   *ds-t*

sleep and shall rise. In the first I made you stewards
brgda od   *torzul. I-li*   *eol*   *balzarg*

and placed you in seats 12 of government, giving
od aala   *thiln os*   *netaab,*   *dluga*

unto every one of you   power   successively   over 456,
    vomsarg   *lonsa*   *capmiali*   *vors cla,*

the true ages of time, to the intent that,
      homil cocasb,   *fafen,*

from the highest vessels and the corners of
              izizop od   *miinoag de*

your governments, you might work my power, pouring down
  g-netaab,   *vaun   nanaeel, panpir*

the fires of life and increase on the Earth continually.
  malpirgi   *Caosg*   *pild.*

Thus you are become the skirts of Justice and Truth.
          Noan   *unalah Balt*   *od Vooan.*

In the name of the same, your God, lift up, I say,
  Dooiap   *MAD, goholor, gohus,*

yourselves. Behold, his mercies flourish, and name
  amiran. Micma,   *iehusoz cacacom, od dooain*

is become mighty amongst us; in whom we say, move,
  noar   micaolz   aaiom;   *casarmg gohia, ZACAR,*

descend and apply yourselves unto us, as unto partakers
uniglag od   imvamar,   *pugo plapli*

of the secret wisdom of your creation.
      ananael   *qaan.*

Fourth Key

I have set my feet in the south, and
  Othil   *lasdi*   *barbage, od*

have looked about me, saying, are not
  dorpha,   *gohol,*   *gchisge*

the Thunders of Increase numbered 33, which reign
  Avavago   *cormp pd,*   *d-sonf*

in the second angle? Under whom I have placed 9639
    viu-diu?   *Casarmi*   *oali mapm*

whom none hath yet numbered, but one; in whom
sobam ag   *cormpo,*   *crp-l*   *casarmg*

the second beginning of things are and wax strong;
     croodzi   *chis od ugeg;*

which also successively are the number of time: and
   ds-t   *capimali*   *chis*   *capimaon:*   *od*

their powers are as the first 456. Arise, you Sons
    lonshin chis ta   *lo cla. Torgu,*   *Nor*

of Pleasure, and visit the Earth: for
   Quasahi, od F   *caosga: bagle*

I am the Lord your God, which is, and liveth.
     Zir-ena-iad,   *ds-i*   *od*   *apila.*

In the name of the Creator, move, and show yourselves
   Dooaio   *Qaal, ZACAR, od ZAMRAN*

as pleasant deliverers, that you may praise him amongst
     obelisong,   *rest-el*   *aaf*

the sons of men.
   nor-molap.

Fifth Key

The Mighty Sounds have entered into the third
     Sapah   *zimii*   *D*

angle, and are become as olives in the Olive Mount,
 diu, od   *noas*   *ta qaanis*   *Adroch,*

looking with gladness upon the Earth, and dwelling
dorphal   *[ulcinina]*   *Caosg, od faonts*

in the brightness of the heavens as continual comforters;
   [luciftias]   *peripsol ta*   *blior;*

unto whom I fastened pillars of gladness 19, and
    casarm   amipzi   naz-arth   af, od

gave them vessels to water the Earth
  dlugar   zizop   zlida   Caosgi

with her creatures; and they are the brothers
      tol-torgi; od z-chis   esiasch

of the first as of the second, and the beginning
    L   ta   viu   od   iaod

of their own seats, which are garnished
     thild, ds   peral

with continually burning lamps 69636, whose numbers
   [pild]   *hubar peoal, soba cormfa*

are as the first, the ends, and the contents of time.
chis ta   la,   vls, od   q-cocasb.

Therefore come you and obey your creation; visit us
  Ca   niis   od darbs   qaas;   F

in peace and comfort; conclude us as receivers
 etharzi od bliora; iaial   ednas

of your mysteries. For why? Our Lord and Master
    cicles.   Bagle?   Geiad

is all one.
i-l.

Sixth Key

The spirits of the fourth angle are nine, mighty
  Gah   S   diu   em, micalzo

in the firmaments of waters; whom the First hath planted
     pilzin;   sobam El   harg

as a torment to the wicked and a garland
  mir   babalon od   obloc

to the righteous, giving unto them fiery darts to van
    samvelg,   *dlugar*   *marprg*   *ar*

the Earth, and 7699 continual workmen; whose courses
  Caosgi, od acam   *canal;*   *sobol-zar*

visit with comfort the Earth, and are in government
  f-bliard   *Caosgi, od chis anetab*

and continuance as the second and the third.
od miam ta viv od D.

Wherefore, harken unto my voice: I have talked of you
 Darsar, solpeth   *bien:*   *brita*

and I move you in power and presence, whose works
od ZACAM g-micalzo   *sobha-ath*

shall be a song of honor and the praise of your God
trian luiahe   *od*   *ecrin*   *MAD*

in your creation.
    qaaon.

Seventh Key

The east is a house of virgins singing praises
  Raas i-salman   *paradiz oecrimi*

amongst the Flames of the first glory, wherein the Lord
  aao   *Ialpirgah*   *quiin*   *Enay*

hath opened his mouth, and they are become 28
        butmon, od   *i-noas ni*

living dwellings in whom the strength of men rejoiceth;
   paradial casarmg ugear   *chirlan;*

and they are appareled with ornaments of brightness,
od   *zonac*   *luciftian,*

such as work wonders on all creatures; whose kingdoms
cors ta vaul zirn   *tol-hami;*   *soba londoh*

and continuance are as the third and fourth,
od   miam   chis ta   D   od   es,

strong towers and places of comfort, the seats of mercy
    umadea od   pi-bliar   othil-rit

and continuance. O you Servants of Mercy, move,
od   miam.   C-Noquol   Rit,   ZACAR,

appear,   sing praises unto the Creator, and be mighty
ZAMRAN, oecrimi   Qadah,   od   omicaolz

amongst us; for to this remembrance is given power,
    aai-om; bagle   papnor   i-dlugam lonshi,

and our strength waxeth strong in our Comforter.
od   umplif ugegi   Bigliad.

Eighth Key

The midday, the first, is as the third heaven
    Bazme,   lo,   I ta   [D]   piripson

made of pillars of hyacinth 26, in whom the Elders
oln   naz-a-vabh   ox, casarmg   Uran

are become strong; which I have prepared
chis   ugeg;   ds   abramg

for my own righteousness, saith the Lord; whose
        baltoha,   goho   Iad; soba

long continuance shall be as bucklers to the stooping
    miam   trian   ta lolcis   abai

Dragon, and like unto the harvest of a widow. How many
Vovin, od   aziagier   rior.   Irgil

are there which remain in the glory of the Earth,
chis da   ds   paaox   busd   Caosgo,

which are, and shall not see   death, until
 ds   chis, od   ip-uran teloah, cacarg

this house fall and the Dragon sink! Come away, for
oi-salman loncho od   Vovina carbaf! Niiso,   bagle

the Thunders have spoken; come away, for the crowns
Avavago   gohon; niiso   bagle   momao

of the Temple and the coat
Siaion od   mabza

of Him that Is, and Was, and Shall Be Crowned,
Jadoiasmomar,

are divided. Come, appear to the terror of the Earth,
poilp.   Niis, ZAMRAN   ciaofi   Caosgo,

and to our comfort, and of such as are prepared.
od   bliors, od   corsi ta   abramig.

Ninth Key

A mighty guard of fire with two-edged swords
Micaoli bransg prgel   napta

flaming (which have vials 8 of wrath for two times
ialpor   (ds   brin efafafe P vonpho   olani

and a half: whose Wings are of wormwood, and
od   obza: sobca Upaah chis   tatan,   od

of the marrow of salt), have settled their feet
tranan   balye),   alar   lusda

in the west, and are measured with their ministers
soboln, od chis holq   c-noquodi

9996. These gather up the moss of the Earth as
cial. Unal aldon   mom   Caosgo ta

the rich man doth his treasure. Cursed are they
las ollor gnay   limlal.   Amma   chiis

whose iniquities they are! In their eyes are
sobca madrid   z-chis!   ooanoan chis

millstones greater than the Earth, and
  aviny   *drilpi*   *Caosgin, od*

from their mouths run seas of blood. Their heads
          butmoni parm zumvi cnila.   *Daziz*

are covered with diamond, and upon their hands are
    ethamz   *a-childao,*   *od mirc*   *ozol chis*

marble sleeves. Happy is he on whom they frown not.
pidiai collal. Ulcinin   a-sobam   ucim.

For why? The God of Righteousness rejoiceth in them.
Bagle   *Iadbaltoh*   *chirlan   par.*

Come away, and not your vials! For   the time
  Niiso,   *od ip*   *ofafafe! Bagle a-cocasb*

is such as requireth comfort.
i-cors-ta   unig   blior.

Tenth Key

The Thunders of Judgement and Wrath are numbered
  Coraxo   *chis cormp*

and are harbored in the north in the likeness
od   blans   lucal   aziazor

of an oak, whose branches are nests 22 of lamentation
  paeb,   soba   lilonon chis virq op   eophan

and weeping, laid up for the Earth, which burn night
od raclir,   maasi bagle Caosgi, ds ialpon dosig

and day, and vomit out the heads of scorpions and
od basgim, od   oxex   dazis   siatris   od

live sulphur mingled with poison. These be the Thunders
  salbrox cynxir   faboan. Unal-chis   Const

that 5678 times in the 24th part of a moment roar
 ds daox cocasb   ol   oanio   yor

with a hundred mighty earthquakes and a thousand times
    eors   vohim   gizyax   od   matb   cocasb

as many surges, which rest not, neither know any
 plosi   molvi,   ds   page-ip,   larag   om   droln

quiet time. Here one rock bringeth forth 1000
matorb cocasb. Emna L   patralx yolci   matb

even as the heart of man doth his thoughts. Woe, woe,
nomig   monons olora gnay   angelard. Ohio, ohio,

woe, woe, woe, woe, yea, woe be to the Earth, for
ohio, ohio, ohio, ohio, noib, ohio   Caosgon, bagle

her iniquity is, was, and shall be, great. Come away,
    madrid I, zirop,   chiso,   drilpa. Niiso,

but not your noises!
crip ip   nidali!

Eleventh Key

The mighty Seat groaned, and there were 5
    Oxiayal holdo,   od   zirom O

Thunders which flew into the east; and the Eagle
Coraxo   ds   zildar   raasy; od   Vabzir

spake, and cried with a loud voice, Come away! And
camliax od bahal,   Niiso!   [Od

they gathered themselves together and became the house
    aldon   od noas]   salman

of death, of whom it is measured, and it is as
  teloch, casarman   holq,   od t-i ta

they are whose number is 31. Come away, for
 z-chis soba   cormf I ga. Niisa,   bagle

I have prepared for you! Move, therefore, and
    abramg   noncp! ZACARe, ca,   od

show yourselves. Open the mysteries of your creation.
ZAMRAN.   *Odo*   *cicle*   *qaa.*

Be friendly unto me, for I am the servant
    Zorge,   *lap zirdo   noco*

of the same your God, the true worshipper of the Highest.
                    MAD,   *hoath*   *Iaida.*

Twelfth Key

O you that reign in the south, and are 28,
 Nonci   d-sonf   *babage, od chis ob,*

the Lanterns of Sorrow: bind up your girdles, and
    Hubaio   Tibibp: allar   *atraah, od*

visit us. Bring down your train 3663, that the Lord
 ef.   Drix   *fafen mian, ar*   *Enay*

may be magnified, whose name amongst you is Wrath.
            ovof,   soba dooain aai   *I VONPH.*

Move, I say, and show yourselves; open the mysteries
ZACAR, gohus, od ZAMRAN;   *odo*   *cicle*

of your creation; be friendly unto me, for I am
            qaa;   *zorge,*   *lap zirdo*

the servant of the same your God, the true worshipper
    noco   *MAD,*   *hoath*

of the Highest.
    Iaida.

Thirteenth Key

O you Swords of the south,[7] which have 42 eyes
    Napeai   babagen,   ds-brin   vx ooaona

to stir up wrath of sin, making men drunken which
 lring   vonph doalim, eolis   ollog orsba   ds

are empty: behold the promise of God and his power,
chis affa: micma   isro   MAD od lonshi-tox,

which is called amongst you a bitter sting. Move, and
ds   i-umd   aai   GROSB. ZACAR, od

show yourselves; open the mysteries of your creation;
ZAMRAN;   odo   cicle   qaa;

be friendly unto me, for I am the servant
  zorge,   lap zirdo   noco

of the same your God, the true worshipper of the Highest.
    MAD,   hoath   Iaida.

Fourteenth Key

O you Sons of Fury, the Daughters of the Just,
  Noromi Bagie,   Pasbs   Oiad,

which sit   upon 24 seats vexing all creatures
  ds   trint mirc ol thil dods   tol-ham

of the Earth with age; which have under you 1636:
    Caosgo   homin; ds brin oroch   quar:

behold the voice of God, promise of Him
micma   bial   Oiad, aisro   Tox

which is called amongst you Fury (or Extreme Justice).
  ds-i-um   aai   [Bagie (q]   Baltim).

Move   and show yourselves; open the mysteries
ZACAR od ZAMRAN;   odo   cicle

of your creation; be friendly unto me, for I am
    qaa;   zorge,   lap zirdo

the servant of the same your God, the true worshipper
  noco   MAD,   hoath

of the Highest.
  Iaida.

Fifteenth Key

O thou the Governor of the first Flame,
  Ils   *Tabaan*   *L-ialprt,*

under whose Wings are 6739, which weave the Earth
  casarman Upaahi chis darg,   ds   oado   Caosgi

with dryness, which knowest of the great name
      orscor,   ds   omax   monasci

Righteousness and the seal of honor: move   and
Baeovib   *od   emetgis iaiadix: ZACAR od*

show yourselves; open the mysteries of your creation;
ZAMRAN;   *odo   cicle   qaa;*

be friendly unto me, for I am the servant
  zorge,   *lap zirdo   noco*

of the same your God, the true worshipper of the Highest.
        MAD,   *hoath*   *Iaida.*

Sixteenth Key

O thou second Flame, the House of Justice, which
  Ils   Viu-ialprt, Salman   Balt,   ds

hast thy beginning in glory, and shalt comfort
brin   acroodzi   busd, od   bliorax

the just; which walkest on the Earth with Feet 8763
  balit; ds-insi   Caosg   Lusdan emod

that understand and separate creatures: great art
  ds-om   od   tliob   hami: drilpa geh

thou in the God-of-Stretch-Forth-and-Conquer. Move and
ils   Madzilodarp.   ZACAR od

show yourselves; open the mysteries of your creation;
ZAMRAN;   *odo   cicle   qaa;*

be friendly unto me, for I am the servant
   zorge,   *lap zirdo*   *noco*

of the same your God, the true worshipper of the Highest.
         MAD,   *hoath*   *Iaida.*

Seventeenth Key

O thou third Flame, whose Wings are thorns
  Ils   *D-ialprt,*   *soba* *Upaah chis nanba*

to stir up vexation, and hast 7336 Lamps Living going
  zixlay dodsih, *od brint faxs Hubaro*   *tustax*

before thee; whose God is Wrath-in-Anger: gird up
      ylsi; soba   *Iad I*   *Vonpo-unph:* *aldon*

thy loins and harken! Move and show yourselves; open
    daxil od   *toatar! ZACAR od ZAMRAN;*   *odo*

the mysteries of your creation; be friendly unto me, for
    cicle   *qaa;*   *zorge,*   *lap*

I am the servant of the same your God,
zirdo   *noco*   *MAD,*

the true worshipper of the Highest.
     hoath   *Iaida.*

Eighteenth Key

O thou mighty light and Burning Flame of comfort,
  Ils   *micaolz olprit od*   *Ialprg*   *bliors,*

which openest the glory of God to the center
ds   *odo*   *busdir* *Oiad*   *ovoars*

of the Earth, in whom the secrets of Truth 6332 have
   Caosgo, casarmg laiad [Vaoan] eran brints

their abiding, which is called in thy kingdom Joy, and
   cafafam, ds   *i-umd* *a-q-loadohi* *Moz, od*

not to be measured: be thou a window of comfort unto me.
        maoaffs: bolp   como-bliort   pambt.

Move   and show yourselves; open the mysteries
ZACAR od   ZAMRAN;   odo   cicle

of your creation; be friendly unto me, for I am
        qaa;   zorge,   lap zirdo

the servant of the same your God, the true worshipper
    noco   MAD,   hoath

of the Highest.
    Iaida.

Key of the Thirty Aethers

O you Heavens which dwell in (the first Air) are
        Madriax   ds-praf   (LIL)   chis

mighty in the parts of the Earth,   and execute
micaolz   saanir   Caosgo, od   fisis

the judgement of the Highest. To you it is said: behold
    balzizras   Iaida.   Nonca gohulim: micma

the face of your God, the beginning of comfort; whose
    adoian   MAD,   iaod   bliorb;   soba

eyes   are the brightness of the heavens; which
ooaona chis   luciftias   peripsol; ds

provided you for the government of the Earth, and her
abraassa noncf   netaaib   Caosgo, od tilb

unspeakable variety,   furnishing you with a power
adphaht   damploz, tooat   noncf g-micalz

of understanding to dispose all things according
    oma   lrasd   tofglo   marb

to the providence of Him-That-Sitteth-On-the-Holy-Throne,
    yarry   IDOIGO,

and rose up in the beginning, saying: the Earth,
od   torzulp   iaodaf,   gohul: Caosga,

let her be governed by her parts,   and let there be
        tabaord   saanir, od   christeos

division in her, that the glory of her may be always
  yrpoil tiobl,   busdir tilb noaln   paid

drunken and vexed in   itself;   her course,
orsba   od dodrmni   zylna; elzaptilb,

let it run with the heavens, and as a handmaid
    parm-gi   peripsax, od ta   qurlst

let her serve them; one season, let it confound another,
      booapis;   l-nibm,   oucho   symp,

and let there be no creature upon or within her
od   christeos ag-toltorn mirc Q   tiobl

the same; all her members, let them differ
    lel;   ton   paombd,   dilzmo

in their qualities, and let there be no one creature
O   aspian,   od   christeos ag L   tortorn

equal with another;
parach   a-symp;

the reasonable creatures of Earth (or men), let them vex
        cordziz   dodpal

and weed out one another; and the dwelling places,
od   fifalz   l-smnad;   od   fargt,

let them forget their names; the work of man and
        bams   omaoas;   conisbra   od

his pomp, let them be defaced; her buildings,
avavox,   tonug;   orsca-tbl,

let them become caves for the beasts of the field;
      naosmi tabges   levithmong;

confound her understanding with darkness. For why?
unchi   omp-tilb   ors.   Bagle?

It repenteth me I made man. One while let her be known,
   Moooah   ol-cordziz.   L   capimao   ixomaxip,

and another while a stranger: because she is the bed
od   ca-cocasb   gosaa: baglen   pi-i   tianta

of an harlot, and the dwelling place
a-babalond, od   faorgt

of Him-that-is-Fallen. O you Heavens, arise!
   Telocvovim.   Madriiax, torzu!

The lower Heavens underneath you, let them serve you.
      Oadriax   orocha   aboapri.

Govern those that govern; cast down such as fall;
Tabaori priaz   ar-tabas; adrpan   cors-ta dobix;

bring forth with those that increase, and destroy
  yolcam   priazi ar-coazior, od   quasb

the rotten. No place let it remain in one number; add
   qting.   Ripir   paaoxt   saga-cor;   uml

and diminish until the stars be numbered. Arise,
od prdzar cacrg aoiveae   cormpt.   TORZU,

move, and appear before the Covenant of His mouth,
ZACAR, od ZAMRAN aspt   Sibsi   butmona,

which He hath sworn unto us in His justice; open
ds   surzas   Tia baltan; odo

the mysteries of your creation, and make us partakers
   cicle   qaa,   od ozazma plapli

of undefiled knowledge.
      iadnamad.

CHAPTER FIFTEEN

The Spirits of the Thirty Aethers

THE PRINCES OF THE AIRS

The names of the ninety-one Princes, who are the tutelary daemons or genii of the regions of the world, were
delivered to Dee through Kelley by the angels Gabriel
and Nalvage on May 21 and 22, 1584, at Cracow.
Gabriel presided over the process, and Nalvage did the
actual work. It was this hierarchy of geographical spirits
that held the greatest promise of practical utility for
Dee, who hoped to use them to achieve political advan-
tages for his sovereign, Elizabeth I. This desire was not
to be realized, however, because Dee was never granted
permission to invoke them.

Although the names and sigils of these spirits are
clearly set forth, along with the angels by which they
are ruled and their esoteric associations, they constitute
one of the most neglected aspects of Enochian magic.
They were ignored by the Golden Dawn and by Aleister
Crowley. This neglect continues through to the present
day, perhaps because few Enochian magicians know
what to do with them.

The thirty Aethers, or Airs, are described by the
angels as concentric spheres surrounding the Earth.
Each is divided into three parts, except the area closest

Sigils of the Ninety-One Princes on the Original Table

to the Earth, which is divided into four. These parts are inhabited by ninety-one spirits whom Nalvage refers to as "Princes and spiritual Governours." These Princes are all spirits of elemental Air, but each rules a particular region on the surface of the Earth.

Their habitations or Aethers lie between the surface of the Earth and the spiritual fires of the firmament. However, it is a trifle simplistic to conceive of them as occupying physical space. Dimensions or frequencies of vibration are more useful models for these Aethers.

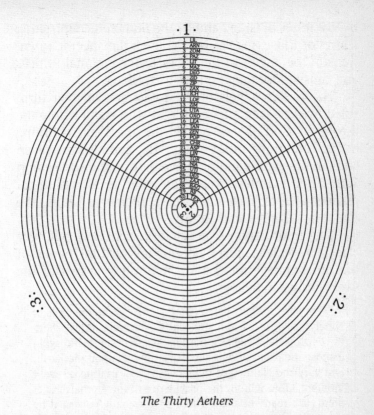

· 1 ·

1 LIL
2 ARN
3 ZOM
4 PAZ
5 LIT
6 MAZ
7 DEO
8 ZID
9 ZIP
10 ZAX
11 ICH
12 LOE
13 ZIM
14 UTA
15 OXO
16 LEA
17 TAN
18 ZEN
19 POP
20 CHR
21 ASP
22 LIN
23 TOR
24 NIA
25 VTI
26 DES
27 ZAA
28 BAG
29 RII
30 TEX

The Thirty Aethers

They lie mingled, yet one above the other, just as the colors of the rainbow are all contained in normal sunlight but may be separated and distinguished by their particular wavelengths.

THE HIERARCHY OF THE AETHERS

The Princes of the regions appear to be receptive rather than active. They are the spiritual identities that reside in, animate, and give particular qualities to their regions. They are ruled by the twelve angels of the twelve tribes of Israel, and by the numerous ministering spirits of those angels, who convey the specific intentions of the angels of the tribes to the regional Princes and cause those intentions to be realized.

The twelve angels of the tribes are, in their turn, ruled by the seven angels of light who stand before the throne of God. These angels are the lamps burning before the throne in *Revelation* 4:5, and also the seven stars in the right hand of heavenly Christ in *Revelation* 1:16. Their manifest expression is the seven traditional planets of astrology—the Moon, Mercury, Venus, the Sun, Mars, Jupiter and Saturn.

This information was set forth concisely but very clearly by Nalvage just before he revealed the names of the ninety-one Princes and their ruling angels of the twelve tribes to Kelley:

> There are 30 Calls yet to come. Those 30 are the Calls of Ninety-one Princes and spiritual Governours, unto whom the Earth is delivered as a portion. These bring in and again dispose the Kings and all the Governments upon the Earth, and vary the Natures of things with the variation of every moment; Unto whom, the providence of the eternal Judgement, is already opened. These are generally governed by the twelve Angels of the 12 Tribes: which are also governed by the 7 which stand before the presence of God. Let him that can see look up: and let him that can here, attend; for this is wisdom. They are all spirits of the Air: not rejected, but dignified; and they dwell and have their habitation in the air diversly, and in sundry places: for their mansions are not alike, neither are their powers equal. Understand therefore, that from the fire to the earth, there are 30 places or abidings: one above and beneath another: wherein these aforesaid Creatures have their aboad, for a time.[1]

The number ninety-one seems oddly unbalanced, but it is based on the formula 7 x 12 + 7 = 91. Seven is the number of the heptarchical Kings and their Princes, while twelve is the number of the angels of the tribes of Israel. In astrology, seven is the number of the planets and twelve is the number of the signs and their houses. It is emphasized by Nalvage, who even goes so far as to make a pun at the end of his speech, that the angels of the Aethers act within the constraints of time. The Princes "vary the Natures of things with the variation of every moment." It is these angels that are responsible for the transformations of the Earth from moment to moment, and for the constantly changing play of thoughts within the human mind.

USE OF THE AETHERS

The geographical genii of each Aether are to be invoked by the Call of the Thirty Aethers, with the name of their particular Aether inserted into the parentheses near the beginning of the Call. This was the practice followed by Aleister Crowley during his 1909 trek through Algeria (though Crowley merely invoked the Airs, not the Princes). First, however, it is probably necessary to perform a general ritual working that involves the vibration of the eighteen distinct Keys, one per night, in reverse order: the Eighteenth Key on the first night, the Seventeenth Key on the second, and so on.

As was pointed out in the previous chapter, the Keys are associated with the directions of the Earth in four sets of four, with each set working its way in one complete circle around the Earth. The Eighteenth Key should be vibrated to the north, the Seventeenth to the west, the Sixteenth to the south, the Fifteenth to the east, and so on. This pattern should continue to the Second Key, which relates to the beam of the Black

Cross on the Great Table of the Watchtowers (the northeast by southwest axis), and the First Key, which relates to the pillar of the Black Cross (the southeast by northwest axis). The unexpressed primordial Key of the Holy Ghost or Great Mother, which is not an explicit part of the working, relates to the intersection of the Black Cross, the fountain of Spirit beneath the throne of New Jerusalem.

After this initial working of the Keys is successfully completed, the Aethers may be tuned in or "keyed" by vibrating the Call of the Thirty Aethers. Then the angels of the tribes may be invoked and commanded by the names of God that lie on the beams of the Great Crosses of the four Watchtowers. Each angel is ruled by the name of God associated with its particular point of the compass.

For example, the second Prince of the third Air, ZOM, is Virooli, the tutelary genius of Thracia (Thrace). He is ruled by the angel Alpudus, who is the angel of the tribe of Issachar. This angel resides in and is invoked from the west-northwest. Alpudus has 3,660 good ministering spirits who serve him. He is invoked and ruled by PDOCE, which is the name of God on the banner of west-northwest and one of the names on the line of Spirit in the Watchtower of the North (on the Original Great Table).

The ritual application of the angel of a tribe to the genius of a region of the Earth is a kind of spiritual copulation that is performed to engender the desired purpose of the Enochian magician. The genius of the place, who is manifestly embodied by his sigil, acts as the receptive medium. The angel of the tribe, acting through his ministers, is the catalyst by which that medium is shaped and quickened.

It should be understood that the tutelary angel of a particular place represents not merely the physical place itself, but also the living spirit of that place. Every region of the Earth has its own distinct character and its own unique power. Through this branch of Enochian magic the spiritual powers of the nations and regions can be harnessed and directed for ritual ends. For example, the spirit of England, symbolized by the goddess Britannia and the hero John Bull, is completely different in its virtues from the spirit of the United States, symbolized by the goddess America and the hero Uncle Sam.

It may be that the full Apocalypse working (if such a thing even exists) will be conducted in this way:

- Vibrating the nineteenth Key for each of the thirty Aethers on thirty successive nights from the First Air to the Thirtieth Air
- Vibrating each of the first eighteen Keys in reverse order, also on successive nights
- Vibrating the primordial, unwritten Key that relates to the center of being
- A final jubilee day of attainment

In this way the Apocalypse working would span fifty days, which is the same period of time the angels say that Enoch toiled. The movement would be from the outer reaches to the center of the Earth. All this is speculation, of course.

THE USE OF THE TABLE OF SIGILS

The accompanying table shows the thirty Aethers, the ancient regions of the Earth they command, the Princes or genii of those regions, the tribes of the Hebrews and the angels of the tribes who rule the genii, the number

	Air	Region	Genius	Tribe	Angel	Min.	Dir.	God N
1	1	Egypt	Occodon	Naphtali	Zarzilg	7209	E-NE	ORO
2	LIL	Syria	Pascomb	Zebulun	Zinggen	2360	W-SW	OIP
3		Mesopotamia	Valgars	Issachar	Alpudus	5362	W-NW	PDOCE
4	2	Cappadocia	Doagnis	Manasseh	Zarnaah	3636	N	ARSL
5	ARN	Etruria	Pacasna	Reuben	Ziracah	2362	S	DIAL
6		Asia Minor	Dialioa	Reuben	Ziracah	8962	S	DIAL
7	3	Hyrcania	Samapha	Naphtali	Zarzilg	4400	E-NE	ORO
8	ZOM	Thracia	Virooli	Issachar	Alpudus	3660	W-NW	PDOCE
9		Gosmam	Andispi	Gad	Lavavot	9236	S-SE	MOR
10	4	Thebaidi	Thotanp	Gad	Lavavot	2360	S-SE	MOR
11	PAZ	Parsadal	Axziarg	Gad	Lavavot	3000	S-SE	MOR
12		India	Pothnir	Ephraim	Arfaolg	6300	N-NW	MPH
13	5	Bactriane	Lazdixi	Dan	Olpaged	8630	E	IBAH
14	LIT	Cilicia	Nocamal	Issachar	Alpudus	2306	W-NW	PDOCE
15		Oxiana	Tiarpax	Zebulun	Zinggen	5802	W-SW	OIP
16	6	Numidia	Saxtomp	Asher	Gebabel	3620	E-SE	AOZPI
17	MAZ	Cyprus	Vavaamp	Ephraim	Arfaolg	9200	N-NW	MPH
18		Parthia	Zirzird	Asher	Gebabal	7220	E-SE	AOZPI
19	7	Getulia	Opmacas	Manasseh	Zarnaah	6363	N	ARSL
20	DEO	Arabia	Genadol	Judah	Hononol	7706	W	TEAA
21		Phalagon	Aspiaon	Zebulun	Zinggen	6320	W-SW	OIP
22	8	Mantiana	Zamfres	Asher	Gebabal	4362	E-SE	AOZPI
23	ZID	Soxia	Todnaon	Dan	Olpaged	7236	E	IBAH
24		Gallia	Pristac	Naphtali	Zarzilg	2302	E-NE	ORO
25	9	Assyria	Oddiorg	Judah	Hononol	9996	W	TEAA
26	ZIP	Sogdiana	Cralpir	Gad	Lavavot	3620	S-SE	MOR
27		Lydia	Doanzin	Naphtali	Zarzilg	4230	E-NE	GAIOL
28	10	Caspis	Lexarph	Zebulun	Zinggen	8880	W-SW	OIP
29	ZAX	Germania	Comanan	Issachar	Alpudus	1230	W-NW	PDOCE
30		Trenam	Tabitom	Naphtali	Zarzilg	1617	E-NE	ORO
31	11	Bithynia	Molpand	Gad	Lavavot	3472	S-SE	MOR
32	ICH	Gracia	Usnarda	Simeon	Zurchol	7236	S-SW	HCTGA
33		Lacia	Ponodol	Judah	Hononol	5234	W	TEAA
34	12	Onigap	Tapamal	Simeon	Zurchol	2658	S-SW	HCTGA
35	LOE	India Major	Gedoons	Benjamin	Cadaamp	7772	N-NE	GAIOL
36		Orchenii	Ambriol	Ruben	Ziracah	3391	S	DIAL
37	13	Achaia	Gecaond	Gad	Lavavot	8111	S-SE	MOR
38	ZIM	Armenia	Laparin	Dan	Olpaged	3360	E	IBAH
39		Nemrodiana	Docepax	Issachar	Alpudus	4213	W-NW	PDOCE
40	14	Paphlogonia	Tedoond	Asher	Gebabal	2673	E-SE	AOZPI
41	UTA	Phasiana	Vivipos	Issachar	Alpudus	9236	W-NW	PDOCE
42		Chaldei	Ooanamb	Ephraim	Arfaolg	8230	N-NW	MPH
43	15	Itergi	Tahamdo	Naphtali	Zarzilg	1367	E-NE	ORO
44	OXO	Macedonia	Nociabi	Gad	Lavavot	1367	S-SE	MOR
45		Garamannia	Tastoxo	Ephraim	Arfaolg	1886	N-NW	MPH

The Table of Sigils: 1–45

	Air	Region	Genius	Tribe	Angel	Min.	Dir.	God N
46	16	Sauromatica	Cucarpt	Reuben	Ziracah	9920	S	DIAL
47	LEA	Ethiopia	Lauacon	Judah	Hononol	9230	W	TEAA
48		Fiacim	Sochial	Ephraim	Arfaolg	9240	N-NW	MPH
49	17	Colchica	Sigmorf	Reuben	Ziracah	7623	S	DIAL
50	TAN	Cireniaca	Avdropt	Dan	Olpaged	7132	E	IBAH
51		Nasamoma	Tocarzi	Naphtali	Zarzilg	2634	E-NE	ORO
52	18	Carthago	Nabaomi	Asher	Gebabal	2346	E-SE	AOZPI
53	ZEN	Coxlant	Zafasai	Issachar	Alpudus	7689	W-NW	PDOCE
54		Adumea	Yalpamb	Ephraim	Arfaolg	9276	N-NW	MPH
55	19	Parstavia	Torzoxi	Ephraim	Arfaolg	6236	N-NW	MPH
56	POP	Celtica	Abriond	Benjamin	Cadaamp	6732	N-NE	GAIOL
57		Vinsan	Omagrap	Zebulun	Zinggen	2388	W-SW	OIP
58	20	Tolpam	Zildron	Asher	Gebabal	3626	E-SE	AOZPI
59	CHR	Carcedoma	Parziba	Judah	Hononol	7629	W	TEAA
60		Italia	Totocan	Issachar	Alpudus	3634	W-NW	PDOCE
61	21	Brytania	Chirzpa	Ephraim	Arfaolg	5536	N-NW	MPH
62	ASP	Phenices	Toantom	Benjamin	Cadaamp	5635	N-NE	GAIOL
63		Comaginen	Vixpalg	Simeon	Zurchol	5658	S-SW	HCTGA
64	22	Apulia	Ozidaia	Ephraim	Arfaolg	2232	N-NW	MPH
65	LIN	Marmarica	Paraoan	Dan	Olpaged	2326	E	IBAH
66		Concava Syria	Calzirg	Ephraim	Arfaolg	2367	N-NW	MPH
67	23	Gebal	Ronoomb	Manasseh	Zarnaah	7320	N	ARSL
68	TOR	Elam	Onizimp	Gad	Lavavot	7262	S-SE	MOR
69		Adunia	Zaxanin	Zebulun	Zinggen	7333	W-SW	OIP
70	24	Media	Orcanir	Manasseh	Zarnaah	8200	N	ARSL
71	NIA	Arriana	Chialps	Gad	Lavavot	8360	S-SE	MOR
72		Chaldea	Soageel	Zebulun	Zinggen	8236	W-SW	OIP
73	25	Serica Populi	Mirzind	Manasseh	Zarnaah	5632	N	ARSL
74	UTI	Persia	Obvaors	Reuben	Ziracah	6333	S	DIAL
75		Gongatha	Ranglam	Ephraim	Arfaolg	6236	N-NW	MPH
76	26	Gorsin	Pophand	Ephraim	Arfaolg	9232	N-NW	MPH
77	DES	Hispania	Nigrana	Benjamin	Cadaamp	3620	N-NE	GAIOL
78		Pamphilia	Bazchim	Ephraim	Arfaolg	5637	N-NW	MPH
79	27	Oacidi	Saziami	Reubin	Ziracah	7220	S	DIAL
80	ZAA	Babylon	Mathula	Manasseh	Zarnaah	7560	N	ARSL
81		Median	Orpanib	Asher	Gebabal	7263	E-SE	AOZPI
82	28	Adumian	Labnixp	Gad	Lavavot	2630	S-SE	MOR
83	BAG	Felix Arabia	Pocisni	Naphtali	Zarzilg	7236	E-NE	ORO
84		Metagonitidim	Oxlopar	Simeon	Zurchol	8200	S-SW	HCTGA
85	29	Assyria	Vastrim	Judah	Hononol	9632	W	TEAA
86	RII	Africa	Odraxti	Manasseh	Zarnaah	4236	N	ARSL
87		Bactriani	Gomziam	Ephraim	Arfaolg	7635	N-NW	MPH
88		Asnan	Taoagla	Ephraim	Arfaolg	4632	N-NW	MPH
89	30	Phrygia	Gemnimb	Manasseh	Zarnaah	9636	N	ARSL
90	TEX	Creta	Advorpt	Judah	Hononol	7632	W	TEAA
91		Mauritania	Doxmael	Simeon	Zurchol	5632	S-SW	HCTGA

The Table of Sigils: 46–91

of good ministers under the angels of the tribes, the direction of the compass where each tribal angel resides, and the Enochian banner name of God associated with that direction. The numbers of the Princes may be used to locate their sigils on the grid of the Original Great Table of the Watchtowers. To convert the sigil display on the Original Great Table into a sigil display on my own Restored Great Table, simply invert the quarters of the west and north (transpose the lower right with the lower left).

Bear in in mind that there are minor variations in the lettering between the Original Great Table and the Revised Great Table of Raphael. My Restored Great Table uses the lettering of the Table of Raphael. The sigils of the Princes of the regions are the same shape on all three versions of the Great Table, but some of the names of the Princes are spelled with slight differences depending on whether the Original or the Revised (and Restored) Tables are used.

To locate a particular sigil on the Original Great Table, take note of the number of the Prince, then find this number on the sigil display near the start of this chapter. The sigil closest to the number is the sigil of the Prince. Compare the sigil display with the lettered version of the Original Great Table in Chapter Twelve. You will be able to trace out the individual letters in the name on the Original Table by following the arrow of the sigil. Each sigil begins with a cross and ends with an arrowhead.

If you wish to locate the name of a Prince on my Restored Great Table, first determine which Watchtower the sigil occupies by comparing the quarters of my Restored Table in Chapter Ten with the quarters of the Original Table. Position that sigil on the Restored Table, and trace out the arrow of its name as before. You will see that some names have slight variations in spelling.

It is evident that the names of the angels of the twelve tribes of Israel are each intended to contain seven letters. However, in Dee's manuscript Lavavoth (the angel of the tribe of Gad) is written with eight letters. This occurs because the final letter in the name is the Hebrew letter Tau, which is written in English Th. Tau is on occasion alternatively transliterated by T, so I have used T to stand for this Hebrew letter in order to give the name of the angel seven letters. The name should be pronounced "Lavavoth."

There are ninety-one Princes of the regions of the Earth, but ninety-two sigils on the Great Table. One of the sigils is not named by the angels. It occurs at the bottom of the MPH, ARSL, GAIOL Watchtower, which on the Original Great Table is the Watchtower of the West (lower right quarter). Laxdizi, the name of this extra spirit, can easily be extracted from its sigil.

This supernummary sigil has caused some confusion. In the magical system of the Aurum Solis, a British occult society with a tradition similar to that of the Golden Dawn, this sigil is numbered 65.[2] But the sixty-fifth Prince is named Paraoan (Paoaoan on the Restored Table), and the letters of his name are not to be found in this sigil. This error appears to have arisen from a misunderstanding of the nature of Paraoan's sigil, which is not one unbroken line on the Great Table, but is composed of three two-letter segments from three of the Watchtowers, and a single letter from the fourth: PA;RA;OA;N (all the letters are capitals). If you examine the sigil grid of the Original Great Table, you will find these short segments and single cell marked with the number 65.

This sigil puzzled Dee, who inquired about it to Ave.

Dee: You bad me chuse out of the Tables the Characters of fewest Letters, and I found them to be OA RA JA and L, you said they are eight, you said there are eight in four: I know not what this meaneth.

Ave: You must make up the name Paraoan.

Dee: What shall become of the L aversed?

Ave: It may be N, or L.

Dee: What must I now do with that name?

Ave: In Exarph there wanteth an L which L is of more force then the N and therefore it is set in the Tables. As far as that N stretcheth in the Character, so far shall that Countrey be consumed with fire, and swallowed in Hell, as Sodom was for wickednesse.

Dee's marginal note: So is not one letter superfluous, or wanting in the Tables.[3]

Five days later, Dee again made inquiry concerning this curious name, but received little satisfaction:

Dee: I beseech you say somewhat of the N in Paraoan, of which you said, so far as that stretched, should sink to hell.

Ave: Every letter in Paraoan, is a living fire: but all of one quality and of one Creation: but unto N is delivered a viol of Destruction, according to that part that he is of Paraoan the Governour.

Dee: It may please you to name that Place, City, or Country, under that N.

Ave: Ask Nalvage, and he will tell you.[4]

Dee did not have the letters of what he calls the "Characters of fewest Letters" correctly gathered, but seems to have understood the explanation of the angel. The three sigil segments of two letters make up the first six letters in the name Paraoan on the Original Table. Ave tells Dee that the final letter in the name may be either the single inverted N or the single inverted L on the Watchtower MPH, ARSL, GAIOL in the western quarter of the Original Great Table. However, the L has greater occult potency, and therefore should be attached at the front of the sigil of the twenty-eighth Prince, whose name is L;exarph. The final six letters of this sigil are to be found at the top of the pillar of the Black Cross (and also at the bottom, since the same letters are inverted there).

The Black Cross, as the name implies, was drawn with solid black ink by Dee in his diagram of the ninety-one sigils of the Princes on the Great Table.[5] Consequently, Dee could not illustrate the three sigils that are located upon the upper half of the pillar and the right side of the beam of the Black Cross, as I have done in the illustration at the head of this chapter. The sigil of the twenty-eighth Prince, L;exarph, is located on the top of the pillar. The sigil of the twenty-ninth Prince, Comanan, wraps around the corner of the southern quarter of the Table and passes through the center of the Black Cross. The sigil of the thirtieth Prince, Tabitom, lies on the right arm of the beam of the Black Cross. Since the letters that make up these names also occur in reversed order on the lower half of the pillar and left arm of the beam, these names may be found wrapping around the northern quarter of the Table.

Because Dee did not represent these three sigils on the Black Cross or number the sigils in his diagram, it was an easy matter to misunderstand the use of the three two-letter segments and two single letter cells that occur on the Great Table. Many of Dee's sigils contain minor mistakes in form. I have corrected these errors in the sigil display at the head of this chapter. Unfortunately, I can offer no insight into the use of the ninety-second sigil of the spirit whose name is Laxdizi. Dee accurately drew the sigil of this spirit on his grid, but did not include its name in his list of Princes of the Aethers.

The Regions of the Earth

After conveying the names of the Princes of the Aethers, Nalvage indicated places on the surface of the Earth to which they correspond. He began by simply pointing to the region ruled by each spirit on a globe of the Earth in the depths of the showstone. Dee protested that this way was too confusing, so the angel adopted a different approach:

> *Kelley:* There appeareth a great thing like a Globe, turning upon two axell-trees.
> *Nalvage:* Turn to the first Air.
> *Dee:* I have done.
> *Nalvage:* The Earth in the first ayre, is this.
> *Kelley:* Pointing on that Globe to it.
> *Dee:* We beseech you to bound or determine the Countries or Portions of the Earth, by their uttermost Longitudes and Latitudes, or by some other certain manner.
> *Nalvage:* Our manner is, not as it is of worldlings: We determine not places after the forms of legs, or as leaves are: neither we can imagin any thing after the fashion of an horn: as those that are Cosmographers do.
> Notwithstanding the Angel of the Lord appeared unto Ptolomie, and opened unto him the parts of the Earth: but some he was commanded to secret: and those are Northward under your Pole. But unto you, the very true names of the World in her Creation are delivered.[6]

Nalvage went on to name the geographical name of the region under each of the Princes of the Aethers. Dee had considerable difficulty understanding the location of some of these places, but was occasionally assisted by Kelley's vision of the places or their inhabitants.

> *Nalvage:* The third [of the seventh Aether], Phalagon.
> *Dee:* I never heard of it.
> *Kelley:* It is toward the North, where the veines of Gold;

and such people appear as before were noted. On this side them a great way appear men with swinish snouts, their visage is so strouted out; but to be perceived to be of humane visage. The women have about their privities very long hair down to their knees. The men have things on their shoulders of beasts skins, so instead of a Jerkin or a Mandillion.[7]

In the course of naming the regions of the Earth, Nalvage also showed Kelley visions of Noah's ark in Armenia and the Garden of Eden. Paradise is apparently overseen by the second Prince of the eighteenth Aether.

Nalvage: The second [of the eighteenth Air]:
Kelley: Now appear many Crocodiles, long necked, scaled on the body, with long tailes.
Nalvage: Coxlant.
Kelley: A great place appeareth, covered about with fire. Many great serpents appear of 200 foot. It appeareth very Eastward. No people appear here.

There cometh from Heaven like a Mist, and covereth a great place about 300 mile long, like a Park, enclosed with fire. It is on a high ground. There come four Rivers out of it, one East, another West, another North, and another South. The pales, or enclosure of it seem to be Arches, beset most richly with precious stones. In the Gate of it stand three men like us, one is in a long Gown with many pleats, the other like in a Cassek. The third in the rough skin of a beast. In the name of Jesus: Is this the Paradise that Adam was banished out of?
Nalvage: The very same; from hence he was turned out into the earth. This is the true Vale of Josaphat.
Dee: Will you give me leave?
Nalvage: Say on.
Dee: It should seem this must be on the earth, not in the aire.
Nalvage: It is upon the earth.
Dee: You said that from hence he was turned out into the earth.

Nalvage: The curse of God in Adam caused the earth, whereinto he was cast to be accursed. For, if Adam had after his fall tarried in Paradise, his wickednesse would have altred the innocency of the place. Therefore is Paradise distinguished from the earth, in respect of her purity: because the earth is defiled, and corrupted with man. The earth is said to be sinfull in respect of the sin of man.

Dee: Till 45 degrees, both Northerly and Southerly, all is known in the most part of the world: But of any such place there is no knowledge nor likelyhood by any History of these days, or of old time.

Nalvage: Therefore this is cunning, and the wisdom of God. There dwelleth flesh in it that shall never die, which were taken up for a testimony of Truth.[8]

Dee was not a man to be easily deceived concerning geography, since it was one of his primary subjects of study. While in England, he had frequently been consulted by the leading explorers and navigators of the day concerning the fabled Northwest and Northeast Passages as well as the geography of Asia and the New World. English mariners followed his charts when they went sailing into unknown waters. His skepticism concerning a physical Eden is obvious, but he did not argue the point further with Nalvage.

PTOLEMY AND AGRIPPA

Dee was perfectly aware that the names of the places of the Earth were those recorded in the *Tetrabiblos* of the Greek astronomer and astrologer Ptolemy. Nalvage himself had stated as much before beginning to name the places. According to Nalvage, the common names for the regions had been revealed to Ptolemy by the "Angel of the Lord," but not the names of the places near the north pole. However, Nalvage promised to Dee and Kelley something greater, "the very true names of the World in her Creation."

Kelley did not understand Nalvage's reference to Ptolemy, but he did vaguely recognize the names. After the angel completed the list and allowed the men to rest overnight, Kelley followed his thread of memory and was able to look up the names in his private library of magical books. He was enraged by what he regarded as a rank deception on the part of the angels, and at first refused to resume the scrying session.

Dee: After half an hour and lesse, he came speedily out of his Study, and brought in his hand one Volume of Cornelius Agrippa his works, and in one Chapter of that Book he read the names of Countries and Provinces collected out of Ptolomeus (as the Author there noteth) Whereupon he inferred, that our spiritual Instructors were Coseners to give us a description of the World, taken out of other Books: and therefore he would have no more to do with them. I replied, and said, I am very glad that you have a Book of your own, wherein these Geographical names are expressed, such as (for the most part) our Instructors had delivered unto us: and that, according to the Tenor and form of my request to him, so to have them expressed: for our most perfect information, by those known names; to understand those 91 unknown and unheard of names, of seven letters every one: whereby they (our Instructors I mean) are very greatly to be thanked, and to be deemed (in all reasonable mens judgements) most friendly, and far from cosenage, or abusing us: And farther I said, that I my self, had here set down on a paper all the 91 names together orderly, as we received them, and that I had here brought the description (Gerardus [Mercator's] Universal Chart of the World) Geographical of the whole earthly Globe: and also Pomponius Mela set forth in English with the Chartes thereunto belonging, fairly described by hand: To the intent that he might see the verity of their words yesterday delivered unto us: for the performance of my request made to them...[9]

Kelley was not mollified. He refused to have anything more to do with the angels for five days.

The reference Kelley made to Agrippa concerns Book One, Chapter Thirty-One of *The Three Books of Occult Philosophy*. Agrippa here summarizes part of the third chapter of the second book of Ptolemy's *Tetrabiblos*, where the regions of the world are categorized under the ruling influence of the stars. Agrippa introduces his brief chapter by saying, "Moreover the whole orb of the Earth is distributed by kingdoms and provinces to the planets, and signs." He then groups the nations of the classical world under each planet and the signs of the zodiac it rules. This list corresponds in many respects with the list of places given by Nalvage.

In closing, Agrippa writes:

> These we have in this manner gathered from Ptolemy's opinion, to which according to the writings of other astrologers many more may be added. But he which knows how to compare these divisions of provinces according to the divisions of the stars, with the ministry of the ruling intelligences, and blessings of the tribes of Israel, the lots of the apostles, and typical seals of the sacred Scripture, shall be able to obtain great and prophetical oracles concerning every religion, of things to come.[10]

The list of places given by Nalvage is more extensive than the lists in Agrippa and Ptolemy. It is difficult to determine which text served Nalvage as a source, if either. These names were common in ancient geographies.

CHAPTER SIXTEEN

The Enochian Invocations of John Dee

"MAKE YOU BUT INVOCATIONS TO SOW THE SEED"

Dee was anxious to learn the details of the initial eighteen-day ritual working by which he would gain access to the ninety-one Princes of the Thirty Aethers, but he was never actually given this information. Ave did tell him that before he could undertake this extended initial working it would be necessary for him to make a Book of Spirits containing the names of the angels and spirits on the Great Table of the Watchtowers.

> *Ave:* You have the corn, and you have the ground: Make you but invocations to sow the seed, and the fruit shall be plentiful.
>
> *Dee:* As concerning our usage in the 4 dayes [and] in the 14 dayes, we would gladly have some information.
>
> *Ave:* You would know to reape, before your corn be sown.
>
> *Dee:* As concerning a fit place and time to call, and other circumstances, we would learn somewhat.
>
> *Ave:* You would know where and when to call, before your invocations bear witnesses of your readinesse.
>
> *Dee:* Then they must be written in verbis conceptis, in formal words.
>
> *Ave:* I—a very easie matter.
>
> *Dee:* What is the Book you mean that I should write?

Ave: The Book consisteth [1] of Invocation of the names of God, and [2] of the Angels, by the names of God: Their offices are manifest. You did desire to be fed with spoones, and so you are.[1]

This is not a very detailed description, but at least it is something to work with, and more practical information than the angels often gave in response to Dee's questions.

Previously, Ave had informed Dee that after the book had been written out he must invoke the God of Hosts (Dee interpreted this to mean Jehovah Sabaoth) for four days, using the twelve names of God that are found on the lines of Spirit in the four Watchtowers. Then for fourteen days Dee must call the angels "by Petition, and by the name of God, unto the which they are obedient." On the fifteenth day, Dee and Kelley were to clothe themselves in white linen and "so have the apparition, use, and practice of the Creatures."

Dee actually created this Book of Spirits, or at least, he created the pattern from which the book was to be made. It appears in his Latin manuscript *Liber Scientiae Auxilii et Victoriae Terrestris* (British Library Sloane MS 3191). It is reproduced in English in Geoffrey James's *The Enochian Magic of Dr. John Dee*, which I strongly recommend to anyone seriously interested in studying Enochian magic. Dee's Book of Spirits consists of these invocations:

1) The Fundamental Obeisance, which is the invocation of the twelve names of God that are written on the lines of Spirit of the four Watchtowers of the Great Table.

—:—

2) Six Seniors of the east whose names are written on the great cross of the Watchtower of the east.

3) Six Seniors of the south.

4) Six Seniors of the west.

5) Six Seniors of the north.

—:—

6) Four good angels of the east who are skilled and powerful in medicine and curing diseases.

7) Four good angels of the south powerful in medicine.

8) Four good angels of the west powerful in medicine.

9) Four good angels of the north powerful in medicine.

—:—

10) Four good angels of the east who are skilled and powerful in metals and precious jewels.

11) Four good angels of the south powerful in metals and precious jewels.

12) Four good angels of the west powerful in metals and precious jewels.

13) Four good angels of the north powerful in metals and precious jewels.

—:—

14) Four good angels of the east who are skilled and powerful in transformations.

15) Four good angels of the south powerful in transformations.

16) Four good angels of the west powerful in transformations.

17) Four good angels of the north powerful in transformations.

—:—

18) Four good angels of the east, each of whom knows the living creatures in one element, and their use.

19) Four good angels of the south knowing the living creatures of one element, and their use.

20) Four good angels of the west knowing the living creatures of one element, and their use.

21) Four good angels of the north knowing the living creatures of one element, and their use.

—:—

22) Four Dispositors of the east who are skilled and powerful in the mixing together of natural substances.

23) Four Dispositors of the south powerful in natural substances.

24) Four Dispositors of the west powerful in natural substances.

25) Four Dispositors of the north powerful in natural substances.

—:—

26) Four Dispositors of the east who are skilled and powerful in transporting from place to place.

27) Four Dispositors of the south powerful in transporting.

28) Four Dispositors of the west powerful in transporting.

29) Four Dispositors of the north powerful in transporting.

—:—

30) Four Dispositors of the east who are skilled and powerful in the mechanical arts.

31) Four Dispositors of the south powerful in mechanical arts.

32) Four Dispositors of the west powerful in mechanical arts.

33) Four Dispositors of the north powerful in mechanical arts.

—:—

34) Four Dispositors of the east who are skilled and powerful in the discovery of the secrets of men.

35) Four Dispositors of the south powerful in the discovery of secrets.

36) Four Dispositors of the west powerful in the discovery of secrets.

37) Four Dispositors of the north powerful in the discovery of secrets.

These divisions of the angels can be most clearly seen in this table, which is reproduced from Chapter Thirteen. It shows the relative positions of these angels on the quarters of a Watchtower. This interrelation is the same on all four Watchtowers.

East 1.	South 2.
Dispositors: Knitting Together	**Dispositors:** Transportation
Good Angels: Teach Medicine and Heal the Sick	**Good Angels:** Precious Metals and Jewels
Evil Angels: Cause Sickness and Death	**Evil Angels:** Counterfeiting and Gambling
North 3.	**West 4.**
Dispositors: Arts and Crafts	**Dispositors:** Secrets of Men
Good Angels: Transformations of Form, not Essence	**Good Angels:** Knowledge of All Elemental Spirits
Evil Angels: Illusions and Deceptions	**Evil Angels:** Evil and Base Uses of Elementals

Offices of the Angels on Any Watchtower

FOUR DAYS AND FOURTEEN DAYS

Unfortunately, the invocations in Dee's Book of Spirits do not total eighteen. If we take them together in groups of angels linked by function, they total ten. Yet Ave states that the period of invocation must be eighteen days, and must be divided into two parts of four days followed by fourteen days.

The first four days are to be devoted to the invocation of the twelve names of God on the lines of Spirit in the Watchtowers.

Ave: Thou hast three names of God, out of the line of the holy Ghost, in the principall Crosse of the first Angle, so has thou three in the second, etc.

268 • Enochian Magic for Beginners

Four dayes (after your book is made, that is to say, written) must you onely call upon those names of God, or on the God of Hosts, in those names.

And 14 dayes after you shall (in this, or on some convenient place) Call the Angels by Petition, and by the name of God, unto the which they are obedient.[2]

Elsewhere Ave tells Dee:

Ave: One book of perfect paper. One labour of a few days.

The calling them together, and the yielding of their promise, the repetition of the names of God, are sufficient.

I have given you Corn: I have given you also ground. Desire God to give you ability to till.[3]

Obviously the names of God in each Watchtower are to be invoked on four individual days that open the eighteen-day working, yet Dee grouped all twelve names in a single opening invocation. It is evident that Dee did not understand Ave's explicit instruction concerning the names of God on the lines of Spirit. Ave further makes plain that the working is divided into two distinct parts: the invocation of the names of God, and the invocation of the angels by the names of God.

"AT NO TIME TO BE CALLED"

It is not so clear to see how the remaining angels may be divided into fourteen groups, with each group receiving one invocation to be voiced on a separate day. Dee gives thirty-six invocations for the Seniors, good angels, and Dispositors. He does not provide any invocations for the evil angels whose names have only three letters, even though he lists these names beside the names of the good angels from which they are extracted. He was expressly forbidden to invoke the evil angels by Ave.

Dee: Then they [the evil angels] are not to be named in the first summoning or invitation.

Ave: At no time to be called.[4]

This is unequivocal and cannot be casually disregarded. Therefore, it becomes necessary to divide the Seniors, Dispositors, and good angels into fourteen groups, each group to be invoked on its own day during the initial eighteen-day working of invocation. Since the angels never actually say how this is to be done, it is impossible to be certain about it. Dee seems to have completely missed the necessity of making this division—at least, he never mentions it in his writings. I cannot be sure the system of division presented here is correct—all I can say is that it is sensible and workable.

THE INVOCATIONS OF THE ANGELS

In my opinion, it is necessary to divide the Seniors into six groups of four, with each group containing a Senior from all four Watchtowers. This selection should probably be made clockwise (following the order in which the names of the Seniors were delivered by Ave) with the first group composed of the names in the left side of the lines of Spirit of the Great Crosses of the Watchtowers, the second group of the names in the upper part of the lines of the Son, the third group of the names in the upper part of the lines of the Father, the fourth group of the names in the right side of the lines of Spirit, the fifth group of the names in the lower part of the lines of the Father, and the sixth group of the names in the lower part of the lines of the Son.

The Dispositors (or good angels) whose names lie above the arms of the lesser crosses should come next, since they appear to be next in authority. These sixty-four angels are divided into four groups of sixteen angels, each group of which contains four angels from each Watchtower. The first group names the sixteen Dispositors of the subquarters of the east, the second the sixteen Dispositors of the subquarters of the south, the third the sixteen Dispositors of the subquarters of the west, and the fourth the sixteen Dispositors of the subquarters of the north.

The same system of division is followed to divide the sixty-four good angels into four groups of sixteen angels, each group of which contains four good angels from each Watchtower.

For each of these groups an invocation is written that contains the names of God or the angels in the group. Each invocation is voiced during one day of the eighteen-day working. Ave says nothing about how many times each invocation is to be repeated, but from other statements it is likely that each invocation is to be repeated in a consecrated place three times: once at sunrise, once at noon, and once at sunset.

If the system of division I have suggested is adopted, it results in the following eighteen invocations:

1) God Names of the eastern Watchtower.
2) God Names of the southern Watchtower.
3) God Names of the western Watchtower.
4) God Names of the northern Watchtower.

5) Seniors of the left side of the lines of Spirit.
6) Seniors of the top half of the lines of the Son.
7) Seniors of the top half of the lines of the Father.
8) Seniors of the right of the lines of Spirit.
9) Seniors of the bottom of the lines of the Father.
10) Seniors of the bottom of the lines of the Son.

11) Dispositors of the mixing of natural substances.
12) Dispositors of transportation from place to place.
13) Dispositors of the mechanical arts.
14) Dispositors of the discovery of human secrets.

15) Good angels of medicine.
16) Good angels of metals and precious jewels.
17) Good angels of transformations.
18) Good angels of the four elements.

THE INVOCATION OF THE THIRTY AETHERS

Although the angels never say so, it may be that a similar working of thirty days is to be conducted following the eighteen-day working. This would serve to establish communication with the angels of the Thirty Aethers by means of thirty invocations, each spoken three times on its appointed day. Both the working of eighteen days and the working of thirty days would be consummated or fulfilled on the days immediately following the workings, so that the entire period of invocation would occupy fifty days.

Dee seems never to have imagined combining the eighteen-day invocation explicitly described by the angel Ave with another invocation period of thirty days. Yet if he was to have the use of the angels of the thirty Aethers, it makes good magical sense for him to first establish communication with them and secure their cooperation through an opening invocation working. There is no reason to suppose that the employment of the angels of the Aethers follows any different process than the employment of the other angels of the Watchtowers.

THE ROLE OF THE ENOCHIAN KEYS

There are eighteen distinct Enochian Keys, and these Keys obviously relate to the subquarters of the Great Table. However, it is unclear whether these Keys are to be voiced during the eighteen-day working that establishes contact with the Enochian angels. At first consideration, this would seem probable. However, the distinct Keys naturally fall into a division of five parts: 2 + 4 + 4 + 4 + 4. It is not clear how this division can be related to the division of the invocations into 4 + 14 that was defined by Ave, or my own conjectured division of 4 + 6 + 4 + 4.

It is possible to relate the eighteen distinct Keys to the eighteen classes of spirits invoked in the initial working by inverting the order of the Keys, placing the Seniors at the end of the working, and dividing the six groups of Seniors into four and two. If this is done, the Keys 18, 17, 16 and 15 may be linked with the four invocations of the names of God; the Keys 14, 13, 12 and 11 may be linked with the four groups of Dispositors; the Keys 10, 9, 8 and 7 may be linked with the four groups of good angels; the Keys 6, 5, 4 and 3 may be linked with the four groups of Seniors from the upper parts of the lines of the Son, the upper parts of the lines of the Father, the lower parts of the lines of the Son, and the lower parts of the lines of the Father, respectively; and, finally, the Keys 2 and 1 may be linked with the groups of Seniors from the left side of the lines of Spirit and from the right side of the lines of Spirit, respectively.

I offer this association of the Keys with the groups of the names of God and angels on the Great Table as a matter of interest to more advanced Enochian magicians, but I am not happy with it. It is my personal view that the Keys are individually associated with the beam and pillar of the Black Cross (Keys 1 and 2), and with the sixteen subquarters of the Great Table (Keys 3 to 18). If this is true, then the Keys are not to be voiced in the initial eighteen-day working that establishes contact with the angels, but are (perhaps) to be used later to command specific sets of angels on individual subquarters of the Great Table.

For example, Key 4 would be used to invoke specifically the Dispositors and good angels on the eastern subquarter of the Watchtower of the South. Key 13 would be used to invoke the Dispositors and good angels on the northern subquarter of the Watchtower of the West. And so for the rest.

The Seniors (if, indeed, it is ever necessary to invoke the Seniors) would probably be invoked by Keys 1 and 2. The First Key, related by me to the pillar of the Black Cross, would also relate to the double pillars of the Great Crosses on the individual Watchtowers, and to the four Seniors whose names are written on each double pillar (the lines of the Son and the Father). The Second Key, related by me to the beam of the Black Cross, would also relate to the beams of the Great Crosses on the individual Watchtowers, and to the two Seniors whose names are written on each beam (the lines of the Holy Spirit).

To understand this assignment, see the illustration in Chapter Fourteen that shows the numbers of the Keys assigned to the sixteen subquarters of the Great Table in four circles of four. It may well be incorrect, but since the angels left no explicit correspondence between the Keys and the angels on the Great Table, we are forced to invent our own systems. Such improvisation was done by the Golden Dawn, as I shall explain in Chapter Seventeen. The correspondence between the Keys and the angels on the Watchtowers represents one of the most original aspects of Golden Dawn Enochian magic.

THE APOCALYPSE WORKING

As I have stated elsewhere, it is also my opinion that the forty-eight expressed Keys (and the first, unexpressed Key) are intended by the angels to be used in a great working, probably of fifty days duration, designed to initiate the period of destructive transformation that is generally known as the apocalypse. This may be linked with the eighteen-day invocation of the angels of the Great Table, as I suggested in my book *Tetragrammaton*, or it may be a completely separate working.

On this subject, it is impossible to be certain. The whole matter of the Apocalypse Working, as I have called it, is murky and is likely to remain so, because it was never explicitly discussed between Dee and the angels. Indeed, many Enochian magicians would probably say that no such Apocalypse Working exists. I put forward the concept based on my own study of the Enochian transcripts, and I believe there is considerable implicit evidence to suggest that the angels intended Enochian magic, and specifically the Enochian Keys, to serve as a trigger for the apocalypse. But this is primarily a personal conviction. You will not find unequivocal references to an Apocalyse working given anywhere by Dee or the angels.

THE FORM OF INVOCATION

When composing the words of the invocations to the angels, Dee was forced to draw upon his background knowledge of Christian and Hebrew prayers, supplemented by the invocations which appear in the medieval grimoires of magic. Kelley may have aided him in this composition, since the alchemist was a practicing ritual magician and had actually used the invocations in the grimoires. Dee also exhibits a knowledge of legal terminology in his invocations, which are worded in such a way that no loopholes are left open to the angels. He must have been familiar with legends of Black Pacts and other tales in which spirits take advantage of ambiguities in the wording of the contract. Since Kelley had some knowledge of property law he may have helped Dee in this area also.

As I mentioned in Chapter Fourteen, the angels were unable to provide Dee with a pattern for his invocations. Invocation, Ave informs Dee, is a faculty of human nature that the angels do not possess.

> *Dee:* As for the form of our Petition or Invitation of the good Angels, What sort should it be of?
> *Ave:* A short and brief speech.
> *Dee:* We beseech you to give us an example: we would have a confidence, it should be of more effect.
> *Ave:* I may not.
> *Kelley:* And why?
> *Ave:* Invocation proceedeth of the good will of man, and of the heat and fervency of the spirit: And therefore is prayer of such effect with God.
> *Dee:* We beseech you, shall we use one form to all?
> *Ave:* Every one, after a divers form.
> *Dee:* If the minde do dictate or prompt a divers form, you mean.
> *Ave:* I know not: for I dwell not in the soul of man.[5]

According to Ave, invocation arises from human free will and ecstatic inspiration. It is a creative process. Angels cannot create. They are instruments, or extensions, of the will of God. The human power to compose invocations and the human power to assign names (used by Adam in the Garden of Eden—see *Genesis* 2:19–20) have a similar source—the spark of divine fire that lies within every human being.

THE PRAYER OF ENOCH

The angels did provide a model invocation that Dee was free to follow when composing his own set of original invocations. This was the prayer spoken by Enoch to God during the fifty days Enoch spent creating his magical tables of stone. Although Dee chose not to follow the pattern of this prayer, it clearly was intended by the angels to have an application in Enochian magic, although they never explicitly said this to Dee. It may have been intended as a model for the Apocalypse Working.

Since the prayer of Enoch, delivered by Ave on July 7, 1584, is of such great importance in the matter of Enochian invocation, I will reproduce it here.

> *Dee:* Afterward, [Ave] he came again, and (after a pause) said as followeth.
>
> *Ave:* My brother, I see thou dost not understand the mystery of this Book, or work thou hast in hand. But I told thee, it was the knowledge that God delivered unto Enoch. I said also, that Enoch laboured 50 days. Notwithstanding, that thy labour be not frustrate, and void of fruit, Be it unto thee, as thou hast done.
>
> *Dee:* Lord I did the best that I could conceive of it.
>
> *Ave:* I will tell thee, what the labour of Enoch was for those fifty dayes.
>
> *Dee:* O Lord I thank thee.
>
> *Ave:* He made (as thou hast done, thy book) Tables, of Serpasan and plain stone: as the Angel of the Lord appointed him; saying, tell me (O Lord) the number of the dayes that I shall labour in. It was answered to him 50.

Then he groaned within himself, saying, Lord God the Fountain of true wisdom, thou that openest the secrets of thy own self unto man, thou knowest mine imperfection, and my inward darknesse: How can I (therefore) speak unto them that speak not after the voice of man; or worthily call on thy name, considering that my imagination is variable and fruitlesse, and unknown to my self? Shall the Sands seem to invite the Mountains: or can the small Rivers entertain the wonderful and unknown waves?

Can the vessel of fear, fragility, or that is of a determined proportion, lift up himself, heave up his hands, or gather the Sun into his bosom? Lord it cannot be: Lord my imperfection is great: Lord I am lesse than sand: Lord, thy good Angels and Creatures excell me far: our proportion is not alike; our sense agreeth not: Notwithstanding I am comforted; For that we have all one God, all one beginning from thee, that we respect thee a Creatour: Therefore will I call upon thy name, and in thee, I will become mighty. Thou shalt light me, and I will become a Seer; I will see thy Creatures, and will magnifie thee amongst them. Those that come unto thee have the same gate, and through the same gate, descend, such as thou sendest. Behold, I offer my house, my labour, my heart and soul, If it will please thy Angels to dwell with me, and I with them; to rejoyce with me, that I may rejoyce with them; to minister unto me, that I may magnifie thy name. Then, lo the Tables (which I have provided, and according to thy will, prepared) I offer unto thee, and unto thy holy Angels, desiring them, in and through thy holy names: That as thou art their light, and comfortest them, so they, in thee will be my light and comfort. Lord they prescribe not laws unto thee, so it is not meet that I prescribe laws unto them: What it pleaseth thee to offer, they receive; So what it pleaseth them to offer unto me, will I also receive. Behold I say (O Lord) If I shall call upon them in thy name, Be it unto me in mercy, as unto the servant of the Highest. Let them also manifest unto me, How, by what words, and at what time, I shall call them. O Lord, Is there any that measure the heavens, that is mortal? How, therefore, can the heavens enter into mans imagination? Thy creatures are the Glory of thy countenance: Hereby thou glorifiest all things, which Glory excelleth and (O Lord) is far above my understanding. It is great wisdom, to speak and talke according to understanding with Kings: But to command Kings by a subjected commandment, is not wisdom, unlesse it come from thee. Behold Lord, How shall I therefore ascend into the heavens? The air will not carry me, but resisteth my folly, I shall fall down, for I am of the earth. Therefore, O thou very Light and true Comfort, that canst, and mayst, and dost command the heavens: Behold I offer these Tables unto thee, Command them as it pleaseth thee: and O you Ministers, and true lights of understanding, Governing this earthly frame, and the elements wherein we live, Do for me as for the servant of the Lord: and unto whom it hath pleased the Lord to talk of you.

Behold, Lord, thou hast appointed me 50 times; Thrice 50 times will I lift my hands unto thee. Be it unto me as it pleaseth thee, and thy holy Ministers. I require nothing but thee, and through thee, and for thy honour and glory: But I hope I shall be satisfied, and shall not die, (as thou hast promised) until thou gather the clouds together, and judge all things: when in a moment I shall be changed and dwell with thee for ever.

These words, were thrice a dayes talk betwixt Enoch and God: In the end of 50 dayes, there appeared unto him, which are not now to be manifested nor spoken of: he enjoyed the fruit of God his promise, and received the benefit of his faith. Here may the wise learn wisdom: for what doth man that is not corruptible?[6]

When Ave tells Dee "be it unto thee, as thou hast done," he is saying that even though Dee's version of the Book of Spirits is incorrect, the angels will acknowledge it so that Dee's sincere efforts to construct the book will not have been wasted.

THE JUBILEE

The number of Enoch's tables is not stated in the prayer. Presumably they are the same as the forty-eight number/letter squares that make up Dee's Book of Enoch, plus the first occult table that was too holy to reveal to Dee. The last day of the fifty was probably the day of fulfillment, when Enoch's work of the previous forty-nine was brought to fruition by God. Concerning the number fifty, Cornelius Agrippa writes:

> The number fifty signifies remission of sins, of servitudes, and also liberty. According to the [Jewish] Law, on the fiftieth year they did remit debts, and everyone did return to his own possessions. Hence by the year of Jubilee [see *Leviticus* 25:10], and by the psalm of repentance [psalm 50 of the Vulgate] it shows a sign of indulgency, and repentance. The Law also, and the Holy Ghost are declared in the same: for the fiftieth day after Israel's going forth out of Egypt, the Law was given to Moses in Mount Sinai: the fiftieth day after the resurrection, the Holy Ghost came down upon the apostles in Mount Sion; whence also it is called the number of grace, and attributed to the Holy Ghost.[7]

Just as God gave Moses the tablets of the commandments on the fiftieth day, so are the tables of Enoch to be perfected on the fiftieth day of his ritual working. Just as the Holy Ghost descended upon the apostles of Christ fifty days after the resurrection, so are the tables of Enoch to be activated and empowered by the holy Spirit on the fiftieth day.

There seems to be a connection between the number of times Enoch speaks his prayer to God, and the "hundred and fifty Lions, and spirits of wickednesse, errour, and deceit" that God sends among the unrighteous people to sow confusion as punishment for their misuse of

Enoch's wisdom. However, there is not enough space in this book to consider this matter at length.

"LORD I AM LESSE THAN SAND"

Two things to notice about Enoch's prayer are his abasement of himself before God ("Lord my imperfection is great, Lord I am lesse than sand"), and his stated intention not to attempt to command the angels to perform other than their appointed offices: "Lord they prescribe not laws unto thee, so it is not meet that I prescribe laws unto them: What it pleaseth thee to offer, they receive; So what it pleaseth them to offer unto me, will I also receive." By taking this approach Enoch ensures that his magic will never be in violation of divine law. He places himself firmly below the angels in the hierarchy of intelligent beings.

At first impression, this appears contrary to much of the magical practice of the Western world, which has in large part descended from the magic of ancient Egypt through the philosophers and magicians of the Greeks and Romans. The ancient Egyptians believed themselves able to command not only spirits, but gods as well. (This power did not extend to the First Mover, however.) The gods commanded by the Egyptians were capable of independent actions. It was a case of their will being matched against the will of the magician.

The angels of Enoch are not independent beings, but mere messengers or agents of the God of Hosts. Thus, in commanding the angels Enoch would have been in the uncomfortable position of attempting to defy the will of God, since any action the angels might commit that was not of their office would be in defiance of God's will. Conversely, there was no need for Enoch to command the angels to perform their offices, since they would do this in any case.

This raises the question, what good are the tables of Enoch (and by extension, the tables of Dee) if they can only cause the angels to do what they would do anyway? Although the angels perform their natural offices, tables or no tables, presumably through the use of the tables it is possible to call down that angelic grace. For example, an angel of good fortune will always produce good fortune since this is its appointed office, but the magician can control *where* that good fortune occurs, whether in his or her life or the life of another person.

It was probably the human arrogance of attempting to use the magic of Enoch for base personal ends in violation of the natural offices of the angels that provoked God to sow the Earth with the 150 spirits of deceit who taught goetic magic. Through the proliferation of goetic magic the original wisdom of Enoch was gradually forgotten and lost from the world. At any rate, this is the myth presented to Dee and Kelley by the angels.

CHAPTER SEVENTEEN

Enochian Magic in the Golden Dawn

FRÄULEIN SPRENGEL AND THE CIPHER MANUSCRIPT

The Hermetic Order of the Golden Dawn was a secret Rosicrucian society, modeled after Freemasonry, that flourished in England at the end of the Victorian era. It was founded in London in 1888 by three Freemasons: Samuel Liddell "MacGregor" Mathers, Dr. William Wynn Westcott, and Dr. William Robert Woodman. Woodman died in 1891, leaving the Golden Dawn to be run by Westcott and Mathers. Westcott was the solid, respectable cornerstone of the Order; Mathers its brilliant but erratic guiding star.

The genesis of the Order is said to be Westcott's discovery in 1887 of a brief occult manuscript in cipher, found in a book shop between the pages of a book. When translated, the cipher contained the outline of five esoteric Masonic rituals and a letter by a German Rosicrucian adept calling herself Fräulein Sprengel. Westcott enlisted the aid of Mathers to expand the rituals, and wrote to Sprengel, who authorized him to found an English branch of the German occult order Die Goldene Dämmerung. At least, this is the story. A more likely explanation is that the cipher manuscript was a forgery, and that Westcott and Mathers cooked up the original rituals between themselves.

Nevertheless, the Golden Dawn was an important and unusual organization for two reasons. First, it taught a complete system of practical ritual magic solidly based in the history of Western occultism. Second, it admitted women members as equals. In both these innovations, daring for the day, it was influenced by the Theosophical Society founded by Helena Petrovna Blavatsky in New York in 1875.

"THE EXTRAORDINARILY DEVELOPED SYSTEM"

An important part of the advanced teachings of the Golden Dawn was Enochian magic—probably the result of research carried out by Mathers in the reading room of the British Museum Library. It is impossible to be certain about the authors of many Golden Dawn papers because they circulated anonymously among members of the order and were copied and recopied by hand. There may well have been other contributors. Since Enochian words of power appear in the mysterious cipher document,[1] it is evident that Mathers was working on Enochian magic prior to 1887 (presuming the cipher manuscript to be Mathers' forgery, and presuming it to have been forged prior to the establishment of the Isis-Urania Temple).

Israel Regardie, who published the order papers of the Golden Dawn between 1938–40, and who was, along with his teacher Aleister Crowley, one of the two men most responsible for the continuing dominance of Golden Dawn magic in modern Western occultism, regarded Enochian magic as one of the greatest achievements of the Golden Dawn:

So far as we are able to make out, however, the System originated by means of the ceremonial skrying of Dr. John Dee and Sir Edward Kelly towards the close of the 16th century. The original diaries of Dr. John Dee, recording the development of the system, may be found in Sloane Manuscripts 3189-3191 in the British Museum. But this stands out very clearly, that in these diaries is a rudimentary scheme which bears only the most distant relation to the extraordinarily developed system in use by the Order. Whoever was responsible for the Order scheme of the Angelic Tablets—whether it was Mathers and Westcott or the German Rosicrucian Adepts from whom the former are supposed to have obtained their knowledge—was possessed of an ingenuity and an understanding of Magic such as never was in the possession either of Dee or Kelly.[2]

As you will have gathered from the preceding chapters, this is a very unjustified slur against Dee and Kelley, who understood very clearly those portions of Enochian magic which the angels chose to reveal. Regardie is not to be blamed for this attitude. His knowledge of Dee's manuscripts appears to have been quite limited, despite his claim to have obtained "a good deal of information" about "Enochiana" through private meditation and studies at the British Museum. Crowley, Regardie's mentor in magic, suffered from the same shallow understanding of Dee's magical diaries, and also boasted of a much more extensive experience with the Enochian system than he actually possessed.

What the System Contains

The Enochian magic of the Golden Dawn is almost entirely based on the English and Enochian texts of the Enochian Keys, along with a curious compound version of the four Watchtowers arranged in the pattern they form on the Great Table of Raphael. The Black Cross is not used by the Golden Dawn to join the Watchtowers together into a single Great Table. Instead, the Watchtowers are treated as separate entities, and the letters in the Black Cross are gathered into the small magic square that appears in Casaubon,[3] which is called in the Golden Dawn the Tablet of Union.

The Keys are used to invoke or evoke the angels whose names appear written on the four Watchtowers. The methods for extracting the names of these angels, and the names of power that summon and commend the angels, are accurately presented (for the most part) by the Golden Dawn. The names of the Thirty Aethers, or Airs, also appear in the Order papers, but not the names or sigils of the ninety-one geographical spirits, or Princes, who rule the regions of the Earth. That omission is probably why Crowley evoked the Aethers, but not the tutelary genii of the Aethers.[4]

What the System Omits

Omitted from the Enochian magic of the Golden Dawn is any direct mention of the mystical heptarchy of planetary angels, along with their tables and sigils, which form the underlying basis of all Enochian magic. No mention is made of the Table of Practice or the rest of the ritual furniture of the Table, which are derived from the heptarchical system. Nor is anything said about the central importance of a scrying stone in Enochian magic. Westcott does refer to the Sigillum Aemeth in passing when writing about the seals of the Watchtowers, saying: "This 'Liber AEmeth sive Sigillum Dei' that is the Book of Truth, or the Seal of God, entereth not into the knowledge of a Zelator Adeptus Minor"[5] (nor, we may suspect, into the knowledge of anyone else in the Golden Dawn at that time, save possibly Mathers and Westcott).

Less surprising is the silence of the Golden Dawn concerning the Enochian Book of Spirits, which is never clearly described in Casaubon (probably the primary source for Golden Dawn Enochian magic). There is no awareness in the Golden Dawn of the necessity for making initial contact with the angels of the Great Table through an eighteen-day ritual that employs original invocations composed by the magician. The angels are simply summoned by means of the Keys.

A notable void in the Enochian magic of the Order is the silence concerning Kelley's Great Vision of the Watchtowers, and the golden talisman constructed by Dee that depicts this vision. Neither is anything written about the Vision of the Round House, although this may be forgiven since the importance of this vision is still not understood by Enochian scholars. It should also be mentioned that the Enochian alphabet used by the Golden Dawn is faulty in several respects. Unfortunately, the influence of the Order has been so profound over the last hundred years that these defects are universally reproduced in books about Enochian magic. As I mentioned earlier, I have corrected the alphabet in the present work.

In view of these many omissions, the reader may be forgiven for wondering why Regardie was so impressed with the Enochian system of the Golden Dawn. The great virtue of this system is its consistency. Faced with many gaps in his knowledge of the Enochian magic received by Dee and Kelley, Mathers was forced to supply his own material. It was also necessary for him to fully integrate his personal system of Enochian magic into the magic of the Golden Dawn, which he was undoubtedly in the process of creating at the time he researched Enochian magic.

THE MODEL OF THE PENTAGRAM

The primary model used by Mathers to structure the Enochian system of the Golden Dawn was the relationship between the four elements and the four lower points of the pentagram, which is used in Golden Dawn magic to invoke or banish elemental forces. The assignment of the elements to the pentagram, in turn, was conditioned by the elemental associations of the four Fixed signs of the zodiac. These zodiac associations are very ancient, and served as the basis for the Golden Dawn understanding of the elements. If the lower points of the pentagram are imagined to form a square, this may be laid over the wheel of the zodiac to achieve the following Golden Dawn arrangement.

Mathers' Model of the Pentagram

Mathers and his associates made the fundamental mistake of linking the four Watchtowers to the four elements in the relationship that appears on the four lower points of the Golden Dawn pentagram and in the Fixed signs of the zodiac. He chose the ordering of the Watchtowers upon the Revised Great Table of Raphael as his starting point and simply laid the square of the elements on top of the Watchtowers.

The existence of a second, earlier version of the Great Table, where the Watchtowers occupy different quarters, was never mentioned in the Golden Dawn documents. Mathers must have known about the Original Table, since he gathered all the letter variations that appear in the five extant examples of the Great Table and incorporated them into the Golden Dawn Great Table. As a result, some cells of the Golden Dawn Table have two letters, some have three, and some have four.

The version of the Golden Dawn Watchtowers (they cannot really be called a Great Table since they are unconnected) presented on pages 290–291 is what appears in Regardie's *Golden Dawn*. I have allowed the inaccuracies in lettering and capitalization to stand. It is interesting to speculate what the original members of the Golden Dawn made of the apparently random capital letters in the tables. The ninety-one spirits of the Aethers, whose seven-letter names are capitalized by the angels on the Watchtowers, are never enumerated. Westcott merely writes: "Of the letters on the Tables, some be written as capitals. These are the initial letters of certain Angels' names drawn forth by another method, not now explained, and the offices of these do not concern a Z[elator] A[deptus] M[inor]."[6]

There is also no notice made by Mathers of letters on the Watchtowers that are inverted right to left in Dee's transcript. These held the highest importance for the angels, but exactly what that importance was is never clearly stated (except that the inverted letters at the ends

Eastern Watchtower of Air

r	Z	i	l	a	f	A	y_u	t	l_i	p	a
a	r	d	Z	a	i	d	p	a	L	a	m
c	z	o	n	s	a	r	o	$_vY$	a	u	b
T	o	i	T	t	z_x	o	P	a	c	o	C
S	i	g	a	s	o	n_m	r	b	z	n	h
f	m	o	n	d	a	T	d	i	a	r	l_i
o	r	o	i	b	a	h	a	o	z	p	i
t_c	N	a	b	r_a	V	i	x	g	a	s_z	d
O	i	i	t	T	p	a	l	O	a	i	
A	b	a	m	o	o	o	a	C	u_v	c	a
N	a	o	c	O	T	t	n	p	r	u_a	T
o	c	a	n	m	a	g	o	t	r	o	i
S	h	i	a	l	r	a	p	m	z	o	x

Northern Watchtower of Earth

b	O	a	Z	a	R	o	p	h	a	R	a
u_v	N	n	a	x	o	P	S	o	n	d	n
a	i	g	r	a	n	o	a_o	m	a	g	g
o	r	p	m	n	i	n	g	b	e	a	l
r	s	O	n	i	z	i	r	l	e	m	u
i	z	i	n	r	C	z	i	a	M	h	l
M	O	r	d	i	a	l	h	C	t	G	a
R_o	C_O	a_c	n_a n^c_m	h_c	i_h	$i_b^a t$	s_a	o_s	m_o	t_m	
A	r	b	i	z	m	i	i_l	l	p	i	z
O	p	a	n	a	l_B	a	m	S	m	a	T_L
d	O	l	o	P_F	l	n	i	a	n	b	a
r	x	p	a	o	c	s	i	z	i	x	p
a	x	t	i	r	V	a	s	t	r	i	m

T	a	O	A	d	u_v	p	t	D	n	i	m
a_o	a	b_l	c	o	o	r	o	m	e	b	b
T	o_a	g	c	o	n	x_z	m_i	$n{}^{u}_{a}$	l	G	m
n	h	o	d	D	i	a	i	l_a	a	o	c
f_p	a	t_c	A	x	i	v_o	V	s	P	x_s	$y\,{}^{l}_{N\,h}$
S	a	a	i	z_x	a	a	r	V	r	L^c	i
m	p	h	a	r	s	l	g	a	i	o	l
M	a	m	g	l	o	i	n	L	i	r	x
o	l	a	a	D	n_a	g	a	T	a	p	a
p	a	L	c	o	i	d	x	P	a	c	n
n	d	a	z	N	z_x	i	V	a	a	s	a
r_i	i	d	P	o	n	s	d	A	s	p	i
x	r	i_r	n	h	t	a	r	n_a	d	i	L

Western
Watchtower
of Water

d	o	n	p	a	T	d	a	n	V	a	a
o	l	o	a	G	e	o	o	b	a	u_v	a_i
O	P	a	m	n	o	v_o	G	m_n	d	n	m
a	p_b	l	s	T	e	c_d	e	c	a	o	p
s	c	m	i	o	a	n	A	m	l	o	x
V	a	r	s	G	d	L	b_v	r	i	a	p
o	i	P	t	e	a	a	p	D	o	c	e
p	s	u_v	a	c	n	r	Z	i	r	Z	a
S	i	o	d	a	o	i	n	r	z	f	m
d	a	l_b	t	T	d	n	a	d	i	r	e
d	i	x	o	m	o	n	s	i	o	s	p
O	o	D	p	z	i	A	p	a	n	l	i
r	g	o	a	n	O_p	A	C	r	a	r	

Southern
Watchtower
of Fire

of names indicate that the name may be pronounced backward), and since they also apply to the ninety-one spirits of the Aethers, Mathers completely ignored them.

By linking the Watchtowers themselves to the four elements, and by association to the four directions of space which those elements represent in the Golden Dawn system of magic, and by failing to understand that the Watchtowers form a single integrated whole that is the Great Table, Mathers obliterated all traces of the original relationship between the quarters of the Great Table to the four directions. He completely missed the fact that, in the original Enochian magic of Dee and Kelley, it is the quarters of the Great Table that are associated with the directions, and not the Watchtowers that are placed in those quarters.

In the Golden Dawn system of Watchtowers, we have the absurd arrangement of the Watchtower of the East (Air) placed diagonally opposite the Watchtower of the South (Fire), and the Watchtower of the West (Water) placed diagonally opposite the Watchtower of the North (Earth). This is in harmony with the elemental arrangement of the four lower points of the pentagram and the four Fixed signs of the zodiac employed in Golden Dawn magic, but it is completely contrary to Dee's conception of the Great Table, which is a representation of the Earth divided into four quarters.

In Dee's system, the quarter of the east must always be opposite the quarter of the west, and the quarter of the south must always be opposite the quarter of the north. This is the reality of the quarters of the Earth. It is another matter which Watchtowers are assigned these quarters. As we have seen, Dee was never completely certain about his assignment, and after receiving the Revised Great Table of Raphael he was placed in the

quandary of having two arrangements of the Watchtowers on the Great Table in conflict with each other. But
about the Great Table itself Dee was never in doubt.

You will better understand this distinction between the
placement of the Watchtowers into a complex, syncretic
system of magic by the Golden Dawn and their placement
by John Dee if you bear in mind that Mathers was fitting
the Watchtowers according to their elemental associations,
which are of pre-eminent importance to the Golden Dawn,
whereas Dee was receiving, without preconceptions, a
system from the angels that was based upon a fundamental association with the four corners of the Earth.

The association between the four elements and the
four directions is of almost no importance in the original system of Enochian magic. It is possible to infer the
elemental associations from the colors of Kelley's Great
Vision, which are clearly linked with the directions. Red
is almost always the color of fire in magic, and black is
usually the color of earth. The angels related the directions with the colors in this way in Kelley's Great Vision
and in the delivery of the Watchtowers:

East	South	West	North
Red	White	Green	Black
Fire	Air	Water	Earth

The elemental associations of the four directions are
explicitly stated in Kelley's later *Vision of the Round
House*. In this second significant vision the east is the
quarter of fire, the south the quarter of air, the west the
quarter of water and the north the quarter of earth. The
whole question is somewhat confused by the different
application of colors to the directions in the Vision of
the Round House, where the east is white and the south

is red. However, there is no confusion about the correspondence between the directions and the elements.

The Golden Dawn used the following association of colors and elements with the four directions, and simply imposed it upon the Watchtowers of the Revised Table of Raphael:

East	South	West	North
Yellow	Red	Blue	Black
Air	Fire	Water	Earth

In Mathers' defense, a curious coincidence should be noted. The association by the angel Ave of the four elements with the good angels beneath the arms of the lesser cross in the subquarters of the west, when read down from top to bottom (air, water, earth, fire),[7] is the same ordering of the elements that was applied to the quarters of the Great Table by Mathers, following the numbering of the quarters used by the angels: (1)Eastern Watchtower of Air, (2) Western Watchtower of Water, (3) Northern Watchtower of Earth, (4) Southern Watchtower of Fire.[8] I do not think this is anything more than a coincidence, but it is interesting nonetheless.

THE MODEL OF THE NAME OF GOD

The other great organizing principle employed by Mathers on the Watchtowers is also fourfold. It is the association of each square in the Watchtowers with the individual Hebrew letters of Tetragrammaton (יהוה) which was usually written in the Golden Dawn YHVH or IHVH. Mathers took his cue from the way in which the names of the four Dispositors above the arms of the lesser crosses are permuted by the angels. He used the same system to permute the letters of Tetragrammaton on the four Watchtowers, and the four quarters of each Watchtower. The individual letters in the Name of God were applied to the Watchtowers according to the elemental associations of the letters in the Golden Dawn system: I = Fire, 1st H = Water, V = Air, 2nd H = Earth.

Regardie believed it was the Hebrew letters of the name that formed the link between the Watchtowers and the elements. "This Name is the key to the whole of the Enochian attributions of the squares to the Elements."[9] As I have demonstrated, this is not so. It was the elemental relationship of the four Fixed signs of the zodiac that determined Mathers' placement of the elements on the Watchtowers of the Table of Raphael. The placement of the letters of Tetragrammaton was made based on the link between the elements and the Hebrew letters in the Golden Dawn system. In the Golden Dawn, the elements are always paramount.

However, the letters of the Name do determine the elemental associations of each individual letter cell in the Watchtowers, which may have been what Regardie meant. I have given that association in full in the accompanying version of the Great Table, because it is poorly understood even among experience practitioners of Golden Dawn magic. The second H in Tetragrammaton is distinguished by bold type.

The key to understanding the arrangement of the four letters of IHVH on the Watchtowers lies in the outermost cells, or squares, of the lines of the Dispositors —what the Golden Dawn called the Kerubic Squares because each set of four squares was related to the four Fixed signs of the zodiac, the Kerubic signs, by elemental association. The Hebrew letter in each of these outer squares has the same elemental quality as the subquarter to which it belongs. The four letters of the

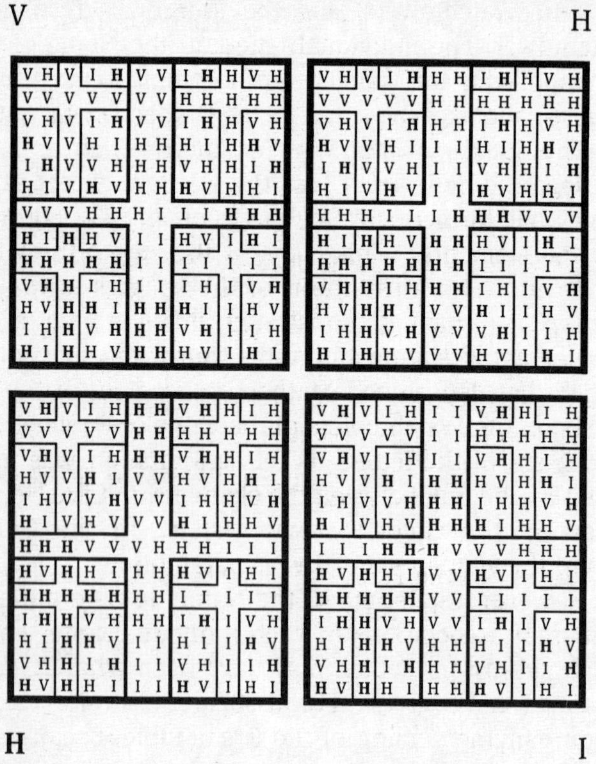

V   **H**

Top-left grid:

V	H	V	I	H	V	V	I	H	H	V	H
V	V	V	V	V	V	V	H	H	H	H	H
V	H	V	I	H	V	V	I	H	H	V	H
H	V	V	H	I	H	H	H	I	H	H	V
I	H	V	V	H	H	H	V	H	H	I	H
H	I	V	H	V	H	H	V	H	H	H	I
V	V	V	H	H	H	I	I	I	H	H	H
H	I	H	H	V	I	I	H	V	I	H	I
H	H	H	H	H	I	I	I	I	I	I	I
V	H	H	I	H	I	I	I	H	I	V	H
H	V	H	H	I	H	H	H	I	I	H	V
I	H	H	V	H	H	H	V	H	I	I	H
H	I	H	H	V	H	H	H	V	I	H	I

Top-right grid:

V	H	V	I	H	H	H	I	H	H	V	H
V	V	V	V	V	H	H	H	H	H	H	H
V	H	V	I	H	H	H	I	H	H	V	H
H	V	V	H	I	I	I	H	I	H	H	V
I	H	V	V	H	I	I	V	H	H	I	H
H	I	V	H	V	I	I	I	H	V	H	I
H	H	H	I	I	I	H	H	H	V	V	V
H	I	H	H	V	H	H	H	V	I	H	I
H	H	H	H	H	H	H	I	I	I	I	I
V	H	H	I	H	H	H	I	H	I	V	H
H	V	H	H	I	V	V	H	I	I	H	V
I	H	H	V	H	V	V	V	H	I	I	H
H	I	H	H	V	V	V	H	V	I	H	I

Bottom-left grid:

V	H	V	I	H	H	H	V	H	H	I	H
V	V	V	V	V	H	H	H	H	H	H	H
V	H	V	I	H	H	H	V	H	H	I	H
H	V	V	H	I	V	V	H	V	H	H	I
I	H	V	V	H	V	V	I	H	H	V	H
H	I	V	H	V	H	H	V	H	I	H	V
H	H	H	V	V	V	H	H	H	I	I	I
H	V	H	H	I	H	H	H	V	I	H	I
H	H	H	H	H	H	H	I	I	I	I	I
I	H	H	V	H	H	H	I	H	I	V	H
H	I	H	H	V	I	I	H	I	I	H	V
V	H	H	I	H	I	I	V	H	I	I	H
H	V	H	H	I	I	I	H	V	I	H	I

Bottom-right grid:

V	H	V	I	H	I	I	V	H	H	I	H
V	V	V	V	V	I	I	H	H	H	H	H
V	H	V	I	H	I	I	V	H	H	I	H
H	V	V	H	I	H	H	H	V	H	H	I
I	H	V	V	H	H	H	I	H	H	V	H
H	I	V	H	V	H	H	V	H	I	H	V
I	I	I	H	H	H	V	V	V	H	H	H
H	V	H	H	I	V	V	H	V	I	H	I
H	H	H	H	H	V	V	I	I	I	I	I
I	H	H	V	H	V	V	I	H	I	V	H
H	I	H	H	V	H	H	H	H	I	I	H
V	H	H	I	H	H	H	V	H	I	I	H
H	V	H	H	I	I	I	H	H	V	I	H

H   **I**

Letters of IHVH on the Watchtowers

Name are written above the arms of each lesser cross according to the placement of this outer letter.

For example, the outer letter in the subquarter (what the Golden Dawn called the "lesser angle") of air on the Watchtower of Air is V (ו), the letter of Tetragrammaton that relates to air. The other three letters in the Name are inserted into the cells above the arms of the lesser cross (what the Golden Dawn called the "Calvary Cross") in order, so that the Name may be read right to left by wrapping it around on itself in the same way that the names of the four Dispositors are formed by wrapping their letters around on themselves.

The permutations of the Name on the four upper subquarters of the Watchtowers of Air and Water are read from right to left, jumping back to the beginning when the end of the Kerubic Squares in each subquarter is reached. The letters of the Name are read in order from left to right on the four lower subquarters. Just the opposite arrangement is used for the Watchtowers of Earth and Fire. On the four upper subquarters of the Watchtowers the Name is read from left to right; on the four lower subquarters the Name is read from right to left.

The order and direction of the letters in the Name on the Kerubic Squares of a subquarter determines the order and direction of the letters in the Name on the squares below the arms of its Calvary Cross. Whereas the letters in the Name are read across on the Kerubic Squares, they are read up and down on the squares of the good angels. For example, on the subquarter of air of the Watchtower of Air, the Name is read from right to left on the row of the Kerubic Squares above the arms of the lesser cross; it is read downwards on the columns of the good angels below the arms of the lesser cross, beginning with the right-hand column. Conversely, on the subquarter of earth of the Watchtower of Air, the Name is read from left to right across the row of the Kerubic Squares; but it is read upwards on the columns of the good angels, beginning with the left-hand column.

The Great Cross of each Watchtower is assigned the letters of the Name in groups of three. The letter that corresponds with the element of the Watchtower is placed on the upper end of the pillar and the left side of the beam of the Cross, and the others follow in order, as they are read from bottom to top and from right to left.

Each triple group of letters is linked with one of the zodiac signs that bears the same elemental association.

The lesser crosses, or Calvary Crosses, of the subquarters are linked with the ten Sephiroth on the Tree of the Kabbalah, because each cross has ten squares. Each cross receives the general elemental association, and thus the letter of the Name, of its own subquarter.

The Golden Dawn made a very complex assignment of the cards of the Tarot, the signs of the zodiac, the planets, the sixteen signs of geomantic divination, the Enochian letters, the Egyptian gods and goddesses, the colors and the five elements (including Spirit) to the individual squares on the Watchtowers. Each square was divided into five sections by drawing it as a truncated pyramid viewed from the top, and different occult correspondences entered into the sections. Unfortunately, this system is too complex to treat in detail. It will be found in Regardie's *Golden Dawn*.[10]

MISTAKES IN THE SYSTEM

There are several very important mistakes, or perhaps I should call them innovations, in the way the names of angels are derived from the Watchtowers by the Golden Dawn. One error is the practice of spelling the names of the Kings of the Watchtowers with eight letters. This results from combining the two letters in the intersection of each Great Cross in a single name, rather than taking them separately and placing them at the ends of two names, one the King is his merciful role (final letter from the line of the Son) and the other the King is his role of severe judge (final letter from the line of the Father). For example, the single form of the name of the King used by the Golden Dawn for the Eastern Watchtower of Air is Bataivah (not, as should be the case, Bataiva for mercy and Bataivh for severity). This practice is in direct contradiction to the instruction of Ave: "You must take but one of them, either the A or the h. A, *comiter,* and h *in extremis Judiciis.*"

Another very important error (or innovation, depending on how you look at it) is the practice of combining the letters in each line of the Tablet of Union with the Dispositors (the Golden Dawn called them "Kerubic Angels") and good angels of its elementally related Watchtower. The Tablet of Union is shown below with its elemental associations.

	Spirit	Air	Water	Earth	Fire
Air	E	X	A	R	P
Water	H	C	O	M	A
Earth	N	A	N	T	A
Fire	B	I	T	O	M

The Tablet of Union

The first line, EXARP, is applied only to the Watchtower of Air. The first letter, E, is prefixed to the names of all sixteen Dispositors above the lesser crosses in the four subquarters of the Watchtower of Air. Regardie called these expanded names "archangelic in character." The second letter, X, is prefixed to the sixteen names of the good angels in the subquarter of air on the Watchtower of Air. The third letter, A, is prefixed to the sixteen names of the good angels of the subquarter of water. The fourth letter, R, is prefixed to the sixteen names of the good angels on the subquarter of earth. The fifth letter, P, is prefixed to the sixteen names of the good angels on the subquarter of fire. And so on for the other three Watchtowers.

You may wonder why there are sixteen angels in each subquarter instead of the four described by Dee. The Golden Dawn employed the same method of permuting the letters of the good angels as was used by Ave to permute the names of the Dispositors. Thus, each line under the arms of the lesser crosses yielded four angels instead of one.

Another point I question is the attribution of the left column of the pillars of the Great Crosses to God the Father and the right column to God the Son.[11] This attribution is never made clear by the Enochian angels, to my knowledge. It is implied that the left column is the line of the Father and the right the line of the Son by the order of their expression. Ave refers to them as "The Father and Son by addition of the [central dividing] line." However, the letter in the center of the Great Cross that lies in the left column is the letter appended to the name of the King to make him merciful, whereas the central letter that lies in the right column is the letter appended to make him severe in judgement. I tend to associate severe judgement with God the Father and mercy with God the Son. This is the arrangement I have followed in this book.

THE KEYS ON THE WATCHTOWERS

One of the most important innovations of the Golden Dawn was the application of the eighteen distinct Keys to various parts of the Watchtowers. The angels never tell Dee how he is to apply the Keys to the Great Table. It is to Mathers' credit that he recognized the necessity of making this association. The system he created has no basis in genuine Enochian magic, but it is still quite impressive.

Keys	Elemental Associations	Invokes Angels of these Places and Names
1	Spirit	Whole Tablet of Union
2	Spirit	Tablet Letters: E, H, N, B
3	Air	EXARP; Watchtower of Air Air of Air: IDOIGO
4	Water	HCOMA; Watchtower of Water Water of Water: NELAPR
5	Earth	NANTA; Watchtower of Earth Earth of Earth: (C)ABALPT
6	Fire	BITOM; Watchtower of Fire Fire of Fire: RZIONR
7	Air	Water of Air: L(I)LACZA
8	Air	Earth of Air: AIAOAI
9	Air	Fire of Air: AOU(V)RRZ
10	Water	Air of Water: OB(L)GOT(C)A
11	Water	Earth of Water: MALADI
12	Water	Fire of Water: IAAASD
13	Earth	Air of Earth: ANGPOI
14	Earth	Water of Earth: ANAEEM
15	Earth	Fire of Earth: O(S)PMNIR
16	Fire	Air of Fire: NOALMR
17	Fire	Water of Fire: VADALI
18	Fire	Earth of Fire: U(V)OL(B)XDO

Association of the Keys to the Great Table

THE SEALS OF THE WATCHTOWERS

The Golden Dawn developed the four seals of the quarters of the Great Table, described by Kelley just prior to the reception of the Watchtowers, into stylized, multicolored emblems for the Watchtowers, while retaining the essential features of the symbols. This was a useful and perceptive innovation. These seals are painted large just above the separate tables of the Watchtowers that adorned Golden Dawn temples, each Watchtower in its Golden Dawn elemental colors.[12]

The outer rim and central T on the seal of the Golden Dawn Watchtower of Air is colored yellow; the background is mauve. The outer rim and central cross, along with the letters and numbers around the cross, on the seal of the Watchtower of Water is blue; the

Golden Dawn Seals of the Watchtowers

background is orange. The outer rim on the seal of the Watchtower of Fire is red; moving from the center outward the concentric circles of the figure are colored green, red, green, red, green; clockwise from the top the twelve flames around the figure are red, yellow, mauve, red, yellow, mauve, red, yellow, mauve, red, yellow, mauve; the background is green. The outer rim on the seal of the Watchtower of Earth is black; clockwise from the top the arms of the cross are colored citrine, olive, black, russet; the center of the cross and the background are both white.

"ELEMENTAL KINGS OF THE ENTIRE TABLET"

From the pattern of each of these seals, a name of power was extracted from the outermost letter ring on Dee's wax Sigillum Aemeth. Each name begins at the capital T with the small 4 above it at the top of Sigillum Aemeth and proceeds by jumps, either clockwise or counterclockwise, with odd letters simply inserted where this was found necessary. Regardie wrote: "The Names yielded by the analysis of the Sigils are to be considered as the Elemental Kings of the entire Tablet."[13] He added that each King who bears one of these names is "purely and intrinsically an elemental force" and should be treated with caution.

The elemental King of the Golden Dawn Watchtower of Air is Tahaoelog. The actual letter formation of his name is shown here.

4	22	20	18	1	og
Th	h	a	o	8	

This is extracted simply by beginning at the top of the circle of letters and numbers around the rim of Sigillum

Aemeth and counting four spaces clockwise for each letter or letter group. Notice that vowels have been inserted into the name to make it easier to pronounce.

The King of the Watchtower of Water is Thaheby-obeaatanun. The extraction of this name is not nearly so simple as the last, but I will give the Golden Dawn explanation, for what it is worth:

> From b.4.6.b grouped about a cross, note that T equals t, (the Cross equals th), is obtained: Cross to h, then b.4., then 6.b., and continue 6:

4	22	b	y	6	6	a	t		
Th	h	4	14	b	A	5	9	14	n
								n	

> yielding the name *Thahebyobeaatanun* for the Water Tablet.
>
> (Four moves from T gives 22.h. b.4. is specially put. y.14 moves to 22 from t. Then 6.b. is special. From 6.b. it is all plain moving by 6 to right [Wynn Westcott]).[14]

The first part of Westcott's explanation is clear enough. However, I'm not sure what he means by "y.14 moves to 22 from t." The square containing y/14 is actually 21 spaces from the uppermost 4/T. The "6.b." is apparently just inserted. However, from the square containing 6/A, the rest proceed clockwise by jumps of six.

The King of the Watchtower of Earth is Thahaaothe. The letters that make up his name are given in this order:

4	22	11	a	o	t	
Th	h	A	5	10	11	h

It is not so obvious how this name is extracted. The Golden Dawn text says: "From the plain Cross, which equals Th4, proceed counting in each case forward as by numbers given." The meaning, poorly expressed, is that you count 4 clockwise from the uppermost capital

T (which is regarded as th). This places you at the square that contains 22/h. You then count 22 clockwise from this square, which places you at the square containing 11/A. You count 11 from this square, which places you at the square containing a/5. Then you must bend back to avoid crossing the uppermost T and count from this square counterclockwise 5 squares, which places you at o/10. Count 10 squares counterclockwise, and you reach t/11. Then count 11 squares counterclockwise to reach the h.

The King of the Watchtower of Fire is Ohooohaatan. The letters in his name are represented in this way:

6		o	o	22	H	6	t	
w	h	8	17	o	12	A	9	n

The W under the 6 is not really a W at all, but is intended to represent the Greek letter Omega, which appears just to the left of the uppermost capital T on the outer ring of the Sigillum Aemeth. You proceed clockwise by jumps of twelve in each case to reach the following letter-number combination. The rationale for this is that the Golden Dawn seal of the Watchtower of Fire has twelve rays radiating out from it (Dee's seal has eleven or nine rays). This time there is no taboo about crossing the 6/W that began the name.

ENOCHIAN CHESS IN THE GOLDEN DAWN

The most interesting idiosyncrasy of Golden Dawn Enochian magic was the invention of Enochian chess. It was probably a purely theoretical exercise. Regardie asserts in *The Golden Dawn* that he never encountered a member who was willing to play a game with him, although some adepts made "fulsome praises of its remarkable divinatory capacity."[15] He further says that the chess pieces he saw were unmounted, and that this was "a clear indication that they had never and could never have been employed."

The board was formed of the sixteen squares of the good angels in each subquarter of a generic Watchtower. The squares of the Great Cross and lesser crosses were simply removed. This resulted in a board of sixty-four squares, the same number as on a regular chess board. Each of these squares was divided with a cross into four triangles, and each triangle painted its associated elemental color (yellow, blue, black and red).

The pieces are Egyptian god forms. A full set numbered twenty men and sixteen pawns (the four kings had no pawn). The game was to be played by four players seated on the four sides of the board. Each received a queen, knight, rook, bishop and king, as well as four pawns to stand before them. The king occupied the corner square, which he shared with his bishop. The elemental association of each set of forces is indicated by colored bases. The forces of the king of air have yellow bases, those of the king of water blue bases, those of the king of earth black bases, and those of the king of fire red bases.

The men move the same way they do in regular chess, with a few idiosyncrasies. The queen can move only three squares in any direction, but she may jump over intervening pieces like the knight. There is no castling. There is no use of *en passant* for the pawns, which move only a single square (they do not have the option of a two-square move at the start). When a pawn reaches the end of its rank, it is promoted to the rank of the piece it guarded (the bishop's pawn is made a bishop

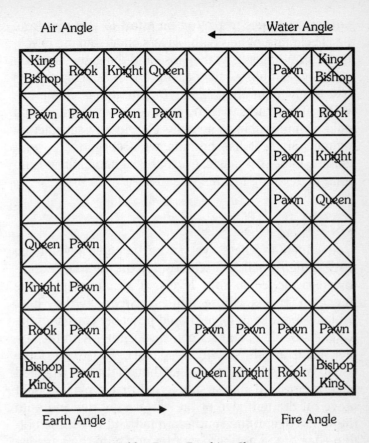

Golden Dawn Enochian Chess

of the same element, for example), even if that piece is still in play. Presumably, additional pieces are needed.

The players play in teams of two, or two players play using two elemental forces that are in harmony with each other (fire and air; water and earth). When stalemate occurs, the player who is stalemated loses his turn until the stalemate is removed. When one player on a team is checkmated, he loses his move and his partner continues to play in an effort to free him from the checkmate. When both players on a team are check-mated simultaneously, they lose and the game is over.

I have simplified the description of Enochian chess that is given in the *Golden Dawn*. It has numerous weird little quirks which, I am quite certain, would make it impossible to actually play in any satisfactory manner. Since it has nothing whatsoever to do with genuine Enochian magic, except by its name, there is no point in devoting much space to it.

TRUE ENOCHIAN CHESS

True Enochian chess (yet to be invented) would be three-dimensional and would play on the four Watch-towers arranged at four levels. It would employ the Enochian angels whose names appear on the Great Table as men. Each force should probably consist of the King, six Seniors, and sixteen Dispositors, with the six-teen good angels serving as pawns. The Great Table would have to be conceived as though it were wrapped back upon itself into a sphere, so that a player could move off the left edge of the eastern quarter and onto the right edge of the southern quadrant, or off the bot-tom edge of the northern quarter and onto the top edge of the eastern quarter.

You are invited to fill in the rest of the rules. I warn you, however, this will be no easy task. It is a fairly simple matter to devise a concept for a board game such as chess. This is all the Enochian chess of the Golden Dawn is—a concept. It is a far more difficult challenge to come up with a set of rules that allows the game to be played as an equal contest to a satisfy-ing conclusion within an agreeable length of time.

Appendix A

Enochian Book of Spirits

A Reconstructed Enochian Book of Spirits

In this appendix, I have attempted to reconstruct the Book of Spirits that is to be used to summon and establish a communication with the angels of the Great Table during the initial eighteen-day working. I have used the structure of the Original Great Table of the Watchtowers as the basis for these invocations because I am presenting the original Enochian magic of Dee and Kelley. Anyone who has understood the exposition of the Great Table previously given can, with little difficulty, alter the text and ordering of the invocations and the spelling of the spirit names to reflect the structure of my own Restored Great Table or (though I do not recommend it) the structure of the Great Table of Raphael.

In this work, I have placed the third cycle of the Dispositors and good angels on the northern subquarters. It would seem more rational to place the cycles successively in a circle clockwise, east, south, west, north. However, it is clear from the Original Table and the Vision of the Round House that the angels intended the cycles of the subquarters to be arranged in two rows in the order east, south, north, west. This in spite of the fact that the individual subquarters of each cycle around the Great Table are unfolded in the order east, south, west, north.

This contradiction between the way the cycles are unfolded around the Great Table (east, south, north, west) and the way the individual subquarters in each cycle are unfolded (east, south, west, north) makes no sense to me. However, I have decided not to second guess the angels on this matter. The arrangement of the subquarters and their four cycles of four are presented as they were delivered by Ave to Dee. For a better understanding of this distinction, see the diagram of the four cycles of the Keys in Chapter Fourteen, which shows the same arrangement.

It should be noted that the Enochian letter Van stands for both U and V in English. Therefore these English letters may be interchanged in the names of the angels where this aids the pronunciation of the names. If you compare the names of the angels below with the letters on the Original Great Table (which I have not altered, except to correct errors) you will see when I have made this substitution. Generally, I have substituted U in place of V when there is no adjacent vowel or when the ease of vibrating the name is greatly improved.

These invocations should be written or typed out by the magician on clean paper, and then bound into the form of a book. Alternatively, they may be written by hand in a new bound journal of blank pages. It is also a good idea to include a table containing all the names of God and the angels in each invocation before the text of that invocation, as Dee did in his own version of the Book of Spirits. One of the reasons is that it allows the inclusion in the book of the names of the evil angels, or cacodemons, formed of three letters. These names are composed of two letters from under the left arms of the lesser crosses coupled with a prefatory letter from the Black Cross on the same line of the Great

Table. The names of these demons are not to be voiced in the invocations, but the angels do not expressly forbid that they be written in the book. Dee included them in his tables.

It is usually the practice in ritual magic to memorize the text of invocations prior to the ritual in which they are to be used. This is always the best course. However, these Enochian invocations are quite complex. Since the Book of Spirits obviously was intended to play a central role in the invocations, it will be acceptable to the angels if the magician reads the text from the book he or she has made. In either case, the book should always be present during the invocations. Each invocation is read three times on its own day: once at sunrise, once at noon, and once at sunset.

These readings must be done in a holy place, a place that has been ritually cleansed and consecrated to its purpose. A flame should be kept burning on the Table of Practice during the invocations. The Table may be used as an altar during ritual as well as a support for the scrying stone. The magician should be dressed in clean white linen, and be physically and mentally pure in the magical sense. A cleansing prayer is recommended before each speaking of an invocation.

A large representation of the Great Table of the Watchtowers that corresponds with the structure of the invocations should also be present. You may wish to adopt the Golden Dawn practice of dividing the Great Table into individual Watchtowers and hanging these on the walls of the ritual chamber in the four directions. Or you may prefer to use my own Enochian cube, a cubic representation of the Great Table that I suggested for Gerald and Betty Schueler's *The Angels' Message to Humanity*. See the Schuelers' book for a description of its making. If the cube is employed, it should be placed on the Table of Practice during the invocations.

It may be that the Book of Spirits is to be used only during the eighteen days of the initial invocation. Its primary purpose is to call forth the angels so that they can be induced to write their sigils or signatures in the Book of Silvered Leaves, using the body of the magician as their writing instrument. On this subject the angel Ave tells Dee:

> *Ave:* You must never use the [linen] Garment after, but that once onely, neither the book.
> *Kelley:* To what end is the book made then, if it be not to be used after.
> *Dee:* It is made for to be used that day onely.[1]

Notice that it is Dee who says the book is to be used only on the nineteenth day of the working, not Ave. The angel says the book and the special linen garment are to be used only once, but this may mean only during the period of the working. Certainly it would seem necessary to refer to the invocations in the Book of Spirits on successive days. Perhaps the linen garment that is worn on the day of consummation may also be worn on the eighteen days of invocation, but never after the working is concluded.

Nor it is completely clear which book Ave refers to, although Dee and Kelley seem to assume that the angel is talking about the Book of Spirits. Ave may mean that the Book of Silvered Leaves is to be used only once, at the time the invoked angels imprint their sigils upon it. If this is so, then no restriction is placed by the angels on the use of the Book of Spirits.

You will find it easier to comprehend the overall pattern of the Book of Spirits in this appendix if you refer to the table near the beginning of Chapter Thirteen, which shows the offices of the various classes of angels on a Watchtower. These groups and their works are the same on all four Watchtowers, but the angels of each Watchtower only function in the corresponding quarter of the Earth.

Some Neopagan practitioners may object to the overtly Christian content of these invocations. They are free to compose their own set of invocations that do not mention the Hebrew names of God or the name of Christ. However, they should consider that Enochian magic functions within the context of Christianity and makes extensive use of Christian, Gnostic, and Kabbalistic symbolism. Indeed, it is scarcely possible to understand Enochian magic without a knowledge of the myths and magic of the Old and New Testaments, as I have demonstrated in my book *Tetragrammaton*. I used as my models Dee's own invocations in *Liber Scientiae* and the prayer of Enoch delivered to Dee by the angel Ave, which I quoted in full in Chapter Sixteen. These paradigms are responsible for the Christian tone.

In composing the following original invocations, I hope that I have managed to do a better job than Dee, and that Ave would not tell me, as he told Dee, "My brother, I see thou dost not understand the mystery of this Book." However, only time and repeated use will prove the worth, or lack of worth, of these invocations.

ANGELS OF THE FIRST DAY		
Quarter	Ruling Name	Names of God
East	Adonai Sabaoth	ORO, IBAH, AOZPI

INVOCATION OF THE FIRST DAY: BANNERS OF THE EAST

Adonai Sabaoth, Lord of Hosts, the fountain of true wisdom, who opens the mysteries of being and not being, who knows the imperfections and inner darkness of men, I, _____, a fragile vessel of the making of your hands, stand here before you and call upon your name. I am less than the sand before your mountain. I am less than the torrents in the springtime before the wonderful and unknown waves of your sea. Yet I call upon your name, and in your name I am become mighty.

Light my soul and make me a seer of visions, that I may see your creatures who are the glory of your countenance. I will praise your names and magnify your works among them. Those who lift their hearts to you in the east ascend by one gate, and through that gate descend your appointed messengers, for we have all one God, all one beginning from you, and all acknowledge you the sole Creator.

I offer and dedicate this table of the Watchtower of the East unto you, and unto your holy angels whose names appear inscribed upon this table and written in this book, desiring their presence in and through your holy names of the east, ORO, IBAH, AOZPI, and your other names having dominion in the east. Let it please your angels to dwell with me, that I may dwell with them; to rejoice with me, that I may rejoice with them; to minister unto me, that I may magnify your names among them.

As you are the light and comfort to your angels, so are they my light and comfort in your names; as it pleases them to receive what you offer, so also I receive with pleasure what they offer unto me; even as they prescribe no laws unto you, O Lord, so shall I prescribe no laws unto them.

Behold, when I call upon them in your names that are in the Watchtower of the East, let it be unto me in mercy as unto the true servant of the Highest. Let them manifest to me in the eastern regions at whatever time or circumstance, and by whatever words, I call them. So also let them depart when I bid them depart. Let them do for me as for the servant of the Lord.

Behold, O Lord, the true light and comfort of the world, the ruler of the heavens, I offer this table of the Watchtower of the East unto you. Command it according to your pleasure. By the Father, the Son, and the Holy Ghost. Amen. Amen. Amen.

ANGELS OF THE SECOND DAY		
Quarter	Ruling Name	Names of God
South	Adonai Malekh	MOR, DIAL, HCTGA

INVOCATION OF THE SECOND DAY: BANNERS OF THE SOUTH

Adonai Malekh, Lord and King, the fountain of true wisdom, who opens the mysteries of being and not being, who knows the imperfections and inner darkness of men, I, _____, a fragile vessel of the making of your hands, stand here before you and call upon your name. I am less than the sand before your mountain. I am less than the torrents in the springtime before the wonderful and unknown waves of your sea. Yet I call upon your name, and in your name I am become mighty.

Light my soul and make me a seer of visions, that I may see your creatures who are the glory of your countenance. I will praise your names and magnify your works among them. Those who lift their hearts to you in the south ascend by one gate, and through that gate descend your appointed messengers, for we have all one God, all one beginning from you, and all acknowledge you the sole Creator.

I offer and dedicate this table of the Watchtower of the South unto you, and unto your holy angels whose names appear inscribed upon this table and written in this book, desiring their presence in and through your holy names of the south, MOR, DIAL, HCTGA, and your other names having dominion in the south. Let it please your angels to dwell with me, that I may dwell with them; to rejoice with me, that I may rejoice with them; to minister unto me, that I may magnify your names among them.

As you are the light and comfort to your angels, so are they my light and comfort in your names; as it pleases them to receive what you offer, so also I receive with pleasure what they offer unto me; even as they prescribe no laws unto you, O Lord, so shall I prescribe no laws unto them.

Behold, when I call upon them in your names that are in the Watchtower of the South, let it be unto me in mercy as unto the true servant of the Highest. Let them manifest to me in the southern regions at whatever time or circumstance, and by whatever words, I call them. So also let them depart when I bid them depart. Let them do for me as for the servant of the Lord.

Behold, O Lord, the true light and comfort of the world, the ruler of the heavens, I offer this table of the Watchtower of the South unto you. Command it according to your pleasure. By the Father, the Son, and the Holy Ghost. Amen. Amen. Amen.

ANGELS OF THE THIRD DAY		
Quarter	Ruling Name	Names of God
West	Elohim Sabaoth	MPH, ARSL, GAIOL

INVOCATION OF THE THIRD DAY: BANNERS OF THE WEST

Elohim Sabaoth, God of Hosts, the fountain of true wisdom, who opens the mysteries of being and not being, who knows the imperfections and inner darkness of men, I, _____, a fragile vessel of the making of your hands, stand here before you and call upon your name. I am less than the sand before your mountain. I am less than the torrents in the springtime before the wonderful and unknown waves of your sea. Yet I call upon your name, and in your name I am become mighty.

Light my soul and make me a seer of visions, that I may see your creatures who are the glory of your countenance. I will praise your names and magnify your works among them. Those who lift their hearts to you in the west ascend by one gate, and through that gate descend your appointed messengers, for we have all one God, all one beginning from you, and all acknowledge you the sole Creator.

I offer and dedicate this table of the Watchtower of the West unto you, and unto your holy angels whose names appear inscribed upon this table and written in this book, desiring their presence in and through your holy names of the west, MPH, ARSL, GAIOL, and your other names having dominion in the west. Let it please your angels to dwell with me, that I may dwell with them; to rejoice with me, that I may rejoice with them; to minister unto me, that I may magnify your names among them.

As you are the light and comfort to your angels, so are they my light and comfort in your names; as it pleases them to receive what you offer, so also I receive with pleasure what they offer unto me; even as they prescribe no laws unto you, O Lord, so shall I prescribe no laws unto them.

Behold, when I call upon them in your names that are in the Watchtower of the West, let it be unto me in mercy as unto the true servant of the Highest. Let them manifest to me in the western regions at whatever time or circumstance, and by whatever words, I call them. So also let them depart when I bid them depart. Let them do for me as for the servant of the Lord.

Behold, O Lord, the true light and comfort of the world, the ruler of the heavens, I offer this table of the Watchtower of the West unto you. Command it according to your pleasure. By the Father, the Son, and the Holy Ghost. Amen. Amen. Amen.

ANGELS OF THE FOURTH DAY		
Quarter	Ruling Name	Names of God
North	Eloah Va-Daath	OIP, TEAA, PDOCE

INVOCATION OF THE FOURTH DAY: BANNERS OF THE NORTH

Eloah Va-Daath, Manifest God, the fountain of true wisdom, who opens the mysteries of being and not being, who knows the imperfections and inner darkness of men, I, _____, a fragile vessel of the making of your hands, stand here before you and call upon your name. I am less than the sand before your mountain. I am less than the torrents in the springtime before the wonderful and unknown waves of your sea. Yet I call upon your name, and in your name I am become mighty.

Light my soul and make me a seer of visions, that I may see your creatures who are the glory of your countenance. I will praise your names and magnify your works among them. Those who lift their hearts to you in the north ascend by one gate, and through that gate descend your appointed messengers, for we have all one God, all one beginning from you, and all acknowledge you the sole Creator.

I offer and dedicate this table of the Watchtower of the North unto you, and unto your holy angels whose names appear inscribed upon this table and written in this book, desiring their presence in and through your holy names of the north, OIP, TEAA, PDOCE, and your other names having dominion in the north. Let it please your angels to dwell with me, that I may dwell with them; to rejoice with me, that I may rejoice with them; to minister unto me, that I may magnify your names among them.

As you are the light and comfort to your angels, so are they my light and comfort in your names; as it pleases them to receive what you offer, so also I receive with pleasure what they offer unto me; even as they prescribe no laws unto you, O Lord, so shall I prescribe no laws unto them.

Behold, when I call upon them in your names that are in the Watchtower of the North, let it be unto me in mercy as unto the true servant of the Highest. Let them manifest to me in the northern regions at whatever time or circumstance, and by whatever words, I call them. So also let them depart when I bid them depart. Let them do for me as for the servant of the Lord.

Behold, O Lord, the true light and comfort of the world, the ruler of the heavens, I offer this table of the Watchtower of the North unto you. Command it according to your pleasure. By the Father, the Son, and the Holy Ghost. Amen. Amen. Amen.

ANGELS OF THE FIFTH DAY		
Quarter	Ruling Names	Senior
East	Bataiva	Abioro
	Bataivh	Habioro
South	Iczhhca	Aidrom
	Iczhhcl	Laidrom
West	Raagios	Srahpm
	Raagiol	Lsrahpm
North	Eldprna	Aetpio
	Edlprna	Aaetpio

INVOCATION OF THE FIFTH DAY: SENIORS OF SPIRIT, LEFT

You four Seniors who stand in the Watchtowers upon the line of Spirit to the left side of the pillar of the Son and the Father, in the name of God who is both one and three, I _____ call upon you to manifest yourselves.

You in the Watchtower of the East who are Abioro, the minister of mercy by God the Son, I call upon in the name of mercy Bataiva; but when you are Habioro, the minister of severity by God the Father, I call upon you by the name of severity Bataivh.

You in the Watchtower of the South who are Aidrom, the minister of mercy by God the Son, I call upon in the name of mercy Iczhhca; but when you are Laidrom, the minister of severity by God the Father, I call upon you by the name of severity Iczhhcl.

You in the Watchtower of the West who are Srahpm, the minister of mercy by God the Son, I call upon in the name of mercy Raagios; but when you are Lsrahpm, the minister of severity by God the Father, I call upon you by the name of severity Raagiol.

You in the Watchtower of the North who are Aetpio, the minister of mercy by God the Son, I call upon in the name of mercy Eldprna; but when you are Aaetpio, the minister of severity by God the Father, I call upon you by the name of severity Edlprna.

I say to you all, descend through the gates I have prepared for your passage and dwell with me. Be manifest unto me in what manner, and by what words, and at what time I call you, so that I may magnify the name of God among you. Be my teachers and guides in the knowledge of all human affairs, and execute faithfully and in a perfect manner whatever task I require of you that falls within your office. Be a light and comfort unto me, for I am the true servant of the Highest, who is the light of heaven and the comfort of the world. Amen. Amen. Amen.

ANGELS OF THE SIXTH DAY		
Quarter	Ruling Name	Senior
East	Bataiva	Aaoxaif
South	Iczhiha	Aczinor
West	Raagios	Saiinou
North	Eldprna	Adoeoet

INVOCATION OF THE SIXTH DAY: SENIORS OF THE SON, ABOVE

You four Seniors who stand in the Watchtowers upon the line of the Son above the line of holy Spirit, in the name of God who is both one and three, I _____ call upon you to manifest yourselves.

You in the Watchtower of the East who are Aaoxaif, the minister of mercy by God the Son, I call upon in the name of mercy Bataiva.

You in the Watchtower of the South who are Aczinor, the minister of mercy by God the Son, I call upon in the name of mercy Iczhhca.

You in the Watchtower of the West who are Saiinou, the minister of mercy by God the Son, I call upon in the name of mercy Raagios.

You in the Watchtower of the North who are Adoeoet, the minister of mercy by God the Son, I call upon in the name of mercy Eldprna.

I say to you all, descend through the gates I have prepared for your passage and dwell with me. Be manifest unto me in what manner, and by what words, and at what time I call you, so that I may magnify the name of God among you. Be my teachers and guides in the knowledge of all human affairs, and execute faithfully and in a perfect manner whatever task I require of you that falls within your office. Be a light and comfort unto me, for I am the true servant of the Highest, who is the light of heaven and the comfort of the world. Amen. Amen. Amen.

ANGELS OF THE SEVENTH DAY		
Quarter	Ruling Name	Senior
East	Bataivh	Htmorda
South	Iczhhcl	Lzinopo
West	Raagiol	Laoaxrp
North	Edlprna	Alndood

INVOCATION OF THE SEVENTH DAY: SENIORS OF THE FATHER, ABOVE

You four Seniors who stand in the Watchtowers upon the line of the Father above the line of holy Spirit, in the name of God who is both one and three, I _____ call upon you to manifest yourselves.

You in the Watchtower of the East who are Htmorda, the minister of severe judgement by God the Father, I call upon in the name of judgement Bataivh.

You in the Watchtower of the South who are Lzinopo, the minister of severe judgement by God the Father, I call upon in the name of judgement Iczhhcl.

You in the Watchtower of the West who are Laoaxrp, the minister of severe judgement by God the Father, I call upon in the name of judgement Raagiol.

You in the Watchtower of the North who are Alndood, the minister of severe judgement by God the Father, I call upon in the name of judgement Edlprna.

I say to you all, descend through the gates I have prepared for your passage and dwell with me. Be manifest unto me in what manner, and by what words, and at what time I call you, so that I may magnify the name of God among you. Be my teachers and guides in the knowledge of all human affairs, and execute faithfully and in a perfect manner whatever task I require of you that falls within your office. Be a light and comfort unto me, for I am the true servant of the Highest, who is the light of heaven and the comfort of the world. Amen. Amen. Amen.

ANGELS OF THE EIGHTH DAY		
Quarter	Ruling Name	Senior
East	Bataivh	Haozpi
	Bataiva	Ahaozpi
South	Iczhhcl	Lhctga
	Iczhhca	Alhctga
West	Raagiol	Lgaiol
	Raagios	Slgaiol
North	Edlprna	Apdoce
	Eldprna	Aapdoce

INVOCATION OF THE EIGHTH DAY: SENIORS OF SPIRIT, RIGHT

You four Seniors who stand in the Watchtowers upon the line of Spirit to the right side of the pillar of the Son and the Father, in the name of God who is both one and three, I _____ call upon you to manifest yourselves. You in the Watchtower of the East who are Haozpi, the minister of severity by God the Father, I call upon in the name of severity Bataivh; but when you are Ahaozpi, the minister of mercy by God the Son, I call upon you by the name of mercy Bataiva.

You in the Watchtower of the South who are Lhctga, the minister of severity by God the Father, I call upon in the name of severity Iczhhcl; but when you are Alhctga, the minister of mercy by God the Son, I call upon you by the name of mercy Iczhhca.

You in the Watchtower of the West who are Lgaiol, the minister of severity by God the Father, I call upon in the name of severity Raagiol; but when you are Slgaiol, the minister of mercy by God the Son, I call upon you by the name of mercy Raagios.

You in the Watchtower of the North who are Apdoce, the minister of severity by God the Father, I call upon in the name of severity Edlprna; but when you are Aapdoce, the minister of mercy by God the Son, I call upon you by the name of mercy Eldprna.

I say to you all, descend through the gates I have prepared for your passage and dwell with me. Be manifest unto me in what manner, and by what words, and at what time I call you, so that I may magnify the name of God among you. Be my teachers and guides in the knowledge of all human affairs, and execute faithfully and in a perfect manner whatever task I require of you that falls within your office. Be a light and comfort unto me, for I am the true servant of the Highest, who is the light of heaven and the comfort of the world. Amen. Amen. Amen.

ANGELS OF THE NINTH DAY		
Quarter	Ruling Name	Senior
East	Bataivh	Hipotga
South	Iczhhcl	Lhiansa
West	Raagiol	Ligdisa
North	Edlprna	Arinnap

INVOCATION OF THE NINTH DAY: SENIORS OF THE FATHER, BELOW

You four Seniors who stand in the Watchtowers upon the line of the Father below the line of holy Spirit, in the name of God who is both one and three, I _____ call upon you to manifest yourselves.

You in the Watchtower of the East who are Hipotga, the minister of severe judgement by God the Father, I call upon in the name of judgement Bataivh.

You in the Watchtower of the South who are Lhiansa, the minister of severe judgement by God the Father, I call upon in the name of judgement Iczhhcl.

You in the Watchtower of the West who are Ligdisa, the minister of severe judgement by God the Father, I call upon in the name of judgement Raagiol.

You in the Watchtower of the North who are Arinnap, the minister of severe judgement by God the Father, I call upon in the name of judgement Edlprna.

I say to you all, descend through the gates I have prepared for your passage and dwell with me. Be manifest unto me in what manner, and by what words, and at what time I call you, so that I may magnify the name of God among you. Be my teachers and guides in the knowledge of all human affairs, and execute faithfully and in a perfect manner whatever task I require of you that falls within your office. Be a light and comfort unto me, for I am the true servant of the Highest, who is the light of heaven and the comfort of the world. Amen. Amen. Amen.

ANGELS OF THE TENTH DAY		
Quarter	Ruling Name	Senior
East	Bataiva	Autotar
South	Iczhhca	Acmbicu
West	Raagios	Soaiznt
North	Eldprna	Anodoin

INVOCATION OF THE TENTH DAY: SENIORS OF THE SON, BELOW

You four Seniors who stand in the Watchtowers upon the line of the Son below the line of holy Spirit, in the name of God who is both one and three, I _____ call upon you to manifest yourselves.

You in the Watchtower of the East who are Autotar, the minister of mercy by God the Son, I call upon in the name of mercy Bataiva.

You in the Watchtower of the South who are Acmbicu, the minister of mercy by God the Son, I call upon in the name of mercy Iczhhca.

You in the Watchtower of the West who are Soaiznt, the minister of mercy by God the Son, I call upon in the name of mercy Raagios.

You in the Watchtower of the North who are Anodoin, the minister of mercy by God the Son, I call upon in the name of mercy Eldprna.

I say to you all, descend through the gates I have prepared for your passage and dwell with me. Be manifest unto me in what manner, and by what words, and at what time I call you, so that I may magnify the name of God among you. Be my teachers and guides in the knowledge of all human affairs, and execute faithfully and in a perfect manner whatever task I require of you that falls within your office. Be a light and comfort unto me, for I am the true servant of the Highest, who is the light of heaven and the comfort of the world. Amen. Amen. Amen.

ANGELS OF THE ELEVENTH DAY				
Quarter	Ruling Name	Dispositors	From the Cross	
			letter	name
East	Erzla	Rzla Zlar Larz Arzl	I	IAON
South	Eboza	Boza Ozab Zabo Aboz	A	AONI
West	Ataad	Taad Aadt Adta Dtaa	O	ONIA
North	Adopa	Dopa Opad Pado Adop	N	NIAO

INVOCATION OF THE ELEVENTH DAY: DISPOSITORS OF JOINING

You sixteen Dispositors who stand above the arms of the eastern lesser crosses of the four Watchtowers and are potent and skilled in the joining together and destruction of natural substances, in the name of God who is both one and three, I _____ call upon you to manifest yourselves.

You four lights of understanding and truth who dwell in the Watchtower of the East, standing above the arms of the lesser cross of the east, and have your office in the eastern part of the world, Rzla, Zlar, Larz and Arzl, I call upon you in the fourfold name of the cross IAON, and in the name of God particular to your office, Erzla.

You four lights of understanding and truth who dwell in the Watchtower of the South, standing above the arms of the lesser cross of the east, and have your office in the southern part of the world, Boza, Ozab, Zabo and Aboz, I call upon you in the fourfold name of the cross AONI, and in the name of God particular to your office, Eboza.

You four lights of understand and truth who dwell in the Watchtower of the West, standing above the arms of the lesser cross of the east, and have your office in the western part of the world, Taad, Aadt, Adta and Dtaa, I call upon you in the fourfold name of the cross ONIA, and in the name of God particular to your office, Ataad.

You four lights of understanding and truth who dwell in the Watchtower of the North, standing above the arms of the lesser cross of the east, and have your office in the northern part of the world, Dopa, Opad, Pado and Adop, I call upon you in the fourfold name of the cross NIAO, and in the name of God particular to your office, Adopa.

I say to you all, descend through the gates I have prepared for your passage and dwell with me in harmony. Be manifest unto my senses in what manner, and with what words, and at what time I call you, so that I may magnify the name of God among you. Be my teachers and guides in the arts of joining and loosing, and discharge faithfully and in a perfect manner whatever service I require of you that falls within your appointed office. Be a light and comfort unto me, for I am the true servant of the Highest, who is the light of heaven and the comfort of the world. Amen. Amen. Amen.

ANGELS OF THE TWELFTH DAY				
Quarter	Ruling Name	Dispositors	From the Cross	
			letter	name
East	Eutpa	Utpa Tpau Paut Autp	L	LANU
South	Ephra	Phra Hrap Raph Aphr	A	ANUL
West	Atdim	Tdim Dimt Imtd Mtdi	N	NULA
North	Aanaa	Anaa Naaa Aaan Aana	U	ULAN

INVOCATION OF THE TWELFTH DAY: DISPOSITORS OF TRANSPORTING

You sixteen Dispositors who stand above the arms of the southern lesser crosses of the four Watchtowers and are potent and skilled in transporting from place to place, in the name of God who is both one and three, I _____ call upon you to manifest yourselves.

You four lights of understanding and truth who dwell in the Watchtower of the East, standing above the arms of the lesser cross of the south, and have your office in the eastern part of the world, Utpa, Tpau, Paut and Autp, I call upon you in the fourfold name of the cross LANU, and in the name of God particular to your office, Eutpa.

You four lights of understanding and truth who dwell in the Watchtower of the South, standing above the arms of the lesser cross of the south, and have your office in the southern part of the world, Phra, Hrap, Raph and Aphr, I call upon you in the fourfold name of the cross ANUL, and in the name of God particular to your office, Ephra.

You four lights of understand and truth who dwell in the Watchtower of the West, standing above the arms of the lesser cross of the south, and have your office in the western part of the world, Tdim, Dimt, Imtd and Mtdi, I call upon you in the fourfold name of the cross NULA, and in the name of God particular to your office, Atdim.

You four lights of understanding and truth who dwell in the Watchtower of the North, standing above the arms of the lesser cross of the south, and have your office in the northern part of the world, Anaa, Naaa, Aaan and Aana, I call upon you in the fourfold name of the cross ULAN, and in the name of God particular to your office, Aanaa.

I say to you all, descend through the gates I have prepared for your passage and dwell with me in harmony. Be manifest unto my senses in what manner, and with what words, and at what time I call you, so that I may magnify the name of God among you. Be my teachers and guides in the arts of transporting from place to place, and discharge faithfully and in a perfect manner whatever service I require of you that falls within your appointed office. Be a light and comfort unto me, for I am the true servant of the Highest, who is the light of heaven and the comfort of the world. Amen. Amen. Amen.

ANGELS OF THE THIRTEENTH DAY				
Quarter	Ruling Name	Dispositors	From the Cross	
			letter	name
East	Hcnbr	Cnbr Nbrc Brcn Rcnb	A	ACMU
South	Hroan	Roan Oanr Anro Nroa	C	CMUA
West	Pmagl	Magl Aglm Glma Lmag	M	MUAC
North	Ppsac	Psac Sacp Acps Cpsa	U	UACM

INVOCATION OF THE THIRTEENTH DAY: DISPOSITORS OF THE SCIENCES

You sixteen Dispositors who stand above the arms of the northern lesser crosses of the four Watchtowers and are potent and skilled in the mechanical arts and sciences, in the name of God who is both one and three, I _____ call upon you to manifest yourselves.

You four lights of understanding and truth who dwell in the Watchtower of the East, standing above the arms of the lesser cross of the north, and have your office in the eastern part of the world, Cnbr, Nbrc, Brcn and Rcnb, I call upon you in the fourfold name of the cross ACMU, and in the name of God particular to your office, Hcnbr.

You four lights of understanding and truth who dwell in the Watchtower of the South, standing above the arms of the lesser cross of the north, and have your office in the southern part of the world, Roan, Oanr, Anro and Nroa, I call upon you in the fourfold name of the cross CMUA, and in the name of God particular to your office, Hroan.

You four lights of understand and truth who dwell in the Watchtower of the West, standing above the arms of the lesser cross of the north, and have your office in the western part of the world, Magl, Aglm, Glma and Lmag, I call upon you in the fourfold name of the cross MUAC, and in the name of God particular to your office, Pmagl.

You four lights of understanding and truth who dwell in the Watchtower of the North, standing above the arms of the lesser cross of the north, and have your office in the northern part of the world, Psac, Sacp, Acps and Cpsa, I call upon you in the fourfold name of the cross UACM, and in the name of God particular to your office, Ppsac.

I say to you all, descend through the gates I have prepared for your passage and dwell with me in harmony. Be manifest unto my senses in what manner, and with what words, and at what time I call you, so that I may magnify the name of God among you. Be my teachers and guides in the mechanical arts and sciences, and discharge faithfully and in a perfect manner whatever service I require of you that falls within your appointed office. Be a light and comfort unto me, for I am the true servant of the Highest, who is the light of heaven and the comfort of the world. Amen. Amen. Amen.

ANGELS OF THE FOURTEENTH DAY				
Quarter	Ruling Name	Dispositors	From the Cross	
			letter	name
East	Hxgzd	Xgzd Gzdx Zdxg Dxgz	A	ASIR
South	Hiaom	Iaom Aomi Omia Miao	S	SIRA
West	Pnlrx	Nlrx Lrxn Rxnl Xnlr	I	IRAS
North	Pziza	Ziza Izaz Zazi Aziz	R	RASI

INVOCATION OF THE FOURTEENTH DAY: DISPOSITORS OF SECRETS

You sixteen Dispositors who stand above the arms of the western lesser crosses of the four Watchtowers and are potent and skilled in the discovery of human secrets, in the name of God who is both one and three, I _____ call upon you to manifest yourselves.

You four lights of understanding and truth who dwell in the Watchtower of the East, standing above the arms of the lesser cross of the west, and have your office in the eastern part of the world, Xgzd, Gzdx, Zdxg and Dxgz, I call upon you in the fourfold name of the cross ASIR, and in the name of God particular to your office, Hxgzd.

You four lights of understanding and truth who dwell in the Watchtower of the South, standing above the arms of the lesser cross of the west, and have your office in the southern part of the world, Iaom, Aomi, Omia and Miao, I call upon you in the fourfold name of the cross SIRA, and in the name of God particular to your office, Hiaom.

You four lights of understand and truth who dwell in the Watchtower of the West, standing above the arms of the lesser cross of the west, and have your office in the western part of the world, Nlrx, Lrxn, Rxnl and Xnlr, I call upon you in the fourfold name of the cross IRAS, and in the name of God particular to your office, Pnlrx.

You four lights of understanding and truth who dwell in the Watchtower of the North, standing above the arms of the lesser cross of the west, and have your office in the northern part of the world, Ziza, Izaz, Zazi and Aziz, I call upon you in the fourfold name of the cross RASI, and in the name of God particular to your office, Pziza.

I say to you all, descend through the gates I have prepared for your passage and dwell with me in harmony. Be manifest unto my senses in what manner, and with what words, and at what time I call you, so that I may magnify the name of God among you. Be my teachers and guides in the arts of discovering human secrets, and discharge faithfully and in a perfect manner whatever service I require of you that falls within your appointed office. Be a light and comfort unto me, for I am the true servant of the Highest, who is the light of heaven and the comfort of the world. Amen. Amen. Amen.

ANGELS OF THE FIFTEENTH DAY				
Quarter	Invoking & Commanding	Good Angels	Invoking & Commanding	Evil Angels
East	IDOIGO	Cz(o)ns	OGIODI	Xcz
		To(i)tt		Ato
	ARDZA	Si(g)as	AZDRA	Rsi
		Fm(o)nd		Pfm
South	ANGPOI	Ai(g)ra	IOPGNA	Xai
		Or(p)mn		Aor
	UNNAX	Rs(o)ni	XANNU	Rrs
		Iz(i)nr		Piz
West	OLGOTA	Ta(g)co	ATOGLO	Mta
		Nh(o)dd		Onh
	OALCO	Pa(t)ax	OCLAO	Cpa
		Sa(a)iz		Hsa
North	NOALMR	Op(a)mn	RMLAON	Mop
		Ap(l)st		Oap
	OLOAG	Sc(m)io	GAOLO	Csc
		Va(r)sg		Hua

INVOCATION OF THE FIFTEENTH DAY: ANGELS OF MEDICINE

You sixteen good angels who stand beneath the arms of the eastern lesser crosses of the four Watchtowers and are potent and skilled in the teaching of medicine and the curing of diseases, in the name of God who is both one and three, I _____ call upon you to manifest yourselves.

You four good angels of light who dwell in the Watchtower of the East, serving the lesser cross of the east, and have your office in the eastern part of the world, Czns, Tott, Sias and Fmnd, I call upon you in the sixfold name of the pillar of your cross, Idoigo, that you show yourselves and manifest perceptibly to my awareness; I command you in the fivefold name of the beam of your cross, Ardza, to fulfill all my stated purposes that fall within the function of your office. And when the need for your services is extreme, your names shall be expressed Czons, Toitt, Sigas and Fmond.

You four good angels of light who dwell in the Watchtower of the South, serving the lesser cross of the east, and have your office in the southern part of the world, Aira, Ormn, Rsni and Iznr, I call upon you in the sixfold name of the pillar of your cross, Angpoi, that you show yourselves and manifest perceptibly to my awareness; I command you in the fivefold name of the beam of your cross, Unnax, to fulfill all my stated purposes that fall within the function of your office. And when the need for your services is extreme, your names shall be expressed Aigra, Orpmn, Rsoni and Izinr.

You four good angels of light who dwell in the Watchtower of the West, serving the lesser cross of the east, and have your office in the western part of the world, Taco, Nhdd, Paax and Saiz, I call upon you in the sixfold name of the pillar of your cross, Olgota, that you show yourselves and manifest perceptibly to my awareness; I command you in the fivefold name of the beam of your cross, Oalco, to fulfill all my stated purposes that fall within the function of your office. And when the need for your services is extreme, your names shall be expressed Tagco, Nhodd, Patax and Saaiz.

You four good angels of light who dwell in the Watchtower of the North, serving the lesser cross of the east, and have your office in the northern part of the world, Opmn, Apst, Scio and Vasg, I call upon you in the sixfold name of the pillar of your cross, Noalmr, that you show yourselves and manifest perceptibly to my awareness; I command you in the fivefold name of the beam of your cross, Oloag, to fulfill all my stated purposes that fall within the function of your office. And when the need for your services is extreme, your names shall be expressed Opamn, Aplst, Scmio and Varsg.

I say to you all, descend through the gates I have prepared for your passage and dwell with me in harmony. Be manifest unto my senses in what manner, and with what words, and at what time I call you, so that I may magnify the name of God among you. Be my teachers and guides in the practice of curing diseases, injuries and infirmities, and discharge faithfully and in a perfect manner whatever service I require of you that falls within your appointed office. Be a light and comfort unto me, for I am the true servant of the Highest, who is the light of heaven and the comfort of the world. Amen. Amen. Amen.

ANGELS OF THE SIXTEENTH DAY				
Quarter	Invoking & Commanding	Good Angels	Invoking & Commanding	Evil Angels
East	LLACZA	Oy(a)ub	AZCALL	Xoy
		Pa(c)oc		Apa
	PALAM	Rb(z)nh	MALAP	Rrb
		Di(a)ri		Pdi
South	ANEEM	Om(a)gg	MEEANA	Xom
		Gb(e)al		Agb
	SONDN	Rl(e)mu	NDNOS	Rrl
		Ia(m)hl		Pia
West	NELAPR	Ma(l)gm	RPALEN	Mma
		Le(a)oc		Ole
	OMEBB	Us(p)sn	BBEMO	Cus
		Ru(r)oi		Hru
North	VADALI	Gm(d)nm	ILADAV	Mgm
		Ec(a)op		Oec
	OBAUA	Am(l)ox	AUABO	Cam
		Br(i)ap		Hbr

INVOCATION OF THE SIXTEENTH DAY: ANGELS OF METALS AND STONES

You sixteen good angels who stand beneath the arms of the southern lesser crosses of the four Watchtowers and are potent and skilled in the finding and working of metals and precious stones, in the name of God who is both one and three, I _____ call upon you to manifest yourselves.

You four good angels of light who dwell in the Watchtower of the East, serving the lesser cross of the south, and have your office in the eastern part of the world, Oyub, Paoc, Rbnh and Diri, I call upon you in the sixfold name of the pillar of your cross, Llacza, that you show yourselves and manifest perceptibly to my awareness; I command you in the fivefold name of the beam of your cross, Palam, to fulfill all my stated purposes that fall within the function of your office. And when the need for your services is extreme, your names shall be expressed Oyaub, Pacoc, Rbznh and Diari.

You four good angels of light who dwell in the Watchtower of the South, serving the lesser cross of the south, and have your office in the southern part of the world, Omgg, Gbal, Rlmu and Iahl, I call upon you in the sixfold name of the pillar of your cross, Anaeem, that you show yourselves and manifest perceptibly to my awareness; I command you in the fivefold name of the beam of your cross, Sondn, to fulfill all my stated purposes that fall within the function of your office. And when the need for your services is extreme, your names shall be expressed Omagg, Gbeal, Rlemu and Iamhl.

You four good angels of light who dwell in the Watchtower of the West, serving the lesser cross of the south, and have your office in the western part of the world, Magm, Leoc, Ussn and Ruoi, I call upon you in the sixfold name of the pillar of your cross, Nelapr, that you show yourselves and manifest perceptibly to my awareness; I command you in the fivefold name of the beam of your cross, Omebb, to fulfill all my stated purposes that fall within the function of your office. And when the need for your services is extreme, your names shall be expressed Malgm, Leaoc, Uspsn and Ruroi.

You four good angels of light who dwell in the Watchtower of the North, serving the lesser cross of the south, and have your office in the northern part of the world, Gmnm, Ecop, Amox and Brap, I call upon you in the sixfold name of the pillar of your cross, Vadali, that you show yourselves and manifest perceptibly to my awareness; I command you in the fivefold name of the beam of your cross, Obaua, to fulfill all my stated purposes that fall within the function of your office. And when the need for your services is extreme, your names shall be expressed Gmdnm, Ecaop, Amlox and Briap.

I say to you all, descend through the gates I have prepared for your passage and dwell with me in harmony. Be manifest unto my senses in what manner, and with what words, and at what time I call you, so that I may magnify the name of God among you. Be my teachers and guides in the discovery and use of metals and precious stones, and discharge faithfully and in a perfect manner whatever service I require of you that falls within your appointed office. Be a light and comfort unto me, for I am the true servant of the Highest, who is the light of heaven and the comfort of the world. Amen. Amen. Amen.

ANGELS OF THE SEVENTEENTH DAY				
Quarter	Invoking & Commanding	Good Angels	Invoking & Commanding	Evil Angels
East	AIAOAI	Ab(a)mo	IAOAIA	Cab
		Na(o)co		Ona
	OIIIT	Oc(a)nm	TIIIO	Moc
		Sh(i)al		Ash
South	CBALPT	Op(a)na	TPLABC	Cop
		Do(l)op		Odo
	ARBIZ	Rx(p)ao	ZIBRA	Mrx
		Ax(t)ir		Aax
West	MALADI	Pa(l)co	IDALAM	Rpa
		Nd(a)zn		And
	OLAAD	Ii(d)po	DAALO	Xii
		Xr(i)nh		Exr
North	VOLXDO	Da(l)tt	ODXLOV	Rda
		Di(x)om		Adi
	SIODA	Oo(d)pz	ADOIS	Xoo
		Rg(o)an		Erg

INVOCATION OF THE SEVENTEENTH DAY: ANGELS OF TRANSFORMATION

You sixteen good angels who stand beneath the arms of the northern lesser crosses of the four Watchtowers and are potent and skilled in the transformation of forms, in the name of God who is both one and three, I _____ call upon you to manifest yourselves.

You four good angels of light who dwell in the Watchtower of the East, serving the lesser cross of the north, and have your office in the eastern part of the world, Abmo, Naco, Ocnm and Shal, I call upon you in the sixfold name of the pillar of your cross, Aiaoai, that you show yourselves and manifest perceptibly to my awareness; I command you in the fivefold name of the beam of your cross, Oiiit, to fulfill all my stated purposes that fall within the function of your office. And when the need for your services is extreme, your names shall be expressed Abamo, Naoco, Ocanm and Shial.

You four good angels of light who dwell in the Watchtower of the South, serving the lesser cross of the north, and have your office in the southern part of the world, Opna, Doop, Rxao and Axir, I call upon you in the sixfold name of the pillar of your cross, Cbalpt, that you show yourselves and manifest perceptibly to my awareness; I command you in the fivefold name of the beam of your cross, Arbiz, to fulfill all my stated purposes that fall within the function of your office. And when the need for your services is extreme, your names shall be expressed Opana, Dolop, Rxpao and Axtir.

You four good angels of light who dwell in the Watchtower of the West, serving the lesser cross of the north, and have your office in the western part of the world, Paco, Ndzn, Iipo and Xrnh, I call upon you in the sixfold name of the pillar of your cross, Maladi, that you show yourselves and manifest perceptibly to my awareness; I command you in the fivefold name of the beam of your cross, Olaad, to fulfill all my stated purposes that fall within the function of your office. And when the need for your services is extreme, your names shall be expressed Palco, Ndazn, Iidpo and Xrinh.

You four good angels of light who dwell in the Watchtower of the North, serving the lesser cross of the north, and have your office in the northern part of the world, Datt, Diom, Oopz and Rgan, I call upon you in the sixfold name of the pillar of your cross, Volxdo, that you show yourselves and manifest perceptibly to my awareness; I command you in the fivefold name of the beam of your cross, Sioda, to fulfill all my stated purposes that fall within the function of your office. And when the need for your services is extreme, your names shall be expressed Daltt, Dixom, Oodpz and Rgoan.

I say to you all, descend through the gates I have prepared for your passage and dwell with me in harmony. Be manifest unto my senses in what manner, and with what words, and at what time I call you, so that I may magnify the name of God among you. Be my teachers and guides in the transformation of forms, and discharge faithfully and in a perfect manner whatever service I require of you that falls within your appointed office. Be a light and comfort unto me, for I am the true servant of the Highest, who is the light of heaven and the comfort of the world. Amen. Amen. Amen.

ANGELS OF THE EIGHTEENTH DAY				
Quarter	Invoking & Commanding	Good Angels	Invoking & Commanding	Evil Angels
East	AOURRZ	Ac(u)ca	ZRRUOA	Cac
		Np(r)at		Onp
	ALOAI	Ot(r)oi	IAOLA	Mot
		Pm(z)ox		Apm
South	SPMNIR	Ms(m)al	RINMPS	Cms
		Ia(n)ba		Oia
	ILPIZ	Iz(i)xp	ZIPLI	Miz
		St(r)im		Ast
West	IAAASD	Xp(a)cn	DSAAAI	Rxp
		Va(a)sa		Ava
	ATAPA	Da(s)pi	APATA	Xda
		Rn(d)il		Ern
North	RZIONR	Ad(i)re	RNOIZR	Rad
		Si(o)sp		Asi
	NRZFM	Pa(n)li	MFZRN	Xpa
		Ac(r)ar		Eac

INVOCATION OF THE EIGHTEENTH DAY: ANGELS OF THE ELEMENTS

You sixteen good angels who stand beneath the arms of the western lesser crosses of the four Watchtowers and are potent and skilled in the knowledge and use of the four elements and the elementals that dwell in them, in the name of God who is both one and three, I _____ call upon you to manifest yourselves.

You four good angels of light who dwell in the Watchtower of the East, serving the lesser cross of the west, and have your office in the eastern part of the world, Acca who inhabits the air and understands the qualities and uses of the air and its Sylphs, Npat who inhabits the water and understands the qualities and uses of the water and its Undines, Otoi who inhabits the earth and understands the qualities and uses of the earth and its Gnomes, and Pmox who inhabits the living fire and understands the qualities and uses of fire and its Salamanders, I call upon you in the sixfold name of the pillar of your cross, Aourrz, that you show yourselves and manifest perceptibly to my awareness; I command you in the fivefold name of the beam of your cross, Aloai, to fulfill all my stated purposes that fall within the function of your office. And when the need for your services is extreme, your names shall be expressed Acuca, Nprat, Otroi and Pmzox.

You four good angels of light who dwell in the Watchtower of the South, serving the lesser cross of the west, and have your office in the southern part of the world, Msal who inhabits the air and understands the qualities and uses of the air and its Sylphs, Iaba who inhabits the water and understands the qualities and uses of the water and its Undines, Izxp who inhabits the earth and understands the qualities and uses of the earth and its Gnomes, and Stim who inhabits the living fire and understands the qualities and uses of the fire and its Salamanders, I call upon you in the sixfold name of the pillar of your cross, Spmnir, that you show yourselves and manifest perceptibly to my awareness; I command you in the fivefold name of the beam of your cross, Ilpiz, to fulfill all my stated purposes that fall within the function of your office. And when the need for your services is extreme, your names shall be expressed Msmal, Ianba, Izixp and Strim.

You four good angels of light who dwell in the Watchtower of the West, serving the lesser cross of the west, and have your office in the western part of the world, Xpcn who inhabits the air and understands the qualities and uses of the air and its Sylphs, Vasa who inhabits the water and understands the qualities and uses of the water and its Undines, Dapi who inhabits the earth and understands the qualities and uses of the earth and its Gnomes, and Rnil who inhabits the living fire and understands the qualities and uses of the fire and its Salamanders, I call upon you in the sixfold name of the pillar of your cross, Iaaasd, that you show yourselves and manifest perceptibly to my awareness; I command you in the fivefold name of the beam of your cross, Atapa, to fulfill all my stated purposes that fall within the function of your office. And when the need for your services is extreme, your names shall be expressed Xpacn, Vaasa, Daspi and Rndil.

You four good angels of light who dwell in the Watchtower of the North, serving the lesser cross of the west, and have your office in the northern part of the world, Adre who inhabits the air and understands the qualities and uses of the air and its Sylphs, Sisp who inhabits the water and understands the qualities and uses of the water and its Undines, Pali who inhabits the earth and understands the qualities and uses of the earth and its Gnomes, and Acar who inhabits the living fire and understands the qualities and uses of the fire and its Salamanders, I call upon you in the sixfold name of the pillar of your cross, Rzionr, that you show yourselves and manifest perceptibly to my awareness; I command you in the fivefold name of the beam of your cross, Nrzfm, to fulfill all my stated purposes that fall within the function of your office. And when the need for your services is extreme, your names shall be expressed Adire, Siosp, Panli and Acrar.

I say to you all, descend through the gates I have prepared for your passage and dwell with me in harmony. Be manifest unto my senses in what manner, and with what words, and at what time I call you, so that I may magnify the name of God among you. Be my teachers and guides in the knowledge, command and use of the four elements and the four classes of elemental creatures, and discharge faithfully and in a perfect manner whatever service I require of you that falls within your appointed office. Be a light and comfort unto me, for I am the true servant of the Highest, who is the light of heaven and the comfort of the world. Amen. Amen. Amen.

ORISON OF THE NINETEENTH DAY

O Lord of Hosts, is there any creature that measures the heavens, that is mortal? Can a frail and fearful vessel of flesh lift itself up, heave up its hands, or gather the Sun to its bosom? How shall I therefore ascend into the spheres? The air will not carry me, but mocks my folly. I fall down, for I am the clay of the earth. How, therefore, can the light of heaven enter into man's imagination?

Notwithstanding, I am comforted. In your name I am become mighty. You who are the light of truth and savior of the world can, and shall, and do, command the heavens and all its hosts as it pleases you. I require nothing but by you, and through you, for your greater honor and glory. What it pleases you to offer me, I receive. Behold, I pledge my possessions, my labor, my heart and soul for the fulfillment of this work.

These consecrated tables, shaped and prepared according to your will, I offer up to you and to your holy angels, desiring their attendance in and through your names of power. Command them as you will, O Lord. May it please your angels to dwell with me, that I may dwell with them; to rejoice with me, that I may rejoice with them; to minister unto me, that I may magnify your name. As you are their light and comfort, so they will be my light and comfort; as they receive what it pleases you to offer, so I will receive what it pleases them to offer; as they prescribe no laws to you, so shall I prescribe no laws to them. Yet when I call upon them in your name, O Lord, be it unto me in mercy as unto the servant of the Highest.

I am become a seer in the light of your countenance. I see your shining angels and magnify your name among them. Adonai Sabaoth, I _____ call upon the power of your name. In the power of your mighty name this work of invocation is well and truly fulfilled. Amen. Amen. Amen.

The Vision of the Round House

MONDAY, JANUARY 14, 1585, AT PRAGUE

Kelley: Here is, Dee, one with a Vail afore his face, as it were, a Hair Cloth of Ash-colour: I know him not yet: I see a Garden full of fruit, of divers sorts. In the midst of it is a place higher then the rest. On that place standeth a round House, it hath four corners [within] and 4 Windows: and every Window is round, and hath 4 round partitions, round also. It hath 4 Doores, and at the East Door is one step, at the South 2 steps, and at the North 3, and at the West Door, 4 steps: The first Door is white, like Chrystal, transparent: The South Door is red of an high colour, transparent. The North Door is bright black, not to be through seen, as the rest. The West is green, like an Emerauld Stone: So is the South Door like a Ruby. The Doores be all plain. The House within (as it may be judged by the transparent Doores) seemeth to be white, and empty.

He that hath his face covered, openeth the East Door; and all the House seemeth to be on fire, like a furnace. The fire within doth weve, and move about the House, and by the roofe. Now he openeth the West Door, and there appeareth, as if all the House were a fountain full of water. And there run divers streames, in the same one water, whereof, one doth go and come, as if it ebbed and flowed; which stream doth go about all the rest, by the sides of the House, that is, as if it were the Ocean sea compassing the

353

World. The next stream, within that, moveth from the 4 sides ward, and make (in manner) 4 Triangles, or rather Cones, of water, whose vertices rest cut off (as it were) by the middle stream of water which occupieth the middle or Center of the House, and is in circular form invironed.

An other manner of stream there is, which commeth from the 4 corners of an innermost square: and so run *diametraliter* or *contradictorie* wise, toward that circular middle stream.

The middle stream seemeth to issue out at the very Center of the place, and to mount up, and making an arch of his course, doth seem to fall *circulariter* in one circumference.

Kelley: The fire also had diversity in it.

Dee: I would you had noted the diversity of the fires also.

Levanael: Those that learn truly, learn by parts.

Kelley: The colour of the water in the Center, is most pure white.

The waters of that Saint Andrews Crosse, are like a water somewhat Saffronish coloured. The waters of the Triangles, are somewhat like a watrish blew, which appeareth most, in the top of the arches of their flowing:

For all spring otherwise.

The uttermost water, is of Quick-silver shew, as if it were somewhat mortified.

Dee: In the figure following, you may gather a better and more easie understanding of this Description of the water streams.

Casaubon's Marginal Note: *Here is a blank, or void space in the Original Copie: but no figure.* (I have inserted my own illustrations into the voids in Dee's manuscript—D.T.)

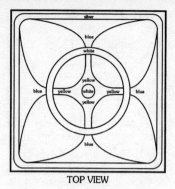
TOP VIEW

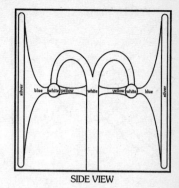
SIDE VIEW

Currents of Water in the Round House

Kelley: Now he openeth the Fire Door againe: And the fire appeareth in a square place. And there appeare 4 fires filling the whole place, leaving nothing vaccuum.

One of these fires seemeth to rise from the Center of the place; and to go in low arches to the 4 corners of the House.

The House seemeth to have 14 foot long in every side.

The arches of these fires seem to come from a trunk of fire, which riseth from about the Center: and seemeth to be 4 foot over in the Diameter.

This Trunk seemeth to be high three quarters of the height of the place; The place seemeth to be as high as it is broad.

On the top of this fiery trunk, seemeth the fire to be in form of a fiery Globe, having 6 foot, his Diameter, which fire reverberateth and rolleth in it self.

From the sides of the Trunk (between the said Globe and the foresaid Arches,) goeth up fire Triangularly, filling all; saving that which remaineth filled, by the flames of fire, which ariseth from the Globe to the 4 corners of the House, filling all the place above the Globe.

Dee: As by the figure annexed, more plainly may appear.

Casaubon's Marginal Note: *Here is a blank, or void space in the Original Copie: but no figure.*

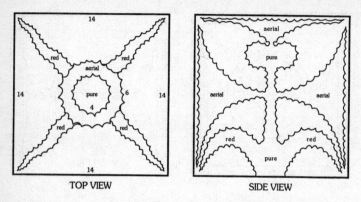

TOP VIEW   SIDE VIEW

Currents of Fire in the Round House

Kelley: Note The colour of the fire of the 4 arches, is very red; The rest are very pure, Aerial, candent, etc.

The Motion of the trunk fire is swiftest.

The Original Center of all these fires, seemeth to be very little.

Now he openeth the red Door.

The House seemeth darkish, of colour of the smoak of a Wax Candle being put out.

Levanael: By it self, it is not, but by the Sunne, it is clear.

Kelley: It hath 4 motions in it also: every one moving more swiftly then the other: All from the middle of the House. Three of them move arch-wise to the sides.

The first and second arise to half the height of the place.

The third occupieth the other half.

The fourth goeth upright to the top of the House.

The second his space (that he striketh against on the Wall) is doubled to the space of the Wall, against which the first smiteth.

Casaubon's Marginal Note: *Here is a blank, or void space in the Original Copie: but no figure.*

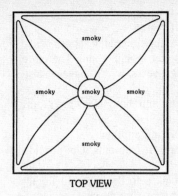 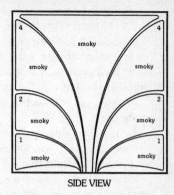

TOP VIEW   SIDE VIEW

Currents of Air in the Round House

Kelley: Now he openeth the black bright Door; and the House there seemeth full of black dust, like Gun-powder colour, or somewhat of Leadish colour.

Now he seemeth to goe down, faire and softly from the House, down the little Hill, and from thence goeth by a water side, to a Rockish Mountain.

He speaketh.

Levanael: Ascend. I am now ready for you: Bring out your Mattocks, Spades, and Shovels. Enig è veri eri.

Kelley: Now come out of that Rock, seven lean men, with Spades, and Shovels, and Mattocks, etc.

Levanael: Follow me.

Kelley: Now they be come up to the foresaid Hill.

Levanael: Come on, Dig till you finde.

Kelley: Every one standeth distinctly one from another, and they dig on the foresaid Hill, which before seemed covered with Earth and Grasse: But now it appeareth to be a Rock, and they dig that the Fire flieth out again of their stroakes, and some have broken their Mattocks, some their Spades, all except two, one with a Shovel, an other with a Pickax.

Workmen: O Lord we labour in vain.

Levanael: So you are sure to do, unlesse you have better Tooles.

Workmen: Alas we labour in vain.

One of them: This is long of you.

Levanael: I had you provide Instruments to labour with, but you asked not me, wherein you should labour. Therefore have you digged away that which you saw, and have repulse with that you know not.

A dark man thou art, and hidden away from men, and so are thy doings.

Kelley: They stood gazing one on another.

Levanael: Have you not better Instruments? Go, provide your selves, and return.

Kelley: They runne a great pace to the foresaid Rocky Cave from whence they came out first. Now they come againe with great Beetles of Iron, and Wedges. They knock their Wedges (as we use in Wood) and so break off great Slakes of Stone, like Slate, and throw it down the Hill.

One of them: What a thing is this, that this Wedg is broken?

Another: We are in worse case then ever we were.

Kelley: Their Wedges are broken, the most part, and the Fire flieth out of the Stone in great abundance.

Levanael: The nature of this Stone is not to cleave: Therefore if you have no other Instruments you must cease.

Kelley: They are in great disquietness among themselves.

Levanael: Those that go a Journey, provide them Cloathes against all weathers: He that is worthy of the Name of a Conqueror, carrieth with him all Engines: Where the Bridges be broken down, he stayeth not, because he is prepared: Behold, he hath victuals for time to come, and his Study is as well the event, as is the mean. So should true Labourers do: considering what they work in. For the Earth is a Monster with many faces: and the receptacle of all variety. Go home, stand not idle. Provide by Arts for the hardnesse of Nature, for the one Sifter weepeth without the other.

Kelley: They go away speedily.

Levanael: They have their Tooles to harden, and their

Steeles to temper. It will be more than an hour space before they return. Therefore may you spend the time in your necessity, and use the time of day as you are acquainted or wonted. I also must over-see them, or else their labour will be without fruit.

Kelley: Now he is gone.

Dee's note: *The same day, after dinner we returned to our former purpose for God his Service, to his Honour and Glory.*

Kelley: He is here. Now the Labourers be comming out; They have Wedges made long and sharp: and Pickaxes with three pikes very short.

Workers: Our trust is, that these tool will serve.

Kelley: They fall to work. They make like square holes, and put in their wedges, and break up the rock or blackish stone (like yron-mine, or Magnes stone) in roundish lumps as big as a two-peny loaf, about two or three inches thick. They pick or dig round about the hole first, and so after use their wedges. The Pickaxes have three heads, each pick thereof bigger then the other. The first is as big as one finger: the second as two: the third as broad as four fingers. And so after the first digging they fetch three or four cakes or pieces out of one hole, and then they go to another. Now one of them is faln into the ground, up to the arm-pits. Now another is faln in, to the knees. Now the house standing thereon beginneth to shake, and waver from one side to the other. Now the men be gotten out of the holes they stuck in.

Levanael: Make an end of your labour.

One of the Workman to the Guide: It behoveth you to find a remedy, or to let us understand what remedy we shall finde, that you may descend thence: for lo, the peril you stand in, is great: for this Rock was nothing else but a shell, whose kernel is a bottomlesse lake, and a myre quickened with some shut up water.

Levanael: You come hither as Labourers, therefore make an end of your work, and stand not idle. If the house, fall, and I sink, then is your labour at an end. For the end of your labour is the fulfilling of my will, and the promise which you have made me.

One of them: We are ready to do our promise; but we are more ready to provide that you may be amongst us; so you may be free from danger.

Levanael: O you of little wit; are you not ashamed? which of you have dwelt within the secrets of this Hill? yea, which of you intendeth to fulfil his promise? Judge not a thing whereof you have no skill, neither be slack in that you have to do: for the one hath his reward of idlenesse, and the other is condemned of rashnesse: For why? It springeth on her mother ignorance.

They say: If we work, it is against reason. Neither do our tools answer to this labour. Therefore we had rather be idle, then to labour about nothing: for to labour in vain, is to do nothing.

If we were determined to work, how should we perform out determination, since the Instruments of working want?

Levanael: Gather up the pieces of your spades, that is wood, and may be joyned together: The older and the baser they are, the fitter they are to turn up such soile.

Kelley: There commeth a Smith by with a budget full of nails.

One of them to the Smith: What hast thou there?

Smith: Nails.

Kelley: They be like Horshooe-nails.

Levanael: Thou cam'st in good time, leave thy nails behind thee, and at thy return I will pay thee for them. See, God is not unmindful of us, for nails are the fittest things to further your work. Joyn therefore your spades and shovels together, and labour.

Kelley: Now they are mending their spades and shovels, the iron of them being all off and broken.

Now they work, and throw away the earth like durty sand, and the skurf of the earth sticketh to their spades and shovels.

One goeth behinde, and maketh a trench to let the water out from the sand.

One of them: How now! Have we found harvest in the midst of winter?

Levanael: Why: what have you there?

One of them: Marry, either Alablaster or Salt.

Kelley: Now one of them knocketh a piece off with his shovel-end, and reacheth it up to his Guide.

Levanael: Did I not tell you, that the Earth hath many faces?

Kelley: They work now easily, and cut up like Salt or Alablaster.

Now they have digged all the hill away, even to the house. Now the house seemeth builded upon that white stuff.

One of them: If we dig any further, we shall undermine the house.

Levanael: Go to your business.

Kelley: They work.

Levanael: Soft, soft. Now labour with your hands as softly as may be. Stand aside.

Kelley: Now he taketh one of the irons of their spades, and seemeth himself to pare the sides of the Foundation under the house, and it seemeth to be a vessel of transparent glasse, and having fire within it.

Levanael: The fear of the Lord is a burning fire, consumeth not, but rectifieth the body; the old dross it wipeth away, and the daily influxion of the flesh and sin it separateth from the soul.

Behold (I say) he liveth not, but unto whom life is given: neither is their any joy, but it is ascending; for the end of joy is glory; but glory is the consummation of desire, and the beginning of felicity. No man entereth into joy, but by life: neither is there any life, but in the fear of God.

Whosoever therefore hath the fear of God, let him draw neer, and come hither. Number exceedeth not, but by unities. Neither is there any multiplication but by order. For the root of number is one. And things that ascend are dignified by order. Out of this vessel go four vents ascending into that Rock, which is the Root, which is this building.

It is said, Behold: let my spirit enter in, let there be Separation made within the house of the North, that the earth may be divided into her members. Cursed be that body, that is not divided, according to proportion, answering to the Division. For she hath yet not cast off the shape of darknesse.

Kelley: There runneth up fire into the house, from out of the round glasse vessel under the foundation of the house. And that fire maketh a great noise (through the black bright or marble door to be hard only.) Now that North door is mightily thrown open, and there appear in the house like kernels of apples, and slime appeareth, and water thinner then slime, and there appeareth pure water, else. Now there commeth together stuff like yellow earth, which the fire wrought out of the black earth: And the pure water runneth into that yellow stuff.

Levanael: Of that take a part.

Kelley: The fire returneth back again among the stuff in that house, and there appear of all Creatures some.

Levanael: Here is Creation, and it is the first.

Kelley: Now he taketh a lump of the earth lying by, which was thrown up, and he breaketh it into six pieces like round Balls.

He taketh a thing like a vessel of iron, and putteth into it that mixture of yellow earth and water. And it looketh now like grasse mingled with water.

Levanael: Thou art strong, and wilt beget a strong Child.

Kelley: Now he putteth out the earth which he put in, and it is a lump of gold. He giveth it him that standeth by.

Levanael: So are the seeds of the earth.

Kelley: Now he taketh the second, and putteth it in.

Levanael: Corruption is a thief, for he hath robbed thee of thy best Ornaments, for thou art weaker in the second.

Kelley: He taketh it out, and it is as if it were pure silver.

Levanael: Where there is double theft, poverth insueth. But, notwithstanding, Thou art true; for thou givest unto every thing as much as he desireth: Thou openest the greatest hability and strength of thy power, not such as it hath been, but such as it is.

Kelley: Now he putteth in the third Ball.

Levanael: Thou must tarry, for thou art of an harder digestion, since thou art the third, Content thy self, for thou art not an Inheritor.

Kelley: He taketh it out, and giveth unto one of them that standeth by, that is a red metal like copper.

Now he taketh up another of the Balls, and holdeth it in his hand.

Levanael: Behold, thy mother, Heat is gone, and the enemy of life entreth; for he that passeth his middle age, decayeth, and draweth to an end.

Behold, thou shalt find a Step-mother, for thou cam'st out of time.

Kelley: Now he putteth it into the vessel.

Levanael: Let cold cover thy face, let the North truly beget thee, for thou art an enemy to thy predecessors. But thou are of great vertue, for of thy excrement shall vertue receive dignity. And thy vertue shall be a garland to Nature; for thou shalt be visible when the other are silent: the Seas shall not hinder thy vertue, notwithstanding, thy vertue shall differ with the Seas: For as they differ, so shalt thou.

Kelley: Now he taketh it out. It is a ragged thing like Smiths cynder of iron, and it hath holes in it, as if it were spongy.

Now he taketh up another Ball of the earth: he putteth it in.

Levanael: Thou are tractable and like unto an obedient daughter: But thou shalt be the fifth in the second and an Instrument to the first.

Kelley: Now he taketh it out, it is like unto a white whetstone, as he shaped it at the putting in, it is like Tynne.

Now he taketh up another Ball, and putteth it in.

Levanael: Thou art the last that hath in himself and by himself his being: Behold thy face is like unto wax, but thy inward bowels are like unto the anger of a Serpent: Many shall have thee, but shall not know thee.

One of them by said: Will you give me nothing?

Kelley: A great cloud covereth them all, the stone and all.[1]

Notes

CHAPTER ONE

1. Casaubon, Meric. *A True & Faithful Relation of What passed for many Yeers Between Dr. John Dee (A Mathematician of Great Fame in Q. Eliz. and King James their Reignes) and Some Spirits: Tending (had it Succeeded) To a General Alternation of most STATES and KINGDOMES in the World.* London: 1659. Reprinted in facsimile by The Antonine Publishing Co., Glasgow, 1974, page 174.

   This work is a reproduction of a portion of Dee's magical diaries, along with plates of some of the more important Enochian symbols such as the Table of Practice and the Golden Talisman. It should be noted that the pagination in this work is faulty. The pages jump (for no obvious reason) from 256 to 353, and continue at this higher level. I have adhered to the page numbering that appears in the original.

2. Ibid., p. 184.

3. Ibid., p. 145.

4. Ibid., p. 64.

5. Ibid., pp. 159–160.

6. For an example of a typical book of spirits, see Francis Barrett's *The Magus* (London: 1801), the plate facing page 105 of Book II.

7. *True and Faithful Relation*, p. 184.

8. Ibid.

9. Ibid., p. 189.

10. See references to the importance of Monday in the Enochian communications in *A True and Faithful Relation*, pp. 23 and 114.

11. Ibid., pp. 145-6.

12. Ibid., p. 161.

13. Ibid., p. 394.

14. Ibid., p. 373.

15. Ibid., p. 61.

16. Ibid., p. 209.

Chapter Two

1. Deacon, Richard. *John Dee: Scientist, Geographer, Astrologer and Secret Agent of Elizabeth I.* London: Frederick Muller, 1968, pp. 15–16. Deacon is quoting from Dee's *Compendious Rehearsall*.

2. Ibid., p. 4.

3. Ibid., p. 3.

4. Smith, Charlotte Fell. *John Dee: 1527–1608*. London: Constable and Company, 1909, pp. 23-4.

5. Ibid., p. 77.

6. Ibid.

7. Waite, Arthur Edward. *The Alchemical Writings of Edward Kelly*. London: James Elliott & Co., 1893, pp. xvi-xix. Concerning Waite's account of the finding of the powders, Charlotte Fell Smith commented that it was "largely an imaginary story based upon Lenglet du Fresnoy's (1742) and Louis Figuier's in *L'Alchemie et les Alchemistes* (Paris, 1856)." (*John Dee: 1527–1608*, pp. 77–78, note 1)

8. *John Dee: Scientist, Geographer*, etc., p. 132.

9. Ashmole, Elias. *Theatrum Chemicum Britannicum*. London: 1652, p. 481.

10. *John Dee: 1527–1608*, p. 77.

11. Unpublished manuscript. British Library, Sloane MS. 3188, fol. 9.

12. Halliwell, James Orchard, ed. *The Private Diary of Dr. John Dee*. London: Camden Society, 1842, p. 11.

13. Ibid., p. 12.

14. *Private Diary*, p. 11.

15. *John Dee: 1527–1608*, p. 68.

16. *Private Diary*, p. 13.

17. *John Dee: 1527–1608*, pp. 68–69.

18. *Private Diary*, p. 14.

19. Ibid., pp. 14–15.

CHAPTER THREE

1. *True and Faithful Relation*, pp. 28–29.

2. Ibid., p. 30.

3. *John Dee: Scientist, Geographer,* etc., p. 168.

4. Ibid.

5. Ibid.

6. *True and Faithful Relation*, p. 30.

7. Ibid., p. 31.

8. Ibid., p. 231.

9. Ibid., p. 396.

10. *True and Faithful Relation*, p. 396.

11. Ibid., p. 9 of the Actio Tertia section.

12. Ibid., p. 11.

13. Ibid., p. 12.

14. Ibid., p. 13.

15. Ibid., p. 20.

16. Ibid., p. 21.

17. *John Dee: 1527–1608*, p. 202. See also Casaubon, p. 32, the marginal note.

18. *John Dee: Scientist, Geographer,* etc., p. 274.

19. *True and Faithful Relation*, p. 164.

Chapter Four

1. *True and Faithful Relation*, p. 20 of the Actio Tertia section.

2. Ibid., p. 11.

3. Ibid., p. 161.

4. *Liber Scientiae et Victoriae Terrestris* is part of British Museum manuscript Sloane 3191. It is entirely in Latin, written in Dee's own hand.

5. James, Geoffrey. *The Enochian Magick of Dr. John Dee.* Minnesota: Llewellyn Publications, 1994, pp. 1-2.

6. *True and Faithful Relation*, p. 170.

7. Ibid., p. 145.

8. Ibid., p. 146.

9. Ibid., p. 188.

10. Ibid., p. 82.

11. Ibid., p. 396.

CHAPTER FIVE

1. *John Dee: 1527-1608*, p. 80.

2. *True and Faithful Relation*, the 44th page in the unpaginated Preface.

3. *John Dee: Scientist, Geographer,* etc, p. 275.

4. *True and Faithful Relation,* 44th page in the Preface.

5. *John Dee: Scientist, Geographer,* etc., p. 274.

6. Ibid., p. 275.

7. *John Dee: 1527-1608,* p. 82.

8. French, Peter. *John Dee: The World of an Elizabethan Magus* [1972]. London: Ark Paperbacks, 1987, p. 13. Ashmole's epitome of Enochian magic is preserved in the Bodleian manuscript Ashmole 1790.

9. Crowley, Aleister. *The Confessions of Aleister Crowley* [1969]. London: Arkana Books, 1989, p. 387.

10. Ibid., p. 618.

11. Ibid., p. 612.

12. Crowley, Aleister. *The Book of the Law* [1904; first published 1937]. Quebec: 93 Publishing, pp. 10-1 (this is on pages 2–3 of ch. 1 of Crowley's manuscript version).

13. Ibid., p. 37 (manuscript p. 5 of ch. 2).

14. Tyson, Donald. *Tetragrammaton.* St. Paul: Llewellyn, 1995, p. 231.

15. *Book of the Law,* pp. 47-8 (ms. pp. 15-6 of ch. 2).

16. Ibid., p. 57 (ms. p. 1, ch. 3).

17. Ibid., p. 61 (ms. p. 5, ch. 3).

18. *Tetragrammaton*, pp. 230–231.

19. *Book of the Law*, p. 70 (ms. p. 14, ch. 3).

20. Ibid., p. 22 (ms. p. 14, ch. 1).

21. Ibid., p. 72 (ms. p. 16, ch. 3).

22. Denning, Melita & Osborne Phillips. *Mysteria Magica.* Book V of the *Magical Philosophy*. St. Paul: Llewellyn, 1981, pp. 174-250.

CHAPTER SIX

1. *John Dee: Scientist, Geographer, etc.,* the second plate following p. 214.

2. *John Dee: 1527–1608*, p. 69.

3. Ibid., p. 72.

4. *The Enochian Magick*, p. 26.

5. Ibid., p. 27.

6. Ibid.

7. Turner, Robert. *The Heptarchia Mystica of John Dee* [1983]. Wellingborough: The Aquarian Press, 1986, p. 76.

8. Tyson, Donald. *Three Books of Occult Philosophy* Written by Henry Cornelius Agrippa. St. Paul: Llewellyn, 1993, pp. 477, 482.

9. *The Enochian Magick*, p. 29.

10. *Heptarchia Mystica*, pp. 80–81 (see also Smith, p. 63).

11. Ibid., p. 80.

12. *True and Faithful Relation*, p. 231.

13. Ibid., p. 382.

14. *John Dee: 1527–1608*, p. 72.

15. *The Heptarchia Mystica*, p. 102.

16. Ibid., p. 82.

17. *John Dee: 1527–1608*, p. 74.

18. *Heptarchia Mystica*, p. 87.

19. Laycock, Donald C. *The Complete Enochian Dictionary.* London: Askin Publishers, 1978, p. 36. Laycock is quoting from Kelley's manuscript version of *Liber Logaeth*, which is British Library Sloane MS 3189.

20. *John Dee: The World of an Elizabethan Magus*, p. 116.

21. *True and Faithful Relation*, p. 172.

22. *Heptarchia Mystica*, p. 92.

23. *Heptarchia Mystica*, p. 88.

24. McLean, Adam. *A Treatise On Angel Magic.* Grand Rapids: Phanes Press, 1990, pp. 30-40.

25. *Heptarchia Mystica*, p. 25.

26. *The Enochian Magick*, p. 37.

27. Ibid., p. 36.

28. *Complete Enochian Dictionary*, p. 24. See also French, p. 117.

29. *Occult Philosophy*, p. 532.

30. *John Dee: 1527–1608*, p. 73.

31. *John Dee: Scientist, Geographer*, etc., p. 226.

32. *Occult Philosophy*, p. 553.

33. *The Enochian Magick*, p. 40.

34. Ibid., p. 32.

35. *The Enochian Magick*, p. 29. See also Turner, p. 40.

36. *Heptarchia Mystica*, p. 35.

37. *The Enochian Magick*, p. 32.

38. *Heptarchia Mystica*, p. 44.

Chapter Seven

1. *True and Faithful Relation*, pp. 92–93.

2. *The Enochian Magick*, pp. 11–12.

3. *Complete Enochian Dictionary*, p. 27.

4. *Liber Logaeth* is preserved in British Museum MS Sloane 3189.

5. *Heptarchia Mystica*, p. 102.

6. *Complete Enochian Dictionary*, p. 44.

7. Ibid., p 43.

8. Regardie, Israel. *The Golden Dawn*. St. Paul: Llewellyn Publications, 1989, (6th edition), pp. 629–630.

9. Ibid., p. 650.

10. Ibid.

11. Ibid., p. 669.

12. *Complete Enochian Dictionary*, pp. 45–47, 59–62, 66–67.

CHAPTER EIGHT

1. *Tetragrammaton*, Appendix A.

2. *Heptarchia Mystica*, p. 95–96.

3. Ibid., p. 81.

4. Ibid., p. 103.

5. *The Enochian Magick*, p. 184.

6. *Heptarchia Mystica*, p. 84.

7. Ibid., pp. 61-2.

8. Ibid., p. 63.

9. Ibid.

CHAPTER NINE

1. *Heptarchia Mystica*, p. 59.

2. *The Enochian Magick*, p. 29.

3. *Heptarchia Mystica*, p. 50.

4. Ibid., p. 67. Dee is not explicit, saying only of this

spirit: "thou preservest me (through the mercy of God) from the power of the wicked: and wast with me in extremity. Thou wast with me thoroughly." The reference is perhaps to the events of September 23, 1583. When Dee and Kelley were disembarking from a Danish flyboat into a small fishing boat, the rigging of the fishing boat became entangled with that of the flyboat and caused the lighter craft to take on water. Kelley bailed the boat using a gauntlet and was able to keep it from foudering in the rough sea until they made land at Queenborough, Kent (see Casaubon, p. 33). This incident took place a year after the reception of the Heptarchia, but perhaps the portion of Dee's manuscript that contains the reference to the spirit Mares was written at a later date.

CHAPTER TEN

1. *True and Faithful Relation*, p. 77.

2. Ibid., p. 145.

3. *Exodus* 39.

4. These diagrams of the tribes in relation to the gates are reproduced in Geoffrey James' *The Enochian Magick of Dr. John Dee*, Llewellyn Publications, 1994, p. 103. James has reproduced them, in a slightly modified form, from Dee's manuscript *Liber Scientiae Auxilii et Victoriae Terrestris*, which forms British Library document Sloane MS 3191.

5. *Exodus* 27:1.

6. Jung, C.G. *Psychology and Alchemy*. New Jersey: Princeton University Press, 1980, pp. 126–127.

7. *The Enochian Magick*, p. 11.

8. Ibid., pp. 1-2.

9. *True and Faithful Relation*, pp. 139–140.

10. Ibid., p. 231.

11. Ibid., p. 181.

CHAPTER ELEVEN

1. *True and Faithful Relation*, pp. 168–169.

2. Ibid., pp. 170–171.

3. Ibid., p. 92.

CHAPTER TWELVE

1. *True and Faithful Relation*, p. 172.

2. *Psychology and Alchemy*, p. 127.

3. *True and Faithful Relation*, p. 173.

4. *True and Faithful Relation*, p. 173.

5. Ibid., pp. 175–176.

6. Ibid., p. 177.

7. Ibid., p. 183.

8. Ibid., p. 355.

9. Ibid., p. 179

10. Ibid., p. 144.

11. Ibid., p. 179.

12. Ibid.

13. Ibid., pp. 13–16 of the "Actio Tertia" section.

CHAPTER THIRTEEN

1. *True and Faithful Relation*, p. 184.

2. Ibid., p. 178.

3. *The Enochian Magick*, p. 120.

4. *True and Faithful Relation*, p. 178.

5. *Tetragrammaton*, pp. 223–224.

6. *True and Faithful Relation*, p. 61.

7. Ibid., p. 180.

8. Ibid., p. 181.

9. Ibid., p. 179.

10. Ibid., p. 181.

11. Ibid., p. 180.

12. Ibid.

13. Ibid., p. 188.

14. Ibid., p. 184.

15. Ibid., p. 183.

16. Ibid., p. 184.

15. Ibid., p. 187.

Chapter Fourteen

1. *True and Faithful Relation*, p. 78.

2. Ibid., p. 79.

3. Ibid.

4. Ibid., p. 81.

5. In British Library Sloane MS 3191. Dee has taken extreme care to reproduce both the Enochian language version (in Latin characters) and the English translation of the Keys in a meticulous printed script.

6. *Complete Enochian Dictionary*, p. 35.

7. It is my strong opinion that the direction in the Thirteenth Key should be west, not south. No mistake was made by Dee and Kelley in transcribing this word, because the English correctly matches the Enochian. "Babagen" does indeed mean south. However, as I have shown in my book *Tetragrammaton* (p. 219) this direction violates the sequence previously and subsequently adhered to in the Keys.

   Beginning with the Third Key, each Key is associated with a direction in four cycles around the Earth that being in the east and move clockwise: 3rd-east, 4th-south, 5th-west, 6th-north; 7th-east, 8th-south, 9th-west, 10th-north; 11th-east, 12th-south, 13th-west (should be), 14th-north; 15th-east, 16th-south, 17th-west, 18th-north.

   I advise anyone working with the Keys to change "Swords of the south" to "Swords of the north," and "babagen" to "sobel."

CHAPTER FIFTEEN

1. *True and Faithful Relation*, p. 139–140.

2. Denning, Melita & Osborne Phillips. *Mysteria Magica*. St. Paul: Llewellyn Publications, 1981, p. 177.

3. *True and Faithful Relation*, p. 183.

4. Ibid., p. 188.

5. *Enochian Magick*, p. 116.

6. *True and Faithful Relation*, p. 153.

7. Ibid, p. 154.

8. Ibid., pp. 156–157.

9. Ibid., pp. 158–159.

10. *Occult Philosophy*, p. 97.

CHAPTER SIXTEEN

1. *True and Faithful Relation*, pp. 188–189.

2. Ibid., p. 184.

3. Ibid., p. 182.

4. Ibid., p. 188.

5. Ibid.

6. Ibid., pp. 196-7.

7. *Three Books of Occult Philosophy*, p. 300.

CHAPTER SEVENTEEN

1. *The Golden Dawn*, p. 624, footnote 2.

2. Ibid., p. 625.

3. *True and Faithful Relation*, p. 179.

4. See Crowley, Aleister.*The Vision and the Voice.* Edited by Israel Regardie. Dallas: Sangreal Foundation, 1972. This material first appeared as a supplement to Volume 1, Number 5 of Crowley's periodical *The Equinox.*

5. *The Golden Dawn*, pp. 657–658.

6. Ibid., p. 656.

7. *True and Faithful Relation*, p. 181.

8. *Golden Dawn*, pp. 631–634.

9. Ibid., p. 638.

10. Ibid., pp. 643–644.

11. Ibid., p. 637.

12. Wang, Robert. *The Secret Temple.* York Beach: Samuel Weiser, 1980, the eighth plate and pages 85-8. This book is an excellent description of the ritual furniture and tools of the Golden Dawn. See also *Golden Dawn*, p. 657.

13. *Golden Dawn*, p. 659.

14. Ibid., p. 658.

15. *Golden Dawn*, p. 683.

Appendix A

1. *True and Faithful Relation*, p. 184.

Appendix B

1. *True and Faithful Relation*, pp. 355–359.

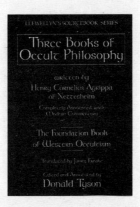

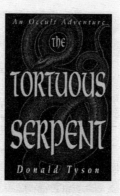

THE ENOCHIAN MAGICK OF DR. JOHN DEE
Geoffrey James

Dr. John Dee's system of Enochian Magick is among the most powerful in the Western tradition, and it has been enormously influential in the practices of the Order of the Golden Dawn. Though long out of print, this book has become an occult classic because it holds all the secrets of Dee's private magical workbooks, just as Dee recorded them in the late 16th century.

This indispensable treasure of Enochian lore offers the only definitive version of the famous Angelical Calls or Keys, conjurations said to summon the angels of the heavenly sphere—as well as all the practical information necessary for the experienced magician to reproduce Dee's occult experiments, with details on how to generate the names of the angels, create Enochian talismans, and set up an Enochian temple. Here readers will find the only available version of Dee's system of planetary and elemental magic, plus other material sure to fascinate a new generation of students of Enochian Magick. Explore the source texts that inspired MacGregor Mathers, Aleister Crowley, Israel Regardie, and a host of others and learn to practice angelic magick!

1–56718–367–0, 6 x 9, 248 pp., illus. $14.95